from

the

pages

of a

finished

PASSPORT

written & produced by:

Patrick DiMarchi

Passenger Name: Bryan _ _ _ _ _ _ _ _ _ _
Country of Origin: _ _ _ _ _ _ _ _ _ _ _ _ _
Flight No.   _ _ _ _ _ _ _ _ _ _ _ _ _
Destination: _ _ _ _ _ _ _ _ _ _ _ _ _

READ IT. REVIEW IT. SHARE IT.

from the pages of a finished PASSPORT

A Palabras by Patrick Production
EXPANDED & REVISED WINTER 2020

Written by: Patrick DiMarchi
Edited by: Stuart Stone & Patrick DiMarchi
Cover Art: Jimmy Ovadia
Graphic Design: Kimia Zadegan

ISBN: 978-1-7341139-1-4 (*paperback*)

Published by Kindle Direct Publishing

Originally Published As:
WHERE THE LIGHTNING STRIKES TWICE

from a 1st time Writer to my 1st time Reader...

First and foremost, thanks for picking up a book. Not just my book, any book really. Though I suppose for this moment I'm especially happy that it's my book you chose. That being said, I know it's a gamble to read from someone you've never heard of before so I promise not to waste your time. If it helps to know I'm one of those people who has been told most of my life that I should write a book. Though I only started giving it any serious thought after I got out of my twenties. At the time I was living up in NYC attempting to create a stand-up comedy routine while surrounding myself with the best of them. In doing so I lived with a few aspiring artists. One in particular who changed my life when he picked up my notebooks and said, *"What do you plan to do with all of these?"* I responded by telling him I was looking for joke ideas, and he pointed out that I had a lot more than funny material in those pages. I took his words to heart and soon enough had started a process that would take me far longer than I planned. Like way longer. No kidding, I told someone it would take me three months to finish this book. Feel this thing. It's soft, right? It took me at least three months to get that right. I was out of my mind. Needless to say, I went beyond my first overly hopeful deadline by nearly two years and even then it took months before the thing was actually printed and ready for readers. Not to say that the changes ended there. Originally I published this book under the title, *Where The Lightning Strikes Twice.* And I went with that title for many reasons, all of which were valid, but none of which made sense as to the mission of letting the reader know what type of story was inside of the book. Hence why I fixed that. I hope my first round of readers will forgive me and know that it was through their excited reviews that I figured out the type of title that would have made them pick up the book even if they didn't know me. So that's that.

I remember all of my hesitations before my first trip, but what I remember most is how quickly they all left me once I finally took off. Now when I went down to Latin America my first time I only knew two things; I would be spending a lot of time in transit, and I would be spending a lot of time alone. With that knowledge I decided to pick up a book that someone told me would get me back into reading, something I had gotten out of touch with since graduating college. And in making this book I hope I've also written something to do the same for someone else. And hopefully it'll inspire someone to travel for the first time.

READ IT. REVIEW IT. SHARE IT.

Which is even easier these days than when I started, as of this writing, there are an average of 140,000 flights per day. With an estimated 64 million take-offs and landings recorded each year.[1] So, if you're able to travel and still haven't, it's a matter of indecision, not lack of options.

Speaking of travel, while writing this book I spent time hopping all over the place, hoping to gain just the right stuff from each set of characters and scenarios I could find. In doing so I managed to touch ground in Spain, Andorra, California, Miami, Washington D.C., New York City, & all ends of the Shenandoah Valley. To anyone who passed by, remarked on my day, or struck me with inspiration, I thank you. And to the peoples of Costa Rica and Panama, I extend my appreciation and endless thanks for the hospitality and amazing times I've had within your borders over the years. A statement which applies to all of the Spanish speaking world as far as I'm concerned. And to all of my friends, family, and loved ones. Thanks for being patient with everything along the way. Much love. In the process of editing this book I had the pleasure of sitting across from one of the most interesting people I've ever met, Mr. Stuart Stone. Sir, for your time, your ears, and the occasional lessons on scotch and language, Obrigado. Couldn't have done it without you. And though he was my main editor, I must also extend my thanks to the many silent editors who wondered through early drafts while providing a variety of feedback along the way. I appreciate you more than you can know. It was a true pleasure to take this journey not just with myself, but with the many who made it possible to get through the unfortunate amount of hours it took to complete this. I hope you enjoy the finality as much as I enjoyed the creation. The outside of this book took just as much work as the inside and for that I must give a big shoutout to my man Jimmy Ovadia for bringing my idea to life. I suppose I should also say don't blame him or anyone else for my choice of font on the original cover. I just happen to like Papyrus. How it looks. How it sounds. Hell. I woulda named the main character Papyrus if I didn't like my own name just a bit better. Anyways, Follow him **@TheArtOfJimmyOvadia**.

As far as why I wrote this, well, for the same reason we all want to write a book, we've got something cool to say. Or so we think. Right? I've been fortunate to make it to some really cool places in my life and nothing has given me more pleasure than sharing the stories of those places with my friends. Given that I figured why not do the same, but for a few more people than I can fit in a circle of couches. Though not to take away from the experience, I hope at the end of the day this all just feels

---

[1] That's what the National Oceanic & Atmospheric Administration says. It's on their website, I promise.
READ IT. REVIEW IT. SHARE IT.

like one really long conversation in which you aren't able to get a word in. Lemme know how I do. And enjoy this adaptation of a sliver of my existence. Once you've finished you can find out more about my writing, stand-up, or whatever else I may decide to do by following me **@PatrickDiMarchi** and checking out my website by visiting www.PalabrasByPatrick.com. And if you wanna read more of these stories sooner please leave a review on whatever platform you see fit AND don't forget to share this book with your friends or anyone who you think may enjoy a story with a little adventure.

DISCLAIMER

Lastly, I feel the need to mention that despite looking like a children's book, the story you're about to read is absolutely not for kids. If it became a movie, it's likely to be rated R. Probably for stuff like crude language[2] and adult situations. You know, one sex scene, lots of drugs, and rock & roll type shit. That sort of thing. If I did this right you should feel like you're with me the entire time. Even a few times I rather wish you weren't. Aside from that minor detail, it's a damn great book and the perfect read for anyone who might be thinking about traveling for the first time or learning another language. And while any art is merely for the enjoyment of the audience, I also hope it encourages you go abroad, pack lightly, stay at a hostel, & mostly, pick up another language. Listed below are a few I've come to be curious about over the years…

English. Espanol. French. PORTUGUESE. German. Dutch. Swedish. Italian. Russian. Mandarin. Korean. JAPANESE. Cantonese. Thai. Vietnamese. Filipino. American Sign Language. Farsi. Arabic. Croatian. Turkish. Corsican. Gaelic. Creole. Urdu. Greek. Amharic. Polish. Bengali. Tagalog. Pashto Navajo, & according to the herd of online sources I could find, about 6,500 more.[3]

Travel Well, Travel Often.
Patrick DiMarchi

---

[2] The so-called 'F-word' is used no less than 108 times, perhaps even a few more.

[3] Sorry for any I left out. It's a long list and paper isn't free. Neither is ink. It's actually absurd. READ IT. REVIEW IT. SHARE IT.

Flight Plan:

READ IT. REVIEW IT. SHARE IT.

This Book Is Dedicated
to all of the travelers
I've met over the years.
To the people, places, books and faces that
made me love the world. To the ones who
spend nights sitting in circles with strangers
talking about nothing. To the people we may
only see once, but whom we shall think of
forever, to all those who continue to put one
foot in front of the other.
Travel Well, Travel Often.

Answering the Interrupter
Washington, D.C.
November 2015

"What's up Señor? Been meaning to hit you up. How much for two weeks of your time? I could use a translator if you're interested…"

"Uh hey, who is this?" - Patrick

"It's Myles. I'm leaving the country for a few weeks and could use some help with my Spanish. You up for it?"

I've known a great many versions of myself, each one stemming from the same desire to be on the go as the next, which is why you may be surprised to hear how close I actually came to passing up his invitation that morning. And I still think I would have done just that if he hadn't caught me at such an awkward moment. See, the city's parking situation had become my new daily annoyance and his message arrived at a moment when the world was making me late for someone who knew me to be a far more punctual person than reality was allowing me to be; one of the many things I've had to get used to after landing my first real job despite graduating college nearly ten years ago. Which isn't to say I hadn't been working in the meantime, it just never felt like *work* was the right word for what I had been doing. And that's probably why a few of my friends had tried talking me out of taking that year to teach English abroad before going to grad school. Seems they knew me more than I knew myself, though I don't think anyone could have guessed that my second time on a plane would springboard me into a decade of living on the go. And while that time abroad may have qualified me for the initiating request, it still struck me as an odd way for someone who hadn't seen me in such a long time to reach out again. Shelving the message in my mind I delayed an answer and went about solving the first real problem in my way that morning. Rounding another block I was still a good ten minutes from where I needed to be I took the first spot I could find and decided to rely more on a clear sidewalk and brief run than the likelihood of another spot opening up. Bundled in a warm jacket I started running and it wasn't until I was halted at a crosswalk minutes later that the crisp November air set in and the choice to run in a pair of dress shoes started to feel like one of the poorer decisions I've made in a while. As patient as one can look with so much on the mind I stood at the edge of the curb until the signals changed in favor of those on foot and the streamline of cars stopped at my toes allowing for access to the final few blocks of my journey. Being the first one to cross I soon arrived under the awning of a cafe at the edge of 14th street in the heart of D.C. where I had agreed to meet Renata earlier that week.

When I made it inside it only took a moment before I spotted Renata and that notorious mane of soft dark curls spiraling down her shoulder and over the collar of a charcoal grey peacoat. Greeting her I took a seat at a small table she had found alongside a bay window decorated in pale holiday lighting and a series of mini-wreaths sown from bright red flowers and deep green thistles. As I took off my coat she did little to hide the void of friendly curiosity behind her attempts at meeting up lately. Once a coworker and fellow wanderer she had recently added helping hand to her resume by linking me up with her boyfriends company when I was looking to get out of teaching. Apparently I was close to netting him some sort of hiring bonus if I stayed around a bit longer. Which I knew she was eagerly awaiting after our last conversation revealed they had decided to combine their savings for a downpayment on a home to be purchased this summer. All before paying for the luxuries one hopes for when dreaming of their still unscheduled wedding. With a glow to her face she looked at me and started where I knew she would.

"Not like you to be late. Work call?" - Renata

"No. Just terrible parking."

"No worries, I didn't know what to order. Still no coffee right?"

"That's right. Just espresso."

"You're ridiculous. I don't see how it's any different. Maybe worse?"

"Don't judge me for being ridiculous after that Halloween latte order you had me get last time. Marcus must keep some sort of cheatsheet you don't know about. And it's way different. Way more caffeine. Less time in the bathroom."

With a roll of her eyes she looked back at me and countered.

"I got a tea this time thank you very much."

"Glad you decided to go with something simple for a change."

"Shut your face. I'm not complicated, you're just annoying. Now look, since you mentioned Marcus. Don't tell him you know, he's really happy about hiring you."

"Always good to have fans."

"Don't be too excited. How are you liking everything? We've barely had a chance to talk lately."

"It's cool. Just taking it day by day."

"Cool? That's all you have to say?"

"I mean it's cool. Just not what I'm used to."

"Which part? Finally making money?"

"I hate you. No. It's just, I know it's a professional environment and all, but the dress code is fucking crazy. They've been annoying the hell out of me lately."

"Yeah. Well you can't be surprised your boss is asking you to dress nice. That's just how it is around here. Plus you look great in a suit. I don't know why you're complaining. Maybe you'll find a girlfriend now that you're always dolled up."

Putting on a grin in response to her thoughts on me in a tie I looked ahead and continued tapping the soles of my feet in accordance with a twitch that had started from an internal disagreement of sorts regarding her other previous statement. Compliments such as that fed one side of my ego while frustrating another. To be frank I never enjoyed that phrase. The *how it is* to life was always a result of how we had made it, but in most places not even *we*, just someone before us. And don't get me wrong I knew they weren't going to let me show up to work in sandals, but it had taken everything in me not to walk out after a few wrinkles on my shirt turned into a few minute lecture about looking more professional. And I didn't understand why it mattered how me or anyone else dressed if we were locked away in our offices all day. I understood when I was working out front, but now that they had me in the back I didn't see why the outfit mattered. And that leads me to something else she should have known without having to ask. I wasn't a fan of the recent change in trajectory which had been assigned to me by her fiancé and his higher ups. Being up front may not have paid the best, but it had been a fun chance to interact with a flood of rotating guests and residents while providing the opportunity to continue using my Spanish at a property located around the corner from embassy row. A location which had given them a primary concern of finding someone who could communicate with as many guests as possible and the only compelling reason I had applied, aside from the assurance of being hired as long as I didn't botch the interview. The thing is, they seemed to be hoping to promote from inside and I felt weird about telling them that I wasn't interested in whatever moves they had planned based on some recent happenings. Nonetheless I knew I was lucky to have found a job so quickly after returning home, especially at a place that wanted to move me up, but that didn't mean I wasn't annoyed by my own fortune once in a while. And while I appreciated the fact that I had someone looking out for me, the burden of appreciation was becoming a bit much.

"Don't you miss when you didn't have anyone breathing down your neck about your outfit all day?"

"All day? Speak for yourself. I've never needed anyone to remind me to dress right and neither should you."

"So much for the sympathy of an old friend."

"I don't have to be nice. You've skipped out on dinner invites from Marcus and I twice now."

"I didn't skip. I was busy."

As the steam danced away from her cup of Chai I moved my attention to the tiny display of espresso at my fingertips and must have kept it in my focus a bit too long for her liking. A point which she kindly made me aware by reaching across the table to push my shoulder and throw me off balance, "What's up with you? Why are you so distracted?"

"Sorry. Just thinking about a text I got on my way in."

"Anything you wanna talk about?"

"No it's nothing like that. Just something outta left field."

"Well don't be like that. Talk to me!"

"Alright chill, this guy I know hit me up on my old international number about taking some type of trip with him. It was weird."

"You still have that?"

"It just forwards to my WhatsApp. I don't even know how he would have gotten that. Or maybe he never deleted it. Who knows?"

"Well where's he wanna go?"

"He didn't say. All he said was a that he needed a Spanish translator. So somewhere south of the border I guess."

"What's the problem then? That sounds awesome."

"I don't know. My head just tells me not to go. He started by saying something about a few weeks. And that just sounds like a lot of time to take off right now regardless of what else he's got to say."

"Well maybe it's an emergency? What does he do for work?"

"Something in solar. Installation last I heard. I can't see any reason he would be venturing out of the country for that though."

"Finally found someone willing to pay you to frolic around in sandals after all. Ya know…my Spanish is still pretty decent. You should keep me in mind for some extra help if you end up going down there."

"I thought you decided not to keep up with Spanish after you left. Isn't Portuguese your thing now? Isn't that why you still take those dance lessons?"

"Well it's not like I forgot everything. I still listen to a lot of the music when I'm at salsa class."

"Ehh even so. I think one translator is enough."

"You don't wanna travel with me? Is that what it is?"

"No. I just don't like to combine my headaches."

"Rude. I'm not a headache!"

"Calm yourself. I know you're not, but traveling with you and traveling with an old friend would be two very different times. Both of which I'm not 100% sure I wanna mix. And you don't wanna travel with two guys anyhow. We're probably harder to deal with than I'd like to admit. I'm my own headache to travel with. Trust me."

"You seem to forget I have kids? I think I can handle two guys."

"Yeah you say that now."

"Well get me onboard and I'll make sure you don't have any problems with Marcus when you gotta take off all of that time. I know how to distract him from his headaches with the schedule."

"Thanks, but you don't need to blackmail *me* to take a vacation. Why don't you just go somewhere with Marcus?"

"Because! He never wants to go anywhere. *Ugh*. He's so boring sometimes. I love him, but just. *Ugh*."

"Then go by yourself. I'm sure you've got plenty of leave."

"No. I'm not doing that. I hate traveling alone."

"Then just keep saving your time and take a long honeymoon, or stay later once he leaves."

"*Ugh*. Why do you have to be like this? I don't wanna wait that long. We haven't even planned our wedding yet."

"That's not my problem."

"Come on. Just ask him and see what he says."

At that I threw in one more roadblock hoping to counter her logic with the emotion of not wanting difficulties down the road.

"Marcus isn't gonna love the idea of you going all that way with some guy he's never met. I don't know that I would do that so close to my wedding if I were you."

With a look of defiance that combined to say a bit of *nobody tells me what to do* and a bit of *whatever*, she glared at me and firmly stated her feelings countering my suggestion.

"He doesn't tell me what to do. And if he won't take me on an adventure, I'll go on my own. Would you *please* just ask your friend if the opportunity presents itself? I can just meet you down there and I'll go off and do my own thing from time to time."

"I'll run it by him and see what he thinks, but I'm not gonna make any promises until I know what he's got in mind."

"Why don't you just give me his number and I'll take your spot."

"Love the enthusiasm, but that'll be a negative Thanks though."

"I'm not paying for your coffee."

We were finally able to get the conversation away from her protesting and back onto business, but she still found time to throw in her interest once more when we got to our goodbyes.

"So lemme know when I need to start packing."

"Yeah yeah. Good seeing ya. We'll talk soon."

When I left I found myself lost in the daydreams of warmer weather as a series of cold gusts shocked every exposed nerve on my face and a light drizzle started coming down without any warning. One which carried a bone chilling moisture just a degree too warm to have been made into snow. The worst of all the precipitations and a harsh reminder of the winters I had gone without for so long. I had missed a lot of things while I was away, but the cold winters promised by the NorthEast had not been one of those things. As I thought about factors other than the weather, two weeks away under such conditions was not something any sane person would normally debate, but my free time had never been harder to come by and if I took it, that would be it for the year. Which in some weird way made me nervous. I hated knowing that I wouldn't have the option to do anything else on my own if I wanted to later on in the year. Something about that felt crippling on it's own and I wasn't sure if I wanted to commit my only free time to someone else's agenda. And even though I had earned that time, I didn't feel like I had been there long enough to ask to use it. As many times before the words of an old neighbor echoed in my mind as I was urged to remember *protect your time, no one else will do it for you.* He had tried drilling that into my head when I was younger, but I never really understood what he meant back then. Nor did I really appreciate the passing of time, so how could I have expected to? But before I could know for sure if I was protecting my time or wasting it I had to see what he thought it was worth.

"Sorry for the delay. It's been a crazy day. "

"No sweat bro. I got your number offline. Hope you don't mind."

"Not at all dude. How goes it?"

"It's good man. Busy working as always. Where you at?"

"Going into work."

"No, I mean what country?"

"Oh. I'm back in the states man. Up around D.C."

"Oh. Ok then. That'll make this even easier."

"So what's up? Lemme hear the details."

"Simple shit dude. I'm looking for someone who can stay at my side while I do some fishing and see some sights. Easy work."

"Where do you want to go?"

"I've always wanted to go to Costa Rica. You been there before right?"

See, this is what I was talking about, he knew I had been there, he even had the postage to prove it. But that didn't mean I knew Costa Rica. I was likely to know more people than towns. The last time I was there I had entered without the proper stamps or the money to leave so I didn't get much time to explore the spots one normally does when they go for the *Pura Vida* experience. Nonetheless, I understood the ways of a coastal Caribbean town enough to feel at home in most of the region. That and I could always trust to know someone somewhere who had been there to help me out if I needed some advice. My delay prompted him to reach out again, but this time with a bit more to say.

"Look man it's cool if you don't wanna go. I can always do a vacation in the Bahamas or something like that, but I figured it would be fun to explore somewhere new and you're the only person I know down there."

"I get that. I just don't know that I'm really qualified."

"Not qualified? You been down there how long now? I'm not asking you to translate a book. I just need someone who can help me get around."

"Well help me understand what we're doing. Are you trying to stay in one place or do you want to do a backpacking trip?"

"Honestly bro, it don't matter. All I know is I got some new fishing rods and I'm fittin' to use them. Maybe we can rent a house near the water."

"That could be fun."

"Exactly. So you comin'? I know we ain't talked in a bit, but I just want someone I trust. Plus I know you'll keep me from stressin' down there."

Although I appreciated the compliment I would never assure someone the luxury of *no stress* in such a situation, but I could promise not to contribute to any that should arise and he knew that. With the mention of his new fishing poles now's probably the time to mention that any equipment he uses is likely to be the best stuff you can find. He wasn't living the life of a Rockefeller or anything, but he had become pretty successful over the years and was never one to spare an expense if it was something he wanted. Which was a quality he supported by working all the time. He was very much a doer. When we were old enough to get jobs he worked his way up in the world of construction through a series of apprenticeships and absorbed a little bit of every trade he could. Eventually he found a combination which struck his interest and became the *go to* man for solar panels in our area. He had started off by getting some of the local turkey farms to convert their homes to solar paneling and soon enough he was leading the charge for farms in the area. Last I heard, he's got a lock on anything within a hundred-mile radius of our hometown. Not too shabby for a boy from the hills. But that same ambition was a bit of what made me hesitant to go in the first place. When we were kids he wasn't just a high speed driver in his life. He was always pushing the dominos in one way or another, whether they were his or not. A trait which had touched my

ce when we ran with the idea of spending a summer making
.. after college. Unfortunately the whole thing went nowhere
beyond some failed plans and unreasonable expectations and when it
was done it created a rift between us which had dragged on since. Not
that my silence was a condition reserved only for him. I kinda fell off the
map with everyone I knew back then and eventually my life was so
scattered that I found it hard enough to relate to the people I met on the
go, let alone those watching from home. And that same lack of
relatability made me hesitant now. Of course it all sounded nice if you
just thought about it on the surface. I was certainly never one to
complain about being in the tropics, but two weeks with the same people
wasn't something I was suited for regardless of relatability. Even my
grandma had once mentioned how much she admired how good I was
at being alone as a child, but I'm not sure she ever realized that trait was
more of a preference than an ability. One which became even more
amplified after college as my life narrowed down a path of seemingly
incoherent decisions. As my night went on I continued down a trail of
thoughts about what to do with his request until another message came
in meant to anchor me in with a different level of persuasion.

"Look. Things are going really well. I can pay you $3,000 plus the cost of
the trip. It'll be easy money. Just come along."

From there the self-corrector inside of me took over did everything it
could to make me realize that I would surely regret it if I turned this
chance down. While also bringing to my attention that it was kind of a
good deal on all fronts. Aside from traveling for free, it would also result
in a doubling of my income over the that two weeks. That is if I
understood the ins and outs of vacation leave. Even more if we're being
honest about what I was making in a usual two week pay period. And
even if the numbers didn't line up I would get to be barefoot and near
the ocean for two weeks. Which was about all I needed to be sold. Surely
basic metrics by most standards, but with four months left before any
relief from winter I felt like the ability to satisfy those needs alone made
the trip worth it. And as far as some time with my friend, I figured it
would be a good chance to catch up with the guy. After all, that gap had
only been strengthened by the passing of time we had both allowed,
nothing else. There was no animosity towards the guy. And I had no
reason to believe there was any from his side either. I just hadn't been
around to make any amends with him or anyone else for a while. And
the truth was I probably needed to start rebuilding more than just the
business side of my life.

That night I sent sent him a text letting him know to count me in, but as my response went unanswered for the next three days I began to wonder if my hesitation had caused him to seek the help of a certified professional. It wasn't til nearly a week later that he finally responded and came back at me with some alterations to our trip made during his delay. Most notably he had expanded the guest list by inviting another friend from home, a guy named Austin who we had both grown up with. I liked the guy plenty and even kept up with him more than most over the years, but still I urged him to consider the realities of traveling as a group in such an unfamiliar atmosphere. As that did not discourage him I figured if he was going to add someone to the trip then that gave me the chance to throw in a few of my own alterations. I had dismissed her suggestions at first, but as the dynamic of the trip shifted I realized it could be fun to have Renata around. Not to mention, I kinda owed it to her. As much as one can owe it to anyone for being a friend. She had done more than could be expected when I decided to return to the states and if all truths were to be told, it wasn't just this last year of my life she had made easier. When we first met in Mexico she was already in her second year of teaching and was more or less operating like a local. It was her tips on getting around town that had helped acclimating to my first year so easy. Which is funny because at first I was the one trying to tell her Mexico couldn't be anything like Brazil had been and she didn't know what she was talking about. Clearly I knew nothing. Truth was, none of us did. That's why she had gone down there after college like the rest of us. No real plan, just an idea for something different. The only difference was her adventure stopped after three years when she decided to head back to the states and take a job in corporate recruiting. That and the birth of two kids kept her anchored from thereon out. While closing my internal debate on inviting her or not I received a final set of messages wrapping up our details.

"I'm shooting to go down somewhere after New Years. That cool?"

"Works for me. Just send me the flight details when you get them. And hey, I might have a friend meet us down there at some point."

"Bring as many people as you want. Just as long as they understand we're not changing any plans to do what they wanna do unless it's somehow cooler than what I wanna do. Which probably ain't happening bro."

I spent the rest of the evening pacing around my apartment as I looked at a collection of mismatched souvenirs accrued during my time away. They were all I had to decorate the place which I now called home. Other than them the place still looked pretty empty. That's why I had jumped at this furnished apartment downtown. Soon enough I would have to look through some boxes and see what I still had to work with for the trip as far as supplies went. Luckily wandering through a tropical setting was the easiest type of existence I knew. One only needed some light clothing and some money for walking around. Perhaps a thing of sunblock if your complexion so desires. The rest was optional. And my optional usually needed no more space than my pockets. I just needed a few notebooks and my passport to be good to go. Speaking of which, this would probably be my last trip with that particular little blue book. And as a man with no tattoos it was the closest thing I had to a collection of ink which spoke to who I was through a series of stamps all imprinted with varying levels of effort. Each time I glanced at those marks I saw a catalogue of my time abroad. I only wish they gave you a passport with a few extra pages between the stamps so you could list not just where you went, but what you saw, what you learned, and where it made you want to go next. Standing there flipping through the pages I couldn't help but try to latch each stamp to a picture in the collage on my living room wall. A tasks which soon led me far from my hesitations about taking any sort of trip.

If I was going to live up to my job as translator I would eventually need to look up a few fishing terms and scribble them down for reference. Even though Spanish had become a part how I thought, it's not like everything was as embedded as it could be. Especially not the things I had never found a reason to learn. That's what happens when you learn via conversation. That being said I knew the simple stuff like *pescado*, and I knew we were looking for them in the *rios*, but if they needed information on some specific type of bait or some odd breed of fish I would likely find myself feeling more than lost than a fish pulled from the water. No worries though, there was still plenty of time to learn the words I needed before take off. In fact that part seemed kind of exciting. At least to me, I was always the type to have a few dictionaries laying around. Only now the stack included a broader set of languages than when I was a kid and now that I had started to make a habit out learning each word in three different tongues, they were getting much more use. It only made sense, I figured once I found the need for a new word in one language I might as well make sure that I had it covered in any others I was learning. Be that as it may, there were still more important tasks to take care of before getting to any new words. And before going to bed I did just that with a quick message to Renata letting her know she was welcome to come along.

"You're gonna need off around the first of January. And so will I. I'll get you the details as soon as I have them. You can thank me later."

La Noche Antes
The Shenandoah Valley, Virginia

O ver the next few weeks I gave little thought to the trip and continued my days without much conversation or action regarding the whole thing. The night before the trip I threw some supplies in the back of my 2-door Volkswagen and drove down from the city to meet up with Myles at his house along the Shenandoah River. As I got off the interstate I ignored my GPS and relied on memory to lead me down a series of backroads and hairpin turns until I made it to the same *Snoopy* mailbox his family had used when we were kids. As I imagined a lot had changed since Myles bought the place from his parents and the closer I got the more I realized the mailbox was the only artifact which had been left unaltered. Among the changes were a stucco guest house off to the right and an awning around the back porch which hung over a pool that was still above ground despite some modern additions. None of this surprised me. He was one of those guys that was somehow able to figure it out without adhering to the attendance of college which had been deemed so necessary by all of our teachers growing up. And figure it out he had. He was truly self-made in that sense. I had heard he was doing really well these days. But by the looks of it even his future was doing well. He had always been able to make a few bucks on the side and this had facilitated for the making of quite the character. He once road a dirt bike cross-country doing odd jobs along the way, but that's a story for another time. He would have been rich no matter what he did.

When I pulled up my lights shined onto the front porch where a cloud of cigarette smoke hovered over a broad figure leaning down as a set of large hands sorted through a series of bags scattered on the hardwood. I turned off the engine and confirmed it was Myles when he turned around and revealed a freshly trimmed beard hiding the bulge of an oversized dip pushing out from his lower lip. He looked a bit more rugged, the type of rugged which comes from hard work and not a hard life, but he did not look any older. He still had the same boyish grin and youthful look in his blue eyes that I had last seen when he spoke excitedly about his future and all he planned to get done in his new venture. His dark black jacket hid the bulky figure underneath, but I could tell he hadn't become a slouch. When I got up the steps he hugged me like a long missed friend and placed one of the small bags in my hand. Inside it was a rolled up *Enos* hammock and a headlamp with a small halogen light, both with the price tags still dangling from them.

"These are for you."- Myles

"Thanks man. You excited?"

"You know it. This seasonal shit got me down."

"I look forward to fixing that."

"Bruh you don't even know. I'm so ready to get my tan on."

"Trust me I feel ya. You coming in?"

"Yeah man. Almost done out here. Just trying to find a few of my things. I got shit from who knows when all over the place. See that shed over there? Fuckin' full of shit I ain't touched in years. Anyways, go check out my spot. Got the kitchen all fixed up finally. I got some food in the fridge if you're hungry."

"Good deal. Love how the place looks."

"Dude. You ain't seen nothing yet. I'll give you a tour when we get back. I think we get back on a weekend. You should stick around after and check out some new things in the area."

"I'll think about it."

I consolidated the items in my hand and walked into the living room where I found Austin digging through a suitcase overflowing with dirty t-shirts and tangled fishing lures. As he stood up I noticed a shaggier head of hair than usual, but the same inflated chest leftover from his days of throwing weights around *Big Phuq's Gym* when we were teenagers. A feature which was now maintained working on the farm where he had gone after marrying his high school sweetheart. He wasn't really a farmer, just a guy who had a knack for fixing things. Proof in the fact, if it weren't for him my first car woulda broken down at least twice before its' final days. Over time he had become embedded through marriage and I had become separated through adventure.

"What up bro?" - Austin

"Long time no see. Time ain't done you wrong."

"Always good to hear. You ready to do some fishing?"

"Yeah I'll cast a few."

"I'm debating bringin' my high waters or not. Watcha think?"

"Do you sir. Do you. You got shit we can cook with?"

"You know it. Check out the spread."

"You look. Uh. Prepared. Perhaps overly? Ya need that many?"

"Fishing rods make friends bro. Plus they all fit in that container. Why not be stocked?"

Walking through the living room I looked around at the scattered mess of outdoor supplies covering the floor around me and was rather impressed by the variety of scenarios they were prepared for. These guys prepped on an entirely different level than I ever would. I always considered weight and packed for mobility, but they had supplies for pretty much anything you could want. Including, but not limited to; night vision goggles, five fishing rods, and enough waterproof-wrapped kindling to keep fires burning for three months. Meanwhile, I had three pairs of shorts, a few shirts, and a hoodie to keep me from the mosquitos at night. As the evening carried on I got the chance to sit down with Myles and talk about what areas he wanted to visit so I could start looking at the bus schedules for our first day. That was when he first told me about the rental.

"I figured we could spend the first few days at the beach. Austin's gonna take all the equipment back when he flies home." - Myles

"He's not staying the whole time?"

"Nah. The wife only gave him a week to play without the kids. So we can fish first and once he's gone we'll go to the city or something. Just gotta have him in San Jose on time."

"Alright. Do you know where you wanna get started?"

"Yeah bro. Down by the Caribbean to start. I got us this badass treehouse to stay in. Here check it out."

He pulled out his phone and showed me a treehouse getaway which looked like the type of place you would imagine the lost boys staying at with Peter Pan. It looked fucking awesome.

"That looks pretty dope. We all got our own rooms?"

"Sure do. And check this out. They got hammocks on the porch!"

"That's actually really cool. So we'll land and head to the coast."

"Yeah dude. I can't fucking wait. I read they have some of the best snorkeling just up the coast from us. Oh and we gotta see a Volcano down there."

"I'll put that on the list. Have you guys scoped out all the fishing spots and everything already?"

A question to which Austin had an answer.

"We sure did. I got a map in my suitcase. Here take a look."

"Why are you taking so much stuff?"

"I need something strong to protect all of this equipment. Here just look at the case this things got."

With that he slammed his suitcase shut and revealed a Samsonite shell that looked like you could pack a body inside and still have room for a weekend away.

"How are you going to carry this thing around?"

"I don't plan to. Plan on keepin' it in the fuckin trunk."

"Trunk? What trunk space do you think we're gonna have?"

At that point Myles interrupted and reached for a piece of paper from his desk.

"Check it out man. Got us a badass rental."

"I thought we decided on traveling by bus."

"Nah. I don't wanna worry about finding bus stops when I'm trying to relax. Here, look, we just gotta pick it up in the morning."

He furthered his point by handing me a piece of paper which revealed a confirmation code and an email indicating that we had a reservation for a mid-sized SUV to be picked up at the Juan Santamaria International airport the next morning. I wanted to protest the choice, but with him paying there was little room for me to argue. And deep down I understood wanting a car. After all, we grew up in a place where it was practically unthinkable not to have one to take you the necessary ten miles or so to the closest store. Although I still couldn't help wanting to avoid the stress of renting a car in the so-called third world again. The few experiences I had in that area of life made me apprehensive about tackling the endeavor if at all avoidable. I guess as long as it's not in my name it's not my headache.

"How we getting to the airport tomorrow?" - Patrick

"You remember Jareds brother?"

"I think so. What about him?"

"Well he's been working for me lately. I invited him along. Which works perfect cuz Jared has this big ole' truck he can take us all in to the airport. Plus I think heeds to get away just as much as I do"

"So there's gonna be four of us?"

"Yeah man. You said the more the merrier."

I decided there was no point in expressing my annoyance when a small amount of internal torture could carry me through the night just fine. And it wasn't like I had a problem with Wes. Hell, all I really remembered about him was how quickly he had picked up snowboarding once he got started taking lessons back in middle school and found his way into our circle. He was our friends tagalong brother back then and now he was another body to find a bed for and another voice in need of translating. Although it's not like it interfered much with anything we had planned. We hadn't really set anything up beyond the plane tickets and apparently a rental. And since Myles had opted out of getting a house I figured we would just find some hostels to hit up along the way. Now I just needed to know what time to be ready.

"What time are we leaving?"

"We're meeting Wes at *Sheetz* around five so we can get some coffee before we hit the road. It's only about twenty minutes from here."

"Alright. Just come grab me when you're up."

When I decided to go to bed they were still scrambling around the house sharpening their knives and organizing supplies. Somehow they had developed the habits of old men before escaping the bodies of the young. As they all continued with the task of extreme organization I gave an Irish goodbye and made my way to the guest house where I spent the rest of the night searching for spots to hang in San Jose the next day. There were a few cool hostels to consider, but I figured we could book that once we got settled at the airport. After all, who knew what mood might strike them once they finally got their feet on the ground.

Falling asleep I began to ponder the weirdness of my situation and the awkwardness I felt in my hometown as this was the first night I had stayed in the area since before I turned twenty-five. From a bed only a few miles down the road I had watched the faces of the Travel Channel showing me a world filled with opportunities each night. I'm sure those evenings created a kid who wanted to make up for a youth spent anchored down by the wills of others often less adventurous than myself. I had loved this area from the very first day we moved here. I was too young to get that I was in a city before then, but I knew I liked it better in the valley. I was lucky to get a bit of both worlds as I grew up. I wanted to just get up and go explore, but I knew the town and the early hours it operated under had not changed. Sadly I wasn't likely to see any of the main streets under the guidance of daylight. Although I had been stateside almost a year now, I had somehow managed to avoid taking a trip back home. Perhaps because my definition of home had changed so much over the years. Which I would say is common for most people who moved around a lot as children. Of course I could always blame the placaters of distraction who were placed in my life over the oddly structured decade which became my twenties. A time in my life which had been built on the basic goal of being on the go. That's all I had always wanted when I was growing up here so many years ago. Not that I felt restricted as a kid, but at a certain age I realized I hadn't done much beyond living an existence of stagnant absorption dictated by the clouds of memorization and repetition which ruled my academic career.

I operated like that until an internship my senior year of college threw me for a loop and showed me how little I knew about what I was getting into while also showing me what other avenues existed. I knew Law school or some equivalent would have served me well, but without an area of specific study to enter I decided to defer my acceptance for a year while I took the time to explore the options I had. That's how I got into teaching. I was just looking for something to do that took me to another country and that was it. I almost felt bad admitting that to myself. But that's how it had been. The other stuff hadn't really mattered to me then. I was just about traveling, and the options were limitless. You would meet someone from some town and the next thing you know you're committed to some far off visit the next time you're free. This seemed to happen all of the time and I never wanted to turn those opportunities down. I just couldn't. Not when I was being granted the chance to travel with a local. That was my favorite way to travel. Because only with a local can you get to know the personality of where you are, not just the location, but the place in time. Otherwise, even the most beautiful places are still just places. This was the type of mindset that got me wrapped up in a rhythm of repetition which I still wasn't sure had been such a bad thing since I was able to pick up something as useful as language for my time. Or enough of a few to get around a good portion of the world. That and a decent network of friends scattered around the world were the two best currencies I had. And maybe those currencies alone made what was seen by some as a lost decade all worth it. Though I was never one to call it that. Before returning to the states I was grateful to had made the decisions I made and was more than happy in the life I was living. Perhaps at times anxious, but never not happy. Living abroad had been filled with excitement and the experience of learning Spanish had been one of the best explorations of my life. It's annoying sometimes to think about how that journey could have started earlier in life if I had just tried. A reality of the fact that I was exposed to foreign languages enough to not have any real excuse for waiting to start until my twenties. I grew up on the outside of a county where one of the towns had their high school announcements in four languages. Only two of which you would ever guess. The others were Russian and Kurdish. From the moment I heard that it fascinated the fuck out of me, but it wasn't until a serving job in college put me around an international staff and showed me how easy it could be to pick up a few phrases with the right help. And while those phrases were useful, it wasn't until living abroad that I saw language was about more than just words. It's everything that opens up to you once you break the barrier beyond those words. It's the people, it's the books, it's the movies, it's the culture. Luckily I had chosen one of the easier barriers for English speakers to break. Not just literally, but figuratively. When it came to language, I had never met a culture or a people more forgiving to my linguistic mistakes than those who spoke Spanish. And in making those mistakes I gained an entirely new world to explore and take part in while also adopting a whole new way to look at my own. It was a portal into another world in a way that only love could ever compare.

Day 1: Departure
Dulles International Airport, Virginia

When I first heard my alarm I sat up uncertain as to why I was awake and glanced around at my unfamiliar surroundings and a set of blinking numbers calling me to move. My confusion was solved a few moments later as Myles came through the door and flipped on the lights in full gear ready to tackle his day.

"Let's go bro. Time to leave."

Oh, that's right. Shocked into a state of sudden alertness I sat up and stretched my arms above my head.

"I'll be right there man."

From there I got moving and gave my face a quick splash of water and brushed my teeth before grabbing my bag and joining the guys at the car. Once everything was loaded we left his house and made it to *Sheetz* where we found Jared and Wes waiting in a silver Suburban with the engine running. As we exchanged our luggage from one trunk to another Wes got out and greeted us with bloodshot eyes and a large backpack at his side. When I first saw him I was immediately struck by how much taller he had gotten and remembered the days when his biggest advantage snowboarding was his low center of gravity. Now I wasn't even sure he could avoid some of the higher branches if he tried the backcountry slopes like we used to. But the rest was the same. The blonde hair, the tan, the blue eyes, everything. It was all the same just more mature. We said hey and exchanged tired glances as we situated ourselves and got our things into the car.

As we drove I tried not to think about the overload I was about to deal with in the next few hours. Between unloading, navigating customs, and picking up transportation I was about to do a lot of talking. A task I was no stranger to, but the addition of three others was likely to compound my output by an unusually high amount compared to the other times I had guided friends through a day or two stop off in whatever city I was in. I had met friends at airports after their arrivals, but I had rarely dealt with the full service travel experience. And because of that travel had become fairly routine and thus far I had avoided the annoyances of cancellations and lost bags. And the out-of-controllable only included one rough landing and two crying babies. Not bad for ten years on the road. And in country changes were always easy because I had so little with me. Even when I had to take all of that camera equipment along I managed to stuff most of it inside with only a portion of the tripod peaking through the top of the same backpack I'd been traveling with for the last fifteen years. Still surprises me that my most reliable piece of outdoor equipment was purchased at an Abercrombie store. I picked it up on a whim and somehow it managed to make it with me through over a dozen countries and nearly two decades of my life. Which is more than I can say about most other things I owned. I hope one day they stop putting holes in jeans and go back to making outdoor equipment as reliable as that backpack.

Not far into the ride I buried myself inside my hoodie and fell into a nap which lasted until we arrived at the airport two hours later. As I got out of the car I danced back and forth in the early morning cold and thanked Jared for the ride up as I tried to hurry myself away and into an environment where the choice to bring only sandals would not punish me so badly. Once I got inside I figured I was a free man until we made it onto foreign soil so I printed my ticket and found a seat along the wall near some outlets as the guys attempted to check their bags. Among the group Austin stuck out the most as he trekked through the terminal maxing-out a pair of heavy rubber boots and a bright fisherman's jacket which he had worn to lighten the weight of his bag. And if the outfit were not enough to call attention he was also carrying an elongated container with the word *BAZOOKA* imprinted on the side. Which despite labeling was merely a resting place for his folded fishing rods. Although its most common use was a portable container for blueprints. Once at the counter the guys received the news that Austin's suitcase was six pounds over weight and that it would be an extra $225 unless they could lighten it up. Austin dismissed the idea and dragged the bag to the end of the line where Myles and Wes followed. As I followed his lead I looked at Austin and gave my thoughts on the matter.

"Open the bag and see what we can wear through security."

"Uh. Yeah, that's a negative."

"Why not? There's no need to pay all that."

"Yeah it ain't about that. Bro. Bags staying closed."

From there Austin creeped in closer and started explaining why he was opting out of re-situating his bag by enlightening me on a few of its contents. And after hearing I'm still not sure if it's because they wanted to be prepared or because they're crazy, but my friends thought it pertinent to bring along a few machetes for the trip. Yes, plural, like we had more than one machete with us. So using good logic Austin decided not to reveal an array of knives to our fellow morning passengers and cause any sort of undue panic. This time he just sucked up the lesson and paid the fee before moving onto security. In many ways I had myself to blame for this. I'm sure I had implanted this in their heads on my one trip home. I guess I had forgotten to tell them how much cheaper a machete was once you got there.

By the time I made it through security Wes and Myles were already done tying their shoes so I let them move along while I made it through the C-terminal and towards our gate. When we got to our gate I found a place to rest while the others left their things with me and went to grab a pre-flight beer. An action with honestly made me a little nervous because the last time any of my friends sidestepped for a pre-flight drink they missed our connection and delayed me in my exploration of Los Angeles for more than half a day. This time I attempted to curb that possibility and got the name of the bar they had found before the guys ran off. From there I lounged around and rested up against a charging terminal while the chairs around me began to fill with the rest of the areas early morning international travelers. I loved airports. They were easily the best place for people watching, and they provided the greatest variety of faces. With my back against my bag I sat there scanning the crowd, relating to the smiles of first time travelers and the discomfort of those sitting slouched on their 10th plus hour of layover. Each possible curve of the face and color of eye passed me by. The shoes were different each way you looked, some laced up for the early morning jog and never changed, others floated in fleece lined slippers ready for a day of extended cabin space. Clusters of friends, family, and business associates crowded the terminal while the gaps between the groups were filled with the brave souls sitting by themselves, relying on the road to provide them with companions along the way. Meanwhile in far off corners those ready for the daily trade perched with their laptops and headphones buried in all the wifi could offer. And much to modern surprise, some still sat, legs crossed, books open, pages flipping, playing one journey in their mind before they took part in another.

After waiting enough time to charge my phone I decided to go down to the bar and found Myles talking with two businessmen as Austin sat with three empty mugs being removed from the counter in front of him. As I approached I saw them doing something I had never been very good at. Or at least not as a combination. I wasn't good at beer and I wasn't great at sitting. When I approached the bar I came up on Austin's side and tried to pull his attention away from the varied shelves of whiskey which had drawn his eyes.

"What's up bro? You excited to get out of the cold?"

He looked up at me from a frosted glass smudged by anxious finger prints and put a serious look on his drunken face.

"Motherfucker, I don't care about the cold. All I care about is how many fish I'm going to catch down there. It can snow in Costa Rica for all it wants."

"Don't worry. We'll be fishing soon enough. How you feeling?"

He peered down into his empty mug of beer and looked back up at me appearing almost to have morphed into the stages of the grinning drunk, clearly unbothered by our delay.

"I'm just glad I don't have to make sense for the next week bruh. Fuckin' that and fishing. This is gonna be awesome."

Austin and I had both started as outsiders to our hometown and as a result had grown up as great friends, always giving each other a ride into town when the other needed it. He was always into fishing and I was always good to chill by a river so we had spent a lot of time exploring the Valley as teenagers. Neither of us had planned to grow up in rural areas, but we made the most of it and eventually you might have even been tricked into thinking we were outdoor guys all along. Once I saw I couldn't steal the guys from the conversations of their new friends I decided to leave and went off to try and find a few things to do on the Pacific side of Costa Rica. While doing this I received word they had eventually made it to beer #4. Not a problem except around that same time I also received a message saying our flight had been delayed by two hours. News which once shared edged them towards beer #5. As I sat there researching a few things Wes reappeared from his venture to the bar and approached me in a series of slurred English.

"Yup, so they're both wasted, and it's fuckin' $35 every round we get. Getting drunk in an airport is stupid."

With that burst of infinite wisdom came the bursting of our bubble echoing loudly throughout the terminal.

"Fight 1410 has been cancelled due to Volcanic ash in the San Jose skies. Please report to Customer Service if this affects your travel plans."

In over a decade of flying I've never faced issues with a delayed flight and there I was about to have my perfect run ruined by an overreaction to ash. What the fuck. And of course none of the guys were in any shape to be making decisions so I had to figure out how I was going to solve a problem which was very much out of my control. Luckily I was already separated from the crowd and started working my way towards the customer service desk at the other end of the terminal before most people had even grabbed their luggage. I was lucky enough to end up as 6th in line and felt pretty good about my odds of fixing the problem. While waiting I googled what to do and the website said to get out of line and call the airline directly so I got the ball rolling and made a call to their hotline. Once someone answered I stepped out of the line and began the process of getting the situation resolved.

On the phone I was met by the voice of a kind woman who was unable to find any promising news until I told her we were open to drive to another airport in the area if she was able to find a flight leaving today. Miraculously she found us another flight taking off in a few hours from Reagan National Airport which was only a forty-five minute drive or so from our current location. I couldn't quite figure out how some other airline was able to get us there despite the conditions in the air, but I didn't bother bring that up with her. If they were going to let us fly I was going to fly, but we still had to gather our things from baggage claim before we could leave. I assumed that the cancelled flight would have alerted them to start returning all of the bags. But I, and pretty much the entire flight, had assumed incorrectly. As we waited for the bags to come the crowd grew impatient and eventually that turned to annoyance as we learned we were not going to receive our luggage soon enough to make it onto our rescheduled flight.

Sitting there I looked up at the departure board as it flashed with a list of familiar cities only a few hours reach of our destination and it got me thinking how Confucius had said an inconvenience was usually an unrecognized opportunity. I had stared at this board many times before with a mind of the endless possibilities I faced arriving at an airport without a plan, but those types of parameters didn't work for the situation I was hoping to fix. I needed to get us in the air and I needed to find a place within a reasonable driving distance to Costa Rica for us to land. The first city to come across my search was Managua, Nicaragua. And while geographically that would have put us closest to the border we needed to cross it was too much of a safety hazard to consider with three novice travelers. I looked and saw another option which my mind had yet to consider, Panama City. A place I had only visited briefly during layovers, but I had been told enough good things about the area to know that we could find something worthwhile so I went over to the help desk and checked on the availability of flights for the day. I then remembered I had a contact from Panama living in the states so I pulled out my phone and sent her a text explaining what I was thinking of doing and asked if she thought we could drive through Panama and into Costa Rica. Crazy at that idea may sound, the idea of improvising and staying on the go became normalized pretty early in my life. I grew up in a family of busy bodies who never spent much time in the same place, whether it be a car or a casa, they stayed moving.

"I need to know one thing, is it feasible? Not do you think it's safe, just do you think it can be done based off what you know of the roads?"

Only minutes later I had a response from Marissa giving me the green light.

"Chico! Of course! You can take the Pacific Coastal Highway and head up to Chiriqui and from there drop your car and cross the border. Lemme know if you have any other questions!"

I took the info from that message and decided that was our best option since it looked like it would be days until we got there if we continued waiting. If that was going to be the case it might as well be controlled by our own wheels so I went up to the guys and proposed the idea. By now they were all beyond tipsy and were thrown off by the initial suggestion to fly to another country. Austin laughed and asked if we would still use Pesos. An issue to address at another time. I didn't have the patience to explain to him what Colones were. To no surprise Wes was agreeable to the sudden change.

"Fuck yeah. We can visit the canal." - Wes

"Ok, Myles what about you? You're cool with this?"

A drunker version of Myles than I had seen in years looked back at me with a pleased grin and a face red with the surges of alcohol and early mornings, "Up to you Pat. What other option we got?"

"We can wait if we want, but the earliest we're getting there is three days from now. Assuming nothing else goes wrong."

"Fuck. Okay. Think we could find new spots to stay?"

"Well yeah. Probably not a treehouse on short notice, but yeah."

"Look. I don't care where we go. I just wanna get moving."

With that one vague parameter I walked away from him and went back to the desk where I was greeted by a tall dark skinned woman with a colorful scarf, the ones used for decorating, not for warmth. I looked at her with one last reach for external confirmation that I was making the best move,

"Excuse me. If we wait here, what are the chances we can get on a flight to San Jose by tomorrow?"

"I'm from an island where this happens from time to time and this type of thing can keep planes grounded for three to four days or it can be as much as a few weeks. Honestly honey it's a gamble no matter what you do."

"Understood. Can we change our destination to Panama City please?"

"Of course, but you understand this only gets you to Panama City right? Your tickets will still require you to depart from San Jose." With a deep breathe I looked at her and nodded my way into the decision, "I understand."

Once the decision had set in I couldn't be sure what had caused me to look at that type of distance so casually. I had driven across North America enough times to make anywhere seem reasonable, but this was a lot of land to cover on vacation. To give you an idea it was comparable to taking a flight from D.C. to Los Angeles and deciding at your layover in Denver to just drive the rest of the way. Something I had done in one sleepless stretch all by myself, but not something I wished on anyone trying to relax. At least this time I would be in a rental and not under the tread of my own tires. And if we do have to rent a car at least now we were getting the most out of it. Since the guys had done their research on the places they wished to visit in Costa Rica it was now on me to be the creator of ideas in this new land we were about to explore. While standing there in thought Austin walked up to me hanging up his phone with a stressed look to his face.

"Well. She's pissed." - Austin

"I thought she was cool with you going."

"Well yeah, when she knew *where* I was going. She had already looked up all of the safety stuff about where we were going."

"Now she has to relocate her spies." - Myles

"She don't gotta worry about me down there unless I get arrested for being naked in a wheelbarrow. Other than that I just gotta be home in time for her brothers visit and she'll be happy."

Apparently Austin had been granted enough time to come along provided that he didn't get too out of control or leave Costa Rica for any reason. Nothing a few phone calls can't fix. From there we waited around as the time dragged on until we were finally able to board our 7 P.M. flight which connected us to Panama City via a quick stop off at JFK airport. As we took off and flew over Washington D.C. I looked down at a long row of red lights slowly making their way down the I-95 funnel and for once found a bit of beauty in the aesthetics of rush hour. From this high up I saw a natural beauty to the landscape of a city which had traded out concrete jungles for parks, monuments, and free museums. Though now all of the trees were void of even the most brittle of leaves they still helped to create a sense of space and the presence of nature as they wove themselves in and out of each neighborhood surrounding the beltway. And in the heart of the evening I appreciated the rare instance in humanity where a city had opted out of towering buildings and instead implemented legislation to limit the heights of any structures to keep the skies open for those living within its limits. Giving a view of the sky rare in most cities.

A concern very opposite of the one by those who had designed the skies we would meet an hour later when the clouds opened up revealing the island of Manhattan. An island stacked to the sky with the many accomplishments of concrete and steel casting century old shadows of glitter and sparkle onto the Hudson River. I looked out trying to appreciate the fullness of historical moments encapsulated before me and was unable to decipher all which I had read in what little I could identify of the towering spectacle below us. This city was only an idea to me. A place only known through hearsay and history books. All I truly knew was that this city had been more than generous in it's interactions with the takers of time and by the number of cranes I saw it didn't look like it was stopping anytime soon. It was the city where my grandparents and many others like them had come to start their humble journey into this blended nation. And at the same time it was also a place with such allowances of power that it had once allowed characters like Robert Moses to become so formidable that it took executive intervention by President Roosevelt to stop the construction of a bridge set to land itself on what we now know as Battery Park. Surely a city with such ranges of opportunity had more stories to share, but those were the only ones I knew. It was a great launching pad for the American experience which is why so many travelers had been surprised to hear that I had turned down a chance to move there after college for Law school. Many of them asked why anyone would sidestep a place like New York and I sometimes wondered that as well, but I'm not sure I could have trusted myself in a place with such a non-stop pace so soon after college. Not if my track record through Latin America was any indicator. I knew at the time I had been more excited at the thought of life in NYC than I had at the thought of going to school. And when it came time to sign up for classes I realized I needed to buy myself some more time before enrolling and closing the decision on my future. And once I sent in my deference I went on and started looking for something to do for a year while I researched the options available after. Which is when I discovered the world of teaching English as a second language. A discovery that led to the mining of similar opportunities over the next decade. Though I only officially taught in the beginning and then the rest of the time I spent working as a tutor of sorts, floating around as I wished.

When we landed I took myself to our gate and left my stuff with Wes while I went to get a snack from one of the kiosks set up around us. Before grabbing some food I walked into a bathroom and spotted Myles entering a stall as I opened the door. It was here that I heard the memories of an old habit finding its way back into the circles of my life as a series of aggressive sniffs came from one of the stalls to my right. I stepped back and tried to examine under the doors to see how many people were with me, but only noticed one set of legs. A moment later Myles exited the stall and patted my bicep as he walked by.

"You good man?" - Patrick

"All good bro. Just some allergies." - Myles

Now I'll never condone or condemn ones choices in dealing with reality and the annoying times it throws at us, but there's no need to bring sand to the beach. And he of all people knew we could find anything we wanted once we made it down there. Not wanting to deal with the issue at the moment I went to get some food and then found my way to a seat next to Wes where he sat asleep and in complete neglect of his baggage watching duties. While he slept I finished an oversized salad and took a moment to write down a few things for once we got there, mainly lists of the spots I had found in my Google searches. As well as the names of a few contacts I had who might still be in the region. The list would always lead me back to my phone, but the whole thing looked a lot more manageable on one tiny piece of paper as opposed to an endlessly scrollable note on a tiny screen. This notebook had been through just as much as my backpack by now, but in way less time. When Wes finally woke up we started catching up and he made a point to let me know how glad he was to be getting out of the country for a while.

"I can't tell you how stoked I am to be here man. All of my trips have been to cool spots, but I've never been anywhere tropical." - Wes

"Good time for it. How did you get tagged along on this anyway?"

"It was just Myles being Myles. He came into my office and asked me if I had a passport. And when I told yeah he just flung this paper plane he made out of our tickets onto my desk."

"Sounds like the guy I know. How much notice did you get?"

"About two weeks."

"Exactly like the guy I know."

"Yeah. Dude's my boss so I didn't have to worry about getting outta work or nothing. Not like he needed to give me more time."

"True. So how long you been working with Myles?"

"I started about the time I graduated last year."

"Good deal. What did you study that steered you towards working with him in solar? Or was it just doing sales?"

"Well I studied Biology. But I needed something to do while I stuck around waiting for my girl to graduate. So I got into sales after a while, but I started just doing installations. It was cool."

"How much longer til she graduates?"

"Doesn't really matter. We broke up over the holidays."

"That's a bitch. What's next?"

"Myles pays well enough to keep you around I imagine?"

"Yeah. The money is nice, but it still pisses me off that I let a girl keep me around that long. I coulda just gone to fucking grad school. Or studied abroad for a semester."

"I learned a long time ago to put shit like that in the *we've all been* there category and get on with it."

"Yeah, but I could already be done with my first year if I had just stuck it out like I planned to."

"You can always go back. If you already know what world you wanna be involved in then you've solved half of the problem."

"I'm planning to. I'm not getting trapped here like some of my friends have."

"Well whether you get trapped somewhere you want to be or somewhere you don't want to be, it's always just a matter of deciding to leave. And your situation isn't that bad if I had to guess."

"True, I don't wanna leave just yet. And it's not like I hate what I'm doing. I studied bio, the environment matters to me, but I'm not sure it's the side I wanna tackle it from."

"Dude, stop delaying. Take some time and sit down to figure that shit out. Or at least get started. You don't have to make the decision. But put it out there and see what happens."

"Oh I'm gonna man. That's what I was getting to. I'm gonna keep making some money for a few more months and then I'm gonna take a trip out west to work a bit and do some cool shit. I'll take some time to get my shit together while I'm out there."

"You don't need six months. Take a day and plan it out. Go enjoy it out there if that's what you want. But don't tell yourself that it's because that's how long a decision about your life is supposed to take."

"I know dude. It's not just that. I want a fucking break. Gonna enjoy some of this. I wanna go do something cool like you and Myles did before I lock it up and put my head down for a while."

"What do you mean like Myles and I did?"

"Well that film you guys made. That was at least a cool trip. And no offense this is cool too, but I wanna go do my own thing for a while. Like by myself."

"I totally feel you on that, but how did you hear about the movie?"

"Myles showed me a few pics of you guys with plane tickets for some island on an old cell phone he had in one of his drawers. He said you guys were doing some documentary thing for a festival right?"

"Yeah, that was the plan," brushing off the need to go further I honed in on something more to my interest, "Damn I'd love to see those. I don't even have any pics from back then. Not anymore at least. Lost all of mine."

"It ain't much. He didn't have any pics from the trip. Just some from you guys at home packing or something."

"Oh. Did you watch any of the video?

"Video? Nah. He didn't show me any of it. Why did you guys have to go out of the country anyway?"

"Well two reasons. One, it was the best spot we could find for what we were trying to do. And two it was somewhere we could bribe our way out of trouble, if it got to that."

With that he started laughing and inquired further.

"Why would you be worried about that?"

From there I took the time to fill Wes in on the specifics of my thoughts and happenings after graduation. I had to remember that he had missed out on our individual peculiarities or any context for our lives beyond whatever skewed view a young kid manages to obtain from the occasional ride up a chairlift. Anyways, those days I was even more a rarity among my friends as the only one who didn't drink when we went out. Well me and this other kid, but he always left early. This was in spite of there being a ceaseless availability of the opportunities and products necessary if I had I wanted to. Of course my friends were always happy to use that reluctance to their advantage when they needed a driver, but Myles never seemed to understand why I wasn't interested in letting loose once in a while. Or why I didn't do it the same way as he did. But even he didn't know about all of my trials and errors. And definitely not about the time a friend from the next county over stole an edible from his brothers stash for my 14th birthday. Nor did he know about the three day coma I had to fight my way out of afterwards. Something which taught me I didn't need to get high unless I actually had time to be high. And for me free time just didn't exist back then. That's really the only thing that ever damned me about it either way, giving up wits or time. Both annoyed me to part with and both were needed on deck most of the day.

Wes was also too young to have known this guy Sebastian who moved in sometime around eighth grade. Surely they knew each other, but it was a small town so we all knew each other somehow. It was only a matter of how well and through whom. Now from the moment he moved in Sebastian had taken a particular liking to Myles and in no time he had wedged himself into our trio. Despite being one of those straight edge kids that Myles never meshed with too well. He was different though. He was pretty good at blending in and even took part in a few stupid stunts as high schoolers to help show us he was down for the group no matter how late he had entered it. Nonetheless, Sebastian wasn't a crazy guy. Although I'm sure that's how it looked to everyone after he died. See he had gotten some ridiculous job offer before graduation and was basically on his way to making 100K a year just because he had spent a few years learning about computers and found out he was a complete wizard behind the keyboard. As a means of celebrating he wanted to go on a Johnny Depp style bender and bought a mound of cocaine with his signing bonus. A gift he invited us over to share, but we were lucky to have been busy that night because the toe-tag it led to was labeled as an overdose induced heart attack. Although calling it that wasn't really fair, it's not like he *overdid* anything. It wasn't the drugs that killed him. It was everything else, at least that's what the autopsy said. In the end the doctors concluded he had gotten a bad batch and from what it looked like the first few lines dropped him. Unfortunately the abundance of leftovers led the authorities to believe he was planning on doing a lot more than keeping it to himself and no one who knew otherwise was gonna speak up about it. It's a shame because he became the easiest target for the locals looking for anyone to blame as the corruptor of their youth. And who better than the dead transplant who died too early to prove anybody wrong about who he was. Little did they know what a good deal he had gotten on it. Nor did we realize he would be the first of many friends to go in the same way.

It wasn't until my first summer home from teaching that I found myself reliving the whole thing with Myles as our friends got together one night. It was there he told me about this idea he had for a documentary involving the whole thing with Sebastian and everything which had happened afterwards. Which seemed like an attempt by Myles to show people what they're really putting in their bodies by buying off the streets. He did his best not to show it, but I really feel like losing our buddy hit him harder than the rest of us. Though we all had our own ways of dealing with it. After he died I briefly became the friend afraid to miss out on anything. Ultimately causing me to go head first into everything and everyone I met. Eventually using the continuation of adventure to mask indecision, or perhaps to extend it. Either way, it cultivated the mindset Myles needed when he approached me about his idea. That combined with my propensity to carry a camera all of the time. A trait no longer novel, but there was once a time when very few moments were captured by the lens. And in those days I was the kid at the party with the camera. Perhaps that's why the whole project was even more than personal for me. Most of my life was always on a track that was strictly academic and in a lot of ways that documentary was the only artistic attempt I ever allowed myself in life.

Synthetics were just starting to hit the market so we got the idea to test stuff around the area and see if anyone was getting what they were paying for. As we brainstormed we decided to figure where along the chain of production the stuff became the most corrupted and to do this we would need to start by testing the differences in potency around the area. I soon discovered Myles had already gone on a silent search to find out where Sebastians specific bad batch had come from, but was unable to get any leads as only a few people had access to such outside sources. We may have been hellions growing up, but neither of us actually knew where Sebastian could had gotten such a large amount and we couldn't start asking around our hometown if we wanted to keep what we were doing hidden. Plus if either of us found the person who had sold it to him it's likely we would have killed him before he gave us what we needed. Even though some of us shared the guilt as the sober facilitators of the late night rides which led to him sparking his first vices.

Since there was no luck in our hometown we soon solved our supply problem by going to a few cities within a days drive to pick up a few samples for comparison. Given our location the easiest choices were the three metropolitans of Washington D.C., Richmond, and Baltimore. A list I have since trembled at after learning they were all neck and neck for being crowned the murder capital of the country at the time we decided to visit. Which totally makes sense now because there was no shortage of dealers once we started looking, but truth be told there wasn't a real big difference between any of the samples once it was all said and done. I mean one batch was total shit, but none of it was lethal. Now during all of this Myles had been doing some research to find out where the purest stuff came from and stumbled across a cluster of islands rumored as a stop off for smugglers making their way through the Caribbean. That's where he wanted to film the second half of his idea. Or at least that's where he decided to send me. He didn't have the time for the trip himself. Which didn't really bother me at first because I planned to go back and work with him after everything anyway. It was only once I was down there that I so drastically altered my course. Who knows what would have happened if he came too. We had the lost boys syndrome back then. I was just the one to lose it last.

"You went to all of those spots by yourself? That's fucking crazy man." - Wes

29

"It wasn't that bad after seeing some of the shit I saw in Mexico. And I had Myles there with me on the streets. He only missed out on the trip to the islands. He was there for the rest. Not like it was some solo mission. To be honest, he was the one making most of the moves. He would sit in a trashcan and film all of the buys. He was so into it. That's why I was so shocked when he dipped out and didn't wanna go."

"How did you know the difference between all of the stuff you bought? Did you have to try it all or test it with some sort of police kit?"

"Well yeah we had actual testing supplies. So factually we could figure those things out. And no, I didn't try it. There was no way I was doing any of the shit from the streets. Myles did, but I was paranoid as fuck about those things then. So I was able to put off doing any of it by telling him I was waiting til we were down in Bocas. And I told him if I was gonna do that I wanted to see him try and go the first week without any cigarettes before I would do a line with him. Man was a feign for Camels back then and I honestly figured he wouldn't be able to make it."

"That's funny. What's a Bocas?"

"Oh. Bocas Del Torro. That's the name of the island chain we found."

"So wait, why did he back out then if it was his idea?"

"Things came up with work before we were supposed to leave."

"Damn. Then why did you bother still go?"

"Well I left thinking he was gonna fly down once everything was settled. Guess I figured I could go down and scope the place out a bit before he arrived. Plus it made sense for what we were trying to find. That was the only place we could get truly pure stuff. We couldn't hope to guarantee that anywhere else we went. The testing had showed us that much."

"So what happened then?"

"It started off fine. I even had a couple of days to make some contacts and buys, but then I ran into some shit I couldn't bribe or buy my way out of."

"What do you mean?"

"Well nobody is really asking for a bribe when they jump you."

"That sucks. How did that happen?"

"Some guys spotted me when I was leaving this bar and grabbed me on my way out."

"What did you do to them? Or did they just see you were by yourself?"

"Not sure. I couldn't really see over the fence until I was already on the other side. And once I stood up from the landing they were practically next to me."

"What were you doing jumping over a fence?"

"I was trying to get a shot of this sunken ship that was by the docks attached to this bar."

"That sounds cool. Was it like treasure ship style?"

"No. I think it sunk somewhere in the last thirty years or so. Looked too new to be a pirate ship. It probably wasn't anything special, but it looked like one of the boats they used for smuggling so I wanted to get some shots without anyone swimming around it."

"That sucks. How did they know you were in there? Did you mess with the security or something?"

"Nah. I don't know. I think they must have seen a flash from my camera or something because they grabbed me the moment my feet hit the ground."

"Were you scared?"

"Didn't have time to be. They literally hit me and just took my stuff. It wasn't anything drastic. I was happy enough to just run back to the hostel when I could stand back up."

"That sucks man. Sounds kinda cool though. I mean ya know, a good story and all since you made it back."

"Oh yeah. Too bad I didn't get it on film. I did get some good shots down there though. I'm pretty sure I even figured out which pier these guys took off from every morning."

"Why didn't you wanna go back and film everything again?"

"What do you mean?"

"Well Myles kinda made it sound like you bailed on him before it was all over."

"I wouldn't call it bailing after dealing with all of that would you? I still had to get back to my plans after the summer was over."

"Yeah, but you know how he can be."

"That I do."

"So did they get your money too? Or just the equipment?"

"They got everything except for a small camera and the thumb drives I had at the hostel."

"Even the laptop?"

"Yup. Even the laptop."

"Damn. You had that with you too?"

"Yeah. Fucking stupid. It's a shame too. I only got one good shot that morning. Damn lighting was terrible."

"That sucks. So what did you do after you ran?"

"I sent him what was left with some instructions and left."

"Where did you go?"

"I went up to Mexico City for a year and then hopped around the countryside for a while."

"Wasn't Mexico dangerous back then?"

"Yes and no. Depends where you went, but there weren't a lot of choices still left by the time I started looking unless I wanted to end up in the middle of nowhere. That's why I would tell you whatever you do next make sure you have your ducks in a row before you do it. Not preparing has fucked me a few times."

"Well I won't be doing anything that extreme."

"What kinda stuff were you thinking?"

"I don't know. I wanna spend a few months camping in the Rockies. Figured that would be a cool place to get my head straight. Just bike and hike while I've got the time."

"What's out there?"

"Nothing in particular. I just thought it would be a cool spot to do some research about which graduate program I'm gonna go and study. That and I just love fucking around in the woods. Figure might as well learn bout the parks while I do that. This Ken Burns documentary I watched got me really into it."

"Dude I saw part of that. When you plan on doing this?"

"Not sure yet. I can only find seasonal positions so far."

"As someone who did that. Whatever you do, set a date to check where you're at in your decision once you get out there. Crazy how a year or two can fly by."

"Oh I will man. I know how to keep an eye on myself."

"Alright good. So have you read up on your options for after working in the parks? Or tried to hit up any spots on the phone and see what they need?"

"Not really. Work has been too busy lately. I've had to put everything on hold for now, but I'm gonna try and get a few things in a row while we're down here. I brought my iPad with me and I got some stuff saved to look at."

"That's good. They got you running around a lot?"

"Non-stop dude. Gotta make the money while it's there."

After some more time talking I found myself drawn to a situation happening a few chairs down as I spotted a girl searching the pockets of her bag for a pen to finish a crossword puzzle sitting on her lap. Wes had mentioned that he was now single so I decided to try and play big brother for a moment.

"Wes, Why don't you go talk to that girl over here. She has no idea her pen fell underneath her chair. Give her this one."

He laughed at the suggestion while taking a first glance.

"Nah man, I'm gonna look like an idiot when she starts talking to me a mile a minute and all I can say back is 'Gracias'. But good choice. She's really cute."

"Come on man."

"Nah, you go do it. My Spanish won't last after hello."

As he took another look he tilted his head and let out a sigh.

"So is that a yes?"

"That's all you man."

Now truth be told. I had assumed he was gonna say yes. And I'm surprised he didn't because I remembered him as a guy with a fair amount of confidence and a track record of success to back it up. But I remember the days when a language barrier seemed like the ultimate barrier. And since that wasn't the case here, I went in her direction and tried to increase my odds with the approach of Spanish.

"You look like you're in need of one of these…"

As she looked up she hesitated a moment and then grabbed a blue .38 *Sarasa* pen from my hand and motioned for me to sit down.

"I'll tear out a few pages for you if you'd like to do some crossword puzzles." - Tall Latina

"No thanks. My brain is done for the day." - Patrick

"That's why you need a puzzle. You can unwind a bit."

"What are you unwinding from?"

"Nothing. I was just saying. I actually use these to help me with my English. They help my vocabulary so much."

"You know what else helps with that? Talking with a native speaker like me."

At her grin I was reminded how I had often thought if you're going to use language you might as well have fun with it. Which is why More often than not I found women to be the more conversationally compelling choice, perhaps it was because they always seemed to have longer attention spans. And enjoying them on all levels it was admittedly nice to add the element of flirtation into conversation, even if the end result was the exchange of a few witty sentences and an air of light playfulness from both parties. Something I had especially missed in Spanish as it was the means by which I had gained my confidence with the language as the years went on as well as my first real confidence with women after college. I was lucky to find early on that the direct nature of their language and overall colorful personalities had mad me easier to understand than Europeans who were often put off by my overly friendly nature. Through a few minutes of talking I found out she wasn't traveling on the same flight as us, but was using our terminal because it was the only one with a charging station open when she first walked by. After which I learned she was originally from Ecuador and was on her way down to Quito to visit her family as a part of delayed holiday celebrations. When our time with formalities had passed I said goodbye and went back to Wes who had been playing on his phone since I left.

"Guess it helps to know more than *Hola where's the cerveza...?* Was she nice?" -Wes

"It has its' advantages. And yeah. She was cool."

"I bet. So Myles said you got some girl meeting us down there. How you know her? She an old girlfriend or something?"

"Hell no. Just a friend I met when I started teaching. We've been talking about traveling together for a while so I figured it would be a fun to have her join us. Plus I kinda have her to thank for being able to take off so much time."

"How's that?"

"Her soon to be husband is basically my boss."

"Nice."

"Yeah. The perks of who you know."

"She meeting us at the airport tomorrow?"

"Nah. She's coming down sometime next week. Then she'll hang out for a few days and then head out when we do."

"Good deal."

As we continued talking Myles and Austin returned carrying a giant box of pizza which bent in the middle as the last two slices exercised their full leverage against the greasy cardboard. Austin was holding his belly with the other hand and extended the box in our direction to reveal what was left of the former deep dished Goliath.

"I'm good. Thanks though."

I wasn't one to normally turn down pizza, but I had already spent enough money and calories at the Duty Free shop to set me straight for the next fiscal year. Instead of sitting in chairs, the guys sprawled out on the floor and soon slipped into food comas which allowed Wes and I to get back to talking until lines of varying priority began forming around our gate. When we walked onto the plane I got myself situated as the guys stowed away their bags and put myself in the seat between Wes and Myles. Once comfortable I looked over to see Austin across the isle already slumping his head into a pillow formed out of a blanket provided by the airline for long trips. At my side Wes leaned over and whispered to me.

"Yo Pat. You gonna use your headphones?"

"Nah. There isn't shit to watch on here."

"Word. Mind if I use them. Mine are bluetooth. I can't hook them up to this fuckin screen."

"Yeah dude. They're in my bag."

"What you gonna watch?"

"I don't know. I just wanna get some noise to fall asleep to."

It didn't take long from there before the humming of the plane slipped me into a dreamless sleep as we rose into the cold night sky.

Day 2: Adjusted Arrival
Panama City, Panama

When I opened my eyes I found myself barricaded by slouching bodies on both sides as my phone remained wedged between my legs still playing a mix from last nights playlist. We had started to descend, but the natural aversion to being awake at 5 A.M. kept my friends and the majority of the cabin motionless long after my ears had started popping. As we drifted below the clouds I looked through the window and saw the Panamanian skyline blanketed in darkness. Unlike the United States where every floor of vacant office buildings remained illuminated throughout the night. In this city the skyscrapers served as dark silos taking up space without taking up sight. I would have appreciated a brighter approach since I wasn't able to get much of an idea of how the city looked beyond the dull spiderweb of lighting working its way away from the outline of an invisible coast.

Once we landed it took slightly over an hour before the boys were able to find their bags amongst the mess at the international baggage claim so I had plenty of time to stretch and get myself ready for the day. As I held my newly minted passport I thought of the exit stamp I neglected to get when I was in Panama many years before and I began to wonder to what extent their system kept up with things like that. Granted this was an entirely different passport, but this was the same me. Of course, regardless of how my passport looked I was bound to be approached with a series of questions to determine my business in their country.

"Now what do you have to declare?"

I wonder if they would have let me list my three friends. All of whom were being reintroduced to the feeling of sobriety while experiencing their first bout with culture shock and strangely worded signs. I made it through immigration and stood there pondering the reputation joining my friends as they presented themselves to the customs agents this morning. Anywhere close to home these guys may have had to be concerned about their reputation the moment they were spotted. As kids their notorious nature had been predominantly localized, but it had not been small. And as far as I knew two of them were still banned from *Universal Studios* which was a good three thousand miles from our hometown. Reputations have always intrigued me that way. They usually affect us to the extent that we stay within the circles who knew us first, but when we leave those circles we are no longer judged by the follies or successes of our youth. Instead we are judged through a filter of historical reference points the new world possesses about our people or some outwardly expressed feature which gives one's brain the ability to identify, label, and then move on. Simple as that. Whether it's a reputation portrayed or a reputation perceived, the two mean no harm. They're just there to help us go about our day faster. Here, we had reached the end of our spheres of recognition and regardless of who we were at home, we were about to be asked why we were there, what we planned to do, and to show that we could conduct ourselves during our visit. We didn't have a place to stay lined up so I made sure to have the guys memorize the name of a hotel downtown before they made it into line. Just in case they asked us for some details. And despite all of my thoughts on the matter, none of it really seemed to matter to the customs officials who hurried them through and stamped their passports welcoming the boys to PANAMA. Which was a cool addition they all readily showed off as they gathered their bags. My reaction was somewhat less enthused as my customs agent sifted through and tried to find an empty page, even seeming annoyed with me for not having the proper blank space for his stamp. He even took it upon himself to let me know his thoughts on the matter.

"Creo que es la hora por un nuevo pasaporte señor."

Since rerouting we needed new rental arrangements so we gathered our things and started moving with the signs directing us to transport and approached the first desk we saw with rental options. I found myself immediately at odds as the woman behind the counter pointed to a sign which informed us they opened at 7. A.M. I looked around and saw that we still had fifteen minutes until anyone was going to be able to help us. This part had always annoyed the hell out of me when I lived down here. Why would anyone not be open once everyone is at the desk? Sure, if you're not there you're not there, but who needs an early morning siesta? Perhaps being raised on the East Coast had instilled me with a different sense of urgency when it came to business, but these workers took relaxation to an entirely different level. When she eventually flipped the sign to *OPEN* we had our forms ready and handed her our information. Unfortunately this became the first time where my job as a translator was unpleasant due to the news which I had to convey.

"They want how much for a deposit?" - Myles

"$3,000. But most of that is refunded once we return car."

"Fuck that."

At this Wes butted in to persuade Myles to just eat the cost.

"I don't know why you're being like this. It's what you got that fancy fucking black card for anyway."

"There's no way I'm letting some tiny ass rental company outside of the country put a hold like that on my card. Fuck that."

"Then what's the point of having it?"

"It's for emergencies bro. Come on. We'll get a better deal."

This led to us checking out a few other rental booths while using Google to find out if we were being screwed or if this was official Panamanian policy for all car rentals as the first desk had tried to inform us. As it turned out there was nothing in the fine print or law about any specific amount so we moved along to the other windows to find a better deal. As this continued I started to see the cycles of frustration adding angst to Myles' mood as we were met with the repetition of one disappointing answer after another. I honestly felt a little embarrassed at this point because I had been enough places to have known better. But the few times I rented a car out of the states I never had any type of issue. I guess I shouldn't have assumed that same ease of transaction would be the policy of each country south of the border. Although we wanted an SUV we started to see that the prices and security deposits they wanted were going a bit beyond the realms of the reasonable. Myles had plenty of money with him and certainly had the credit to cover the cost, but he didn't want to be ripped off when that money could be used for something more exciting during our stay. By now he had found a counter where they spoke English and had opened up a new set of negotiations on his own.

"So why is it still gonna cost so much?" - Myles

"Well sir there's our daily rate plus international insurance."

"Yeah, but I already got this insurance voucher online."

"Yes sir I see that. But your voucher is not valid here. I'm sorry."

"Pat. What if we just Uber everywhere?"

"Dude this country is too long to scale in an Uber. If you wanna pay that we might as well start searching for flights to San Jose from here."

If I were here without three other grown men I would have already gotten out of the airport and be sitting down to a breakfast of eggs, scrambled and topped with hot sauce, but no, instead I continued to stand around waiting on decisions to be made. Which was fine, I knew he wouldn't waste too much time bargaining before giving in or hoping on a bus. My wait continued another ten minutes or so until he made a deal with *Express Car Rental* for $950, $300 of which we were told would be refunded once the car was returned.

"No Dude. We're getting a car and we're doing what we want to do." - Myles

"Alright, then pick one and let's get outta here."

"And they better give me my money back when I return that thing all bright and shiny in San Jose."

"Pardon me sir. But you will actually need to drop off the car at our closest location to the border in Chiriqui. From there you'll need to arrange for transport into Costa Rica on your own. We do not allow our cars to cross international borders." - Clerk

"What the fuck kinda system is this? You mean that $950 only covers a week?" - Myles

"I guess we can forget our Bungalows." - Austin

"We can bunk together if we need." - Wes

"Why you stressing about money? We both know that's not an issue." - Austin

"It's not. But I don't just give it away because someone thinks I'm an idiot. Plus I only brought a card with a few grand on it to keep me from going too crazy."

Myles ultimately had to compromise on a 4-door midsize car, but he said we would get an SUV once we made it to Costa Rica.

"So we just show them this piece of paper and we get our deposit back?" - Myles

"Si Señor."

"Okay guys, vamos. Pat, you got any friends we could stay with?

"Not with four fucking people I don't."

"I thought you knew a ton of people down here."

"Yeah, people, not hosts."

When we got outside we saw a few attendants wiping down a 4-door Hyundai as it idled in the nearest parking spot. It was not the SUV Myles had hoped for, but it still had room for all of our stuff and tinted windows to protect us from the sun which was sure to beat down our necks in the backseat. We approached the attendants and walked around the car to do a quick check of any previous damage, but the whole thing felt very informal. And when it was done I had no reason to believe he actually took note of all the dents we saw on the car, plus the vague grey color made a series of really tiny dings along the drivers door really hard to notice and overall the whole thing just didn't seem right. I mean, the guy didn't even have a clipboard. Once we had signed off I sighed at the thought of which bag was going to end up in the car with us, or how we were even going to manage to get all of our shit in this tiny trunk. A problem Myles managed to take into his own hands.

"Okay. Let's put all of the bags in the trunk, and we'll put the fishing equipment in the backseat with you guys."

It all fit pretty snugly once we managed to Tetris everything into the trunk, minus the *BAZOOKA* case which rode in between Austin and I. Myles decided to take the first swing at driving and used some pent up frustration to maneuver us out of the airport and onto the main highway towards the city center. I normally preferred to be in control of the driving part of my journeys, but Myles was one of the few people I trusted behind the wheel besides myself. He had always taken care his own car growing up, so he had a different knowledge of a vehicle and its capabilities. And I could tell he was less than pleased with how the trip had gone so far, so I figured why not let him take out his frustration on the early morning drivers instead those a bit closer to him.

On the outskirts of the city most buildings were no more than five stories high and the majority resembled a unique mix of Hispanic, Colonial, and Caribbean architecture. All painted with the same brightly shaded pastels which make up the local sea and wildlife floating throughout it. A true sign of a culture coming from mixed peoples of differing ambitions and histories. While zigzagging through the busy morning streets Myles came within inches of motorcycles a time or two, or perhaps they came within inches of us. It's hard to tell in a city that allows them to ride in-between traffic. As we pushed ourselves further from the airport and towards the city Myles drove without GPS and continued in the direction of a series of taller buildings a few miles away. As I looked around the car the guys didn't seem to be experiencing any culture shock for all I could tell. Nor were they put-off by their surroundings. Of course why should they be, it seemed like every mile or so we saw the American influence reanimated by the sight of a newly completed McDonalds or Burger King. It wasn't until we got away from the strip leading to the airport that we started to see street vendors and faded murals taking over the sidewalks on either side of us. Their tiny carts posted up against broken concrete walls and refurbished wooden pallets were the first of many sights which reminded me of the culture shock experienced on my first trip down. Years before I would have been unlikely to travel with these guys for such a long time to any location in the world. Not that they wouldn't have been fun, but I never liked the idea of being someones icebreaker to first time culture shock if it wasn't to my own culture. Luckily Wes had traveled to Eastern Europe and spent his fair share of time around the United States. And even though Austin had only made a one short trip to Canada, he seemed to be at ease in his new environment. As far as my own early exposure, I had culture coming at me in more ways than I can remember when I was younger. One summer in particular sticks out in my head as my family housed a set of Yugoslavian refugees awaiting approval for asylum.

Of all the guys Myles was the biggest wild card with regards to how he would handle his new surroundings. He was as indestructible as they came and operated with an unbearable amount of energy once he got drinking. Where some people may be summed up as coming off as cold, this man would often be described as coming in fiercely hot. I guess that's what you get for growing up in a family with three sisters and four big brothers. It was madness. I recall once walking into their house to borrow a snowboard and having my walk interrupted by one brother body slamming the other onto the ground from the bed oddly placed at my side. These were tough kids. Tough kids bred by patient people. But he was also a silent intellectual at times and was always curious to know about people and places so I figured this would be a good experience for him. He had been one of the only people I could expect to accept an invite on an impromptu trip at midnight when we were teenagers, so that was the type of balance I was working with.

In the back Austin and I observed an odd moment which made us laugh as the driver of a trash truck disposed of his morning coffee cup as he sat stalled at a stop light. It may have been one of the largest acts of exercised laziness I've ever seen. I mean, he didn't even try to toss it behind him and make it land in the back. As much as this confused me I was equally confused as we sped off from the light and the voice of a loud scream came from the front seat.

"HEY BABY NICE BUTT!" - Wes

I looked up front and saw Wes with his head hanging out of the window shouting at a near empty bus stop. At this moment I was glad for two things: first, he was yelling this at a man, and second, it's unlikely that his English was comprehended at such high speeds.

"Patrick, you paying attention? You're not saying anything about what to do." - Myles

"You took the wheel and told me to get in the back seat. I thought you knew where you were going."

"No motherfucker I need directions. That's what you're here for."

"Just keep driving towards those high rises."

"Well I'm wanna find some food. I ain't ate since America."

"Why don't you just stop at one of these street vendors we keep passing. There's food anywhere."

"We been on the road for seventeen hours bro. I'm getting us a real meal."

"I don't know how you're still alive. Wes. Can you see what they got around here?"

Wes got out his phone and opened up his maps to help us find our way as we weaved in and out of the traffic towards the center of the city. The architecture downtown had a surprisingly modern look, even a futuristic way of using glass, at least that was my first thought when I saw the Citibank building. It was a twisting kaleidoscope of large glass plates which left each higher level of offices overhanging outward more and more above a concrete abyss. Glad I wasn't a member of the scaffolding team.

While cruising along the waterfront Wes found *Restaurant Balboa* only a mile away so Myles pulled a U-turn and got us going in the right direction. After navigating the tightest parking garage I've ever encountered we found ourselves being seated in the middle of a Panamanian diner with the rest of the early morning breakfast crowd. Perhaps it was the pale skin of our group, or the fact that two of us were wearing camouflage, I really can't be certain, but the patrons of the restaurant took immediate notice to our presence as we were being seated. Once we were settled in I grabbed the attention of a waitress named Martina as she was passing through the tables. She was a short attractive women in her late forties with a calm smile and a face lightly tanned from a long coastal existence.

"Señora, Puedo un agua por favor?" - Patrick

"No Agua. We're getting coffee. You want it black or with *Lay Chay*?"

In his interruption Myles raised his eyebrows and let out a boyish smile as he showed off the one bit of Spanish he had acquired over the years. I humored him and just responded back.

"Leche." - Patrick

"Dos Por Fay Voor." - Myles

She came back in no time at all and placed a cup down in front of all four of us. Sitting here I thought what a shame it was. I had lived around some of the finer coffee farms in the world for years and still I couldn't identify anything about this coffee except for it being hot. At first sip it was better than any coffee I had consumed in weeks, but it was still just coffee to me. As we continued to sip Myles looked up at our waitress with another request.

"*Trays Lay Chays*, please."

"So that's how we're starting this morning? Dessert before breakfast?"

"I'm fucking starving. I'm eating everything. Order whatever you guys want. I got it."

"Oh now we're using the Amex?"

"Bruh. Don't start with me."

The menu was filled with pictures of delicious looking food and when I glanced at the tables around us it was hard not to find every dish I saw appealing. When Martina came back around I asked her for her recommendation between two dishes and went with her choice, chicken with fried plantains and some homemade bread. After we ordered Austin got up to go find the bathroom. As I watched him walking towards the back I took special note of the confused aim in his steps and saw his eyes darting for any sign as to where to go to next. He was experiencing something I had once dealt with. He must be thinking, *"Clearly the bathroom must be in one of these corners. That's where we keep them at home..."*

"Patrick. They have honey. Think we should offer some to that baby?" - Myles

"Fuck you dude." - Patrick

"What?" - Wes

"Oh ask him. He thinks you should feed honey to babies to see if they're fit enough to live." - Myles

"Oh here we fuckin' go. You know that's not what I said."

"No? When Austin gets back we'll ask him about the time you told my cousin we should help his newborn get over a cough by using some honey."

"That's not what the fuck I said. I said something about honey never hurting a sore throat. And it wasn't a newborn. She was a year and some change."

"Then I told you that it could kill them and *you* said to *give it a go.*"

"Those were not my words."

"Lets just wait and ask Austin what he remembers."

"You're annoying. How's your fucking cake?"

"Delicious bro. You gotta try some."

During this exchange Martina had come by to refill our coffees and dropped off Myles's tres leches as Austin found his way back to his seat. Being the annoying, but generous person Myles could sometimes be he offered us each a bite and instantly instilled a feeling of jealousy for the delicious taste he was going to get to enjoy on repeat. It was rich and fluffy with just the right amount of sweetness for this time of the morning.

"Dude. Lemme get another bite..." - Austin

Austin reached out with his fork towards Myles plate and was deflected by a countering fork from a combination of quick reflexes and the hungry belly of Myles.

"No. Just order another one if you want it. I'll pay for it."

At this time Martina came by to ask us how everything was and I took that opportunity to ask her a few questions I had regarding what to do in the area. She told me that she was from a few hours away but that she had lived in the area long enough to know some great local spots to spend our day. In answering she directed us to Playa Peligrada, a spot she said was less than an hour from the city with beautiful beaches and very few tourists. Once we finished our meal, we thanked her for such great service and all of her suggestions. After leaving our tip we started to walk away when she stopped us to hand over a business card with her phone number and a kind invitation.

"If you and your friends need anything or have any questions while in the city you're welcome to give me a call."

I didn't get the vibe that she was flirting with any of us, but unless she was the city hospitality director, she did express more than the usual amount of friendliness in her goodbye. I'm pretty sure she dug Austin's look.

"Dude we should totally call her. I bet she has some cute cousins she can hook us up with." - Myles

"If you want the number it's all yours. Otherwise I'll hold onto it in case we get into a bind."

As we left Myles took the chance to hand over the driving in my direction and with the help of Wes I navigated us out of downtown and towards Playa Peligrada. As we reached the outskirts of the city we got our first all encompassing view of Panama City in the daylight. In front of us a backdrop of white sky-rises and lightly clouded skies met a bay riddled throughout by small fishing boats and barges, each overcrowded with pelicans greedily lurking to steal the days catch without the days effort. At the sight Myles urged me to pull over for some photos and directed me through a small parking lot to our right. Unfortunately there were no spots open so I dropped them off and then looped around the lot a few times while they got their snapshots. When the boys finished they got back in and we continued our drive up the shore. As we drove the roads became increasingly rural with no lanes for passing, but no traffic to worry about passing. It's amazing how quickly the transition takes place from city to country when the separating barrier is tropic growth. But one transition I was not enjoying was the speed limit. Not the speed, but the process. I love to drive. Always have and always will, but having to convert KPH to MPH while driving was the most annoying thing I've dealt with in a long time. I know it shouldn't be a big deal, but it was. And since I wasn't listed as a driver the last thing I needed was to get pulled over for misreading my velocity. Especially since a traffic stop was the only type of trouble we couldn't run from once it started. Any other situation would allow for the option to escape, but that one always fucked you. Which I wouldn't let happen otherwise. And I had made sure to tell them that before we left as to not need to explain myself if I started to walk away at some point. Not because I was afraid of trouble the way I had been when I was a teacher, I just didn't want the hassle anymore. Whether you had to bribe it out or go down to the station it was always a hassle and I didn't want something like that to interrupt our time. And I knew that no amount of trouble was ever made easier by having more people involved.

Playa Peligrada didn't feel like an hour away, perhaps it was the great scenery that stole the feeling of time from my journey, but I swore it was only fifteen minutes more once we left the city limits. Along the way we saw a series of inlets which invoked Austin to keep complaining that we were not stopping at all of the possible fishing spots.

"Dude, I'd have a prize winning trout by now if you'd just fucking stop at one of these spots we keep passing." - Austin

I ignored his jabs until we got our first glimpse of a large stretch of sand with an inlet and a small parking lot for beachgoers. As I was slowing down to pull in a voice interrupted from the backseat.

"Keep going. Let's see what else is ahead." - Myles

"Come the fuck on man." - Austin

"Chill dude! We got all day. I just wanna check the place out a bit more."

I'd been to enough places to know what else we were going to see, but I had promised myself that I wasn't going to be the blockade of fun if the guys wanted to do something that caught their attention. Even though I knew there wasn't likely to be a more secluded beach ahead, I figured why not adhere to their wishes. Plus I had seen a sign which translated to *Dead End 10KM*, so I knew we wouldn't have to go much further before turning around. We continued to drive until we came upon a small town no larger than two city blocks. Driving through the town I saw something which had become familiar over the years as we passed along an area existing happily in a state of destitution made bearable by a continuously warm climate and festive music. To our left children were running along the sides of a few scattered homes and a group of stray dogs laid quietly on the half broken slabs of concrete which bordered the properties. Along the front of most homes was some sort of small level farming to help sustain the residents, but it was one type of small level farming in particular which struck my friends fancy.

"Oh shit dude did you see that back there?" - Austin

"No what was it?" - Patrick

"That guy had a whole garden of weed growing next to his tomatoes. Badass"

I wasn't exactly thrilled he had noticed his surroundings because I knew his thoughts combined with his observations were leading him to believe that this was the norm for the country we were in. And that's part of the misperception that a lot of people, including myself, had about traveling outside of the United States, that certain laws just don't apply once you're in a poor area. But truth be told, it's often some of the more impoverished areas with the strongest laws against the leisures we associate them with. Not to say they met those same standards when it came to enforcement, but the selective nature of the law was the very thing which concerned me. As the road came to an end we approached a roundabout where a large farm overflowing with freshly trimmed crops was surrounded by a combination of palm trees and short barbed wire fencing. I slowly made my way through the circle and let out a big sigh. It's not like I didn't know I would be asking strangers for sketchy things as we went along, but I was hoping that my icebreaker could happen in some dark city alley, not in the middle of a dealers farm. That being said, when Myles asked me to slow down, I let the car come to a halt and prepared to roll down my window.

"I didn't know this stuff was legal here." - Austin

"It's not. It's pretty grey." - Patrick

"This neighborhood doesn't seem to care much. Pull over and let's ask that guy how much he wants for a couple of bags." - Myles

"Let's just wait til we're in town."

"Why would we do that when it's right in front of us? Let's just ask and see what they say."

We stopped the car next to a fence where a man was using a machete to hack at some plants which he then placed into a satchel hanging from his side.

"Hey man. Any of that for sale?"

He looked at me a moment and started whistling across the street until a man standing around five-foot-five with dark tan skin, no shirt, ripped shorts, a brown bag, and a large machete ducked under the fence and approached the right side of our car. I motioned for him to come around to my side and we got introduced. It's probably best not to know your drug dealers names, but I wanted to appear friendly.

"Hola, cómo te llamas?" - Patrick

"Exxon."

"Exxon?"

"Si."

In my voice there was a sense of hesitation in search of confirmation as he nodded his head at my second attempt of his name and went on to inform me they didn't hold any packages for sale at the farm. However, we were welcomed to go to a house up the road if we wanted him to show us. This had seemed like a much better idea when I was asking a guy to grab me something out of his bag real quick. But once I realized they were gonna have to leave I got a little uneasy. I wasn't about the leave the car there and I couldn't let the guys go off alone so I directed Exxon to get in the back of our car and told him we could drive him to the house he mentioned. My friends looked confused as the shirtless man entered our car without removing his rusty machete and scooted in next to Wes.

"Dude? Uh what the fuck?" - Austin

"You wanted the goods. This is how we get it."

As we got closer to the same town as before I attempted to feign conversation with Exxon and tried to gain some knowledge about the surrounding area, but his slang and the noise from four open windows made it difficult to get much across. He seemed pretty friendly, but the only thing I really understood is that he liked my friends fishing gear. As we approached a cluster of houses he told me to pull off to the left and I parked at his direction in front of a local bus stop. By now it was the middle of the day and there were five women at the bus stop which sat next to a market where a truck was unloading a delivery under the supervision of a man in a military uniform and two store clerks. Wonderful. And behind us was a tiny market with a policeman standing at the door. And then this shirtless little man got out of our car with Myles and they stood in the open doing a cash exchange as I tried to barter the deal without leaving the car. Needless to say I was not a fan of the overall lack of discretion exercised. And while I normally practiced discretion on the go I instead found myself in the middle of some town I shouldn't be in, accompanying locals on errands for illegal favors in broad daylight. And if we were on the other end, it's unlikely to imagine we would be as welcoming to such requests. Nevertheless, there we were.

Exxon ran off and we sat in the car for the next few minutes until he returned and handed us a tiny bag tightly filled with dried up weed. All of which came to a total of $10. I guess for what you deal with in stress you make up for in price. After receiving such a good deal I decided to ask Exxon his thoughts on the area since he seemed more than comfortable to continue standing outside of the car as he got back.

"Hey man, do we need to worry about the police here?"

Laughing at my question he responded.

"No señor, no problemos."

"Patrick, what about the good stuff?" - Myles

"Well you didn't ask me about anything else so neither did I."

"What the fuck man. You know we want some cocaine if they got any. Ask him how much it is."

I had chosen to assume they only wanted to get one kind of high at a time. I had been hopeful. I had not been realistic. I turned to Exxon to thank him and then asked if he could help us some more.

"Hey man you know anyone with some cocaine?"

To no surprise he responded in the affirmative and took a $20 from my hand before running back across the street where he entered the side door of a tiny house after two short knocks. Two-minutes later he returned empty handed and explained that the man who usually supplies him with the cocaine was not around, but said we could come back later if we wanted. I was only half disappointed at this. It just meant that I shall have to ask yet another stranger at another time. But it also meant we were done. Which was good, because we had sat for too long and I could feel the eyes of authority resting on our car from across the street. For that matter I could feel the eyes of everyone around us. Have you ever just zoomed out from your life to look at it from above? As I did this to myself I was not happy with the bird's eye view I was a part of now matter how far out I zoomed. Glancing around my first concern was who was taking more notice, the Army or the police. Sure the women at the bus stop weren't dumb, but they weren't my concern, we'll just serve as some good town gossip for them later. Luckily we were done.

When we arrived back at the farm the setting was the same as before, but this time there were three additional guys chopping away out front. Looping around the road I saw Myles' hand go up with his phone firmly grasped.

"What are you doing?" - Patrick

"Dude this is so cool, I wanna get a shot of this. Put it in the sequel."

"Please don't start snapping photos until this guy is out of the car. After that you can do what you want, don't need his little ass getting paranoid."

"Dude you worry too much."

Exxon got out and went back to his job as we too returned to our original task of finding a beach suitable for fishing. When we got back to the inlet I found a spot amongst the gravel pull off and parked our car away from the others. As the guys got out they opened the trunk and got their beach supplies ready while beginning to change into their swimsuits. Ahead of us was a 100 meter walk or more from where the sand started to water the water washed up. Off the shore was large rock formation probably another 300 yards away with a few plants growing on top. Next to me Myles changed into his bright red speedo, a prop he had brought in order to peacock his way through the beach. He did not need the assistance of a bright red bathing suit, he was already a noticeable contrast to the people around him. His shiny white skin matched that of the sand he walked on and his six-foot figure was greater than most of those around us. Before he left for the beach he looked over at me and calmly said,

"Thanks for coming man. We're gonna have a good time."

"You're welcome man. Glad to be here."

Standing there I looked on as exotic birds of bright colors flew over me and a warm breeze came in from the shore forcing a smile upon my squinting face. The sky was so bright that even my aviators were no match. Something Austin seemed to notice even before I did.

"You need some *Costas* bro." - Austin

"What?"

"Fishing glasses bro, those are classy looking, but you need these."

Austin took off his glasses and tossed them in my direction. I reacted fast enough to catch them as they hit my chest and switched them out with mine to test out their quality. His assertion was correct, they may be the best sunglasses I've ever tried on, but I've never been a fan of thick rimmed tan lines like these would have given me if I kept them on all afternoon. After trying them on I tossed them back in his direction and told him he was right.

"Fuck yes. Found it!" - Austin

"What you got?"

"Fuck, never mind. Well. This will have to do for now."

"What you looking for?"

"I was searching for some dip, but it must be in Myles' bag. I'm just gonna make myself a smoke with this tobacco we got. And while I'm at it, might as well add a bit of our new friends flowers."

He sat down and started to combine the steps needed to make himself a hand rolled cigarette and brushed aside some of the tobacco to make room for his new purchase. I wasn't one to ever keep a pack on me, but I had come to appreciate a cigarette made from the efforts of a skilled roller, which of course Austin was. Knowing that I decided to ask him to make me my own to pull on throughout the day. After which he offered up his recently finished project, a blend of weed and ground up tobacco.

"No man. I'm good."

"What's wrong man? Thought you wanted to smoke?"

"Nah. I still gotta drive us into the city and fucking figure out where we're staying. So for now just make me one with all of that tobacco you're wasting."

"Okay. Gimme a minute to finish these."

Austin continued dispersing his new supply amongst a series of pre-rolled joints and then used all of his discarded tobacco to roll me a large cigarette. Larger than I needed, but it would serve the purpose of extending the life of an outdoor conversation at some point in my journey and I was all about that. I put it in my pocket and grabbed one of the hammocks and started walking towards a favorably separated set of palms off to the left of our car. I am more than happy to have been given such a great gift, but I don't actually have a clue what I am doing as I start hanging up this modern contraption. I know they're supposed to be more resistant to water than cloth but in my ideal world, this hammock would only have two ropes at the end of it. I tie those ropes to a tree, hammock complete, but this thing had cranks and adjustments and just annoyed the shit out of me. The only thing that really resembled a hammock was its general shape once elongated. Which in the end served its purpose, but some things don't require changing.

Between these two trees I found perfect shade and started to enjoy my relaxation, but once the wind blew I discovered why no one had put a hammock between these two perfectly placed trees. The smell which began to engulf me was awful. It was as if all of the winds had drifted from a landfill and right into my nose. Luckily the smell was as temporary as the breeze so I dealt with it for a few more moments until it went away. After lying there about twenty minutes I saw Myles making his way towards my hammock.

"Do you need some water?" - Myles

"Nah I'm good."

"Yo. What the fuck is that smell?"

"Not sure. I am downwind from something bad."

Myles laughed at me and moved himself over to my legs where he started to undo my hammock cranks.

"Dude get up, let's unhook this and get you moved. You can't stay here."

I got up and Myles started to detach the hammock as I followed his lead and began tearing it down from the other palm tree. There weren't many spots left by now that didn't include two to three people lounging around so we had to walk a bit further down the beach to find an opening. Once we found one we put the hammock up and had Myles test out the strength of it by showing me how these new hammocks could be bounced on a bit. As we stood next to my new spot a man came through peddling a bike with a tiny trailer attached to the back. On the trailer was a cardboard stand holding up a selection of sunglasses he had for sale. He seemed to be a common seller of sunglasses, but this didn't look like the spot for someone to find many buyers. The beach may have had a few people, but it looked like the last place to find tourists. As he made another go around he stopped to speak to us and attempted a sale. We were quick to tell him that we weren't in need, but he still seemed curious to ask us about our vacation and how we liked the area. He spent the next few minutes engaging Myles and inquiring about his fishing gear. A thing Myles was happy to brag about.

I decided to take a moment by the water and abandoned my hammock as Myles went off to meet the guys. As I left the shade I felt the sun resting on my freckled shoulders which had now been exposed to the unforgiving rays of the equator long enough to blend freckles and skin into one. A few more cars arrived as I was en route to a far off part of the beach so I glanced back and took a look at my hammock blowing between the two trees wondering briefly if I should move my things. Though my experience had taught me there was nothing to be concerned about so I moved along and explored some further ends of the beach as the guys had their fun attempting to fish. Soon I came upon a few kids kicking a soccer ball around as their father attempted to keep it from going into the water. The father had a skinny figure which barely filled his white muscle-tee. Just up from the kids their mother was tossing a stick back and forth with a dog who looked about a generation or two away from purebred. Which was usually the closest you would get down there as people did not tend to have large or boutique dogs. For that matter no one really *owns* the dogs down here. They just operate in the city and don't bother anyone. They generally wind up living unchained lives of exploring shorelines and storefronts while attracting enough attention from tourists here and there for a cycle of daily snacks. The skinny figure made his way over to me to say hello and asked what my friends were attempting to fish for. I told him I wasn't certain, but that I hoped they had some luck. To which he replied, "Oh there's plenty of fish here. But this time of day is not so good." - Local

"And what time of day is best to fish here?" - Patrick

"Maybe around seven."

I loved my friends, but I had no intention of staying at this beach until after sunset tonight as his information suggested. If we did that we would never find a place to take us by the hour we would get back. After our talk I figured it was time to get up to my hammock and finally rest for a bit, but once I got situated I figured I needed to be listening to something worthwhile as I dozed off. I remembered that I had a few audiobooks downloaded for the trip so I placed my headphones in my ears while I scrolled through the possible listening options. I didn't know whether to chill or to get lost in a story, but either way I was going to take my mind elsewhere. But before drowning out my surroundings, my ears honed in upon layers of evolved mechanics to pick up something which struck a chord deep in my senses. As my brain started to process the far off words I looked around to attach sound and sight and saw a man a few feet to my left leaning up against a palm tree talking on the phone. I thought for a second I had heard wrong, after all, my Spanish wasn't perfect, but further listening confirmed for me that the topic of his discussion was me and my friends. All at once the hair on my arms stood at attention as I heard a new series of confirmation.

"Si, se fueron en el carro con Exxon….Si…coche gris."

I don't know how astute you are with newer languages, but he said, *Yes, they went in the car with Exxon. Yes, the grey one.* My mind quickly eradicated all thoughts of musical distractions as I began to nervously wonder what reason this stranger could have to be talking about us so many miles from where we had picked up Exxon. We hadn't wronged anyone, we had only served as fuel for the local economy. My first instinct was that perhaps he had taken notice of the fishing equipment and thought we had more money than we really did. Or perhaps he was just here to investigate the brash natured men who felt it normal to ride up on a field of drugs and knock on the door. Perhaps somehow dots from years ago had just been connected, but that seemed far less likely than something regarding today.

With my aviators placed on my head I feigned a stretch and glanced to the left to capture a better look at the voice discussing me and my friends. He was slightly taller than me, about six-foot, with darkly tanned skin, buzzed black hair, and wearing an orange shirt with black board shorts. His outfit did not indicate any authoritative nature to his job, but his toned frame reminded me of the soldiers I had seen in town. His muscular build was one from a body sculpted for a purpose, not the act of a normal man, more one of a man on duty. He closed his flip phone and continued to lean on the tree behind him. Now that I took notice of him, he had a suspiciously casual nature to him. Nothing about him said beachgoer except his brightly colored shorts which could have been nothing more than mere props in his uniformed facade. Over the next few moments he kept his attention on the entrance to the inlet where a red car with blacked-out windows was parked. Using the advantage of my sunglasses I tried to get a look at what was going on inside of the car. And though I couldn't be certain, it looked like a guy in the front seat took a picture of our license plate. Which made me even more alarmed than I already was. For a moment I debated bringing my friends in on the situation, but I figured it was ultimately best not to direct their awareness towards trouble until I had an idea of what was really going on. These guys could do enough on their own to bring it in their direction and if the police came they wouldn't be able to understand each other anyway. So let's move forward. I sat there staring at the water a bit as a million thoughts flooded my mind. I hadn't felt that nervous in a long time. More importantly, I hadn't felt a reason to feel that nervous in a while. The irony and annoyance within me grew as I realized this was unfolding in the same country where I had once narrowly avoided arrest under similar circumstances. But this time I would need to assure the safety of three others in any escape. In my moment enslaved by my concerns I neglected to notice Austin coming up behind me.

"Patrick, what the fuck are you doing? You set up the hammock and here you are just standing around."

"Yeah man, I'm good. Just trying not to doze off."

"Do you see that?"

"See what?"

With that Austin pointed to a guy unloading a few buckets from the trunk of a Toyota 4Runner while his friends stood attempting to start a fire in an old trash bin which had been burnt to hell over the years.

"I bet they know something about the fish here. Let's go talk to them."

I was in the mood to do anything that involved getting my head out of the situation I had imagined for myself so I walked with him away from our unknown observer. Who did not follow, but whose attention I never lost. As we approached the 4Runner Austin opened up with a bit of English to break the ice.

"Dude I love how the back window goes down in this thing."

With a puzzled face a tall black man with dreads looked over at us to acknowledge the sounds coming out of his mouth, but he clearly had no understanding so I relayed the message to the driver who responded with a thumbs up in Austin's direction. I attempted to introduce the group to my buddy, but the communication barrier was insurmountable beyond a friendly greeting. False. Communication is always possible, but verbal exchange was not. Despite the lack of words exchanged, the guys were able to take the hint that Austin wanted some food when they saw him eyeing a big bag of oranges they had sitting on top of their roof. They pulled the bag down and offered us as many as we could want. I think it was Bourdain who once said if a local offers you the local, you accept it. And I had lived off of trusting the locals for years, so why stop now? By now Myles and Wes had noticed what was happening and were making their way to enjoy the spoils of diplomacy.

Safety in numbers appealed to me and these guys looked like a group who didn't want trouble with the police either so I figured they would be best suited by our side. Plus, by this time, our little red car from earlier had made several passes and I was beginning to worry my instincts were accurate, but was it instincts or was it an understanding of history? The rest of my group was blissfully unconcerned, absorbing the Reggae and enjoying their citrus treats as we hung out for a while and engaged with our new friends. Austin eventually approached me with his same offer from earlier as he extended me a half-finished joint.

"Do you want a hit?" - Austin

"No. Gracias."

"Why the hell not? We got all the time to relax if we want. And these guys are fucking cool bruh."

"Sorry man. I don't need any more paranoia in my life right now."

"Paranoid? Jeez bro. Maybe I gave you the wrong cigarette already…"

He was right. I could use the relaxation, but I needed to stay alert until I understood more about the unknown inquiries happening around me. Though as I gave my surroundings a look around I could no longer see the man in the orange shirt. Austin sat down on the opened bed of the SUV and brought out a bag of dip, known to some as chewing tobacco, although the two have some clear differences. Upon seeing the strange can the driver of the SUV crouched in his direction and asked me what my friend had.

"Qué es esto?"

"Uh, it's tobacco. Like for your mouth. Well your gums really."

What puzzled the man off the bat was the packaging of my friends tobacco. See back where we're from chewing tobacco is usually consumed via cans of snuff much the size of a drink coaster that we refer to as dip. As I stood there I watched on at one of the more primitive exchanges I had ever seen between two grown men. Without exchanging any words Austin stayed on the ground and opened the can extending it towards the man who was now crouching down to get a smell of the fine black strands halfway gone from a morning of heavy dipping. He peered at the contents of the can and took a waft before pinching off a bit from the top. As I saw him open his mouth I remembered the mistakes of first time users and interrupted him to give a few warnings.

"Hey buddy, make sure you keep spitting. If you swallow that you're going to hate yourself."

He nodded his head yet still looked confused at how he was supposed to ingest the new strange substance. "Here," I took a small pinch and directed it towards the gap between my lip and my bottom teeth, "like this, and then just treat it like a mint". He mimicked my steps and became a portrait of conflicting faces as the tobacco hit his lips and caused his mouth to water while a slight buzz took over his body. He relieved himself by spitting in an amateur fashion and lost half of the dip as he did so. His friends laughed at him and patted him on the back and Myles chimed in, "You got it bro. Now just keep it under your lip until you don't feel it no more". Luckily around this time Austin looked at me and rubbed his stomach mouthing the words, *Lets get the fuck out of here.*" I didn't need much more of a message than that. If the main fisher wanted to leave I'm sure the heat absorbed thus far would convince the others to vacate the beach and head back to the city sooner, leaving our problems and our cultural sins behind us. A goodbye came naturally as Austin started walking toward the car, taking the guys fishing gear along which motivated the others to help him and caused a series of goodbyes to start.

Once the car was packed we all piled in and drove towards the city. I made sure my rear view mirror stayed clear and I broke the silence with the local radio as we cruised along the shore. The songs were light and familiar, reminding me of years before when I was the lost gringo fumbling my way through ordering at a local bar as loud music crowded my ears. For my counterparts of this story, the music playing behind us would not speak to memories, but maybe it would be the start to some understanding. To be honest that's all I did when I started learning Spanish. And it was probably the undertones of latin music while studying which helped me really get a grip on it. At the time I had assumed I was only distracting my brain from following the lyrics, but I guess the whole time it was learning to separate the sounds. Which soon led to a mild understanding of Spanish that was reinvigorated once I took my life abroad. And with that learning came change. Change not just of how I spoke, but of how I saw myself. It was the first time I took the intellect of my English and attempted to add emotion to it. Emotion that the Spanish language had helped me find.

As we neared the highway we saw a sign for the Panama Canal which sparked us to take a left turn in the direction of Mira Flores, the main lochs to the canal. It was almost 5 P.M. and by the time we made it to the main turn off we saw a few cars turning around who stopped us to warn that it had been closed for the day.

"Fuck, I really wanted to see that. Someone in my family was supposedly on the engineering team. Do you think we can make it back tomorrow?" - Wes

"I don't make the decisions here. If you all want to go back I'm down."

"Yeah man, we'll make it there on our way out tomorrow."

"That'd be cool, I wanna see his name on the roster."

"How closely related?"

"Like a great-great-grandfather I think. He was part of the team that rebuilt Richmond after the civil-war. From there he got hired to come down to the canal as support with all of Teddy's guys."

"No shit?"

"Yeah. Bout the only good thing any of my ancestors ever done."

"That is pretty cool. But for now we gotta find a place to stay. I was thinking we get a hostel in the middle of downtown for the night."

At this Austin interjected with some vague hesitation.

"Uh a hostel dude? I don't wanna share a room with a bunch of strangers. Not tonight."

"Stop your worrying man. They're not all like that. We'll find somewhere with private rooms. I saw a bunch of them around the historical side of the city. Just search for anything close to Casco Viejo."

Listening to Austin as he continued, it was hard to think back to a time when my mind possessed the same thoughts and fears about my sleeping arrangements as he was having. As it was far easier to recall the catalogue of good times I had experienced after learning that the stereotype of the dirty dangerous hostel was far from reality. At times even being astonished by the conditions I was able to find for pennies on the dollar. Though in fairness, some hostels were exactly what you expected, minus the murder.

They wanted a spot to party for the night so we found a hostel with a courtyard bar and basement with a dance floor. It looked like the fun place to be by the photos so Wes guided me through the traffic and we wound up at the entrance to Casco Viejo. We took a right and were met with a series of cobblestone streets which took us up to a busy plaza centered around bleach white monuments and bolted down iron benches. Behind the plaza the streets were lined by a combination of tiny apartments decorated in faded pastels and interlocked with half-finished concrete buildings, most with ground level stores or restaurants hidden amongst the chaos. Though even the chaos was brightly colored.

I let the guys out and prepared to park until they called to inform me that they were walking to another place because our first choice was all booked up. When they got to our second choice of the *Hostel Magnolia* they were told there was room enough in a twin bedroom if we were willing to bunk together, but otherwise they were full. It seemed like our best option so we went with it. I was fine with this since we did not plan to stay in the city for long, and we could do well with a place to rest and map out our journey for the next day. The guys already seemed more comfortable than I imagined they would be, which was good because I don't think they realized that they were part of much more today than was apparent.

Myles got us a ground level room with a window giving us sidewalk level views and a three story hike to the rooftop terrace. While Wes and Austin went to wash up I grabbed Myles and told him we should go check out some of the spots in the area to get an idea of what was around for us to do. We left and started walking towards a plaza around four blocks away. From our convening street we were greeted by tall pillars outlining a white marble plaza illuminated with white Christmas lights and clusters of beautiful native flowers. The north end of the plaza was taken up by an upscale hotel made from a Colonial-era complex painted in a coat of light blue and offering a few parking spots nestled among a row of green hedges and a small fountain out front. At the other end was a small stone church with a white rod iron gate and narrow candlelit windows outlined in mosaic portrayals of the Virgin Mary. Covering the other two sides of the street were a series of restaurants and a few shops with some apartments above. As we approached the corner one restaurant in particular caught our eye. One where we could hear loud music surging from a basement dance floor and one where they ushered you towards their door with three gorgeous hostesses standing in a row of matching black skirts and slim fitting red blouses, each covered at the shoulder by a wave of long black hair. Visual marketing at its best.

"Oh yeah, we'll definitely be able to find what we want somewhere like that." - Myles

"Got a hankering for some Panamanian beer?"

"Don't be stupid bro. I'm talking cocaine. We still gotta find some before we go out. Then I wanna hit up a club."

I understood wanting to get loose, but unlike him it was the energy in the city itself which would get me going. As I stood there and hesitated a moment he looked at me and read my face for what it said.

"Why are you so against having fun?" - Myles

"I know as well as anyone what it's like to have too good of a time. I'm sorry you weren't there."

"Oh yeah. You're only fun with *other* people."

"Would you stop. You've seen me do more crazy things than anyone else."

"I can't recall a one."

"You and that memory. You're something else."

"Maybe I am, but do you remember what you said to me when we first talked about doing that documentary and you said you'd do it with me."

"I also said that was predicated on you going a week without smoking. So don't try to bring up some of my words unless you wanna remember the whole conversation. And look, I'll help you get anything you want tonight, but I'm taking it easy for now."

"Yeah. Remember you also said you knew what you were doing. Still waiting to see that one work itself out."

"Whatever."

"You're going to stay sober this whole time aren't you?"

"I'll get drunk with ya once we get up to the mountains or something. But for now I'm here to help get us around."

"Whatever man."

As we walked in Myles directed us to a seat in the back by the AC where we could sit with a facing view of the restaurant entrance. Once we wedged ourselves inside the booth he spun the menu with a page facing open to a long list of beers in my direction. On it I saw a narrow list of the local beers with absurdly low prices lining the page and an asterisk which directed me towards a series of coolers against the wall.

"Well at least have a beer with me." - Myles

"Alright. Lemme check what they got in the cooler."

From there I got up and went to the beer cooler at the edge of the bar and opened a glass door which hid eight shelves of beer each ten bottles across. Their selection was impressive, a ton of European imports, most of which I didn't recognize until a *Leffe* caught my eye. It was a blonde like the one from Antwerp which had stuck in my memory bank as one of the only beers I can ever recall enjoying. I decided to go with it, provided that it was cold, so I grabbed it and was pleased to feel a numbing chill which prompted me to take it out of the fridge. As I grab the bottle it struck me that there must have been a day when you couldn't get the best Belgian beers in Panama. How small has the world gotten when even hops have the ability to cross oceans on a daily basis? We sat there and toasted to finally making our way down there as our waitress Veronica approached us asking if we needed to order any food. Myles shook his head no and then gave me a look.

"We're good on food, but do you know anyone that could help us find some stuff to party tonight?" - Patrick

Veronica looked at us and put on a smile while she held up a finger indicating we would need to wait a moment.

"How much would you like?"

"El Gramo."

" Okay. Un momento."

We waited the next few minutes until she came back from a   series of text messages and requested a $20 bill which Myles happily placed in her hand. From there she left our table and walked out the door and passed by the window before disappearing around the corner to the far side of the restaurant.

"I bet she's meeting one of the cooks and making it look like an outside deal." - Patrick

"I'll get back in that kitchen if I have to."

"Just calm yourself. She'll be back. While she's gone catch me up on things. How's the business and everything going back home?"

"Things are a lot smoother than they used to be."

"You finally trust someone to handle things while you're gone?"

"Yeah. I got an international plan in case he fucks things up though."

"Still trying to grow?"

"Nah. Got too much going on. I can barely keep up."

"Guess that's a good problem to have."

"It has its ups and downs. Need more than this vacation to make up for all of the time I've been giving away to keep things goin."

As the waitress returned she broke between us and placed a black book on the table which we opened to find a tiny baggy, plastic wrapped, and containing a white powder. Myles looked at her with a big smile and dropped another $20 in the checkbook to pay for our drinks as he removed the baggy.

"Alright Pattyboy. Let's go to the bathroom. I wanna make sure they didn't stiff us."

"Dude. Let's just wait until we get back."

"Fuck that. I'm going to the bathroom."

I don't know why I thought my presence would make any difference, but I followed him into the bathroom and stood at the counter as he set up his first line hoping to block the view of any onlooker who may wonder inside. He inhaled his first sample and then laid out another smaller one while gesturing for me to take my turn.

"Come on man. It's barely even half what I did. You're not gonna have a heart attack or nothing." - Myles

"Shut up. I ain't worried about that."

"Then stop delaying man. Just take a bump and we can go."

I stood there with a strange internal predicament at the conflict of promises happening within me as a result of the moment which I had somehow arrived. I had told myself that I was done fucking around after the documentary was over. And until now I had only found myself wanting to backtrack on that promise once before in another tropical bathroom. An odd coincidence I know, but that's not the point right now. The point is, he was right. I had said that it all stayed here. And I had not put a timeline on that statement. And with that I bent down and took in a deep breath inhaling the tiny grains laid out in front of me. Once it was over I reached down and put the rest on my fingertips and rubbed the remaining bits onto my gums.

From there most of my mouth became numb and I stood for a moment as it made its way through my body. With that this anxious tingling took over my fingertips and I wondered if this was how it felt when Popeye gulped down his spinach. And if so I get why he wanted an entire can. As years before I was reminded what it meant to get your money's worth and from the look on his face I could tell Myles was equally pleased. As he bent down for another line I stuck my face in the sink and splashed a bit of water on my forehead to help regain my senses. With cold water trickling down my cheeks my brain became reignited with images of road blocks on the Panamanian border, boats departing in the morning fog, and a skinny man with a brown paper bag swaying back and forth on some forgotten corner of an islanders paradise. I didn't feel bad about doing it. Not now and not the few times between then and now. I had been happy enough with myself to wait til I got out of college to fuck with anything that I though could actually put me out of commission for a few days. And I knew this wasn't one of those drugs. This at worst was going to check me out for the next hour. And check-out wasn't really an accurate way to see it. I would probably be more honed in than usual. Jittery, but honed in if I could shut down that side of my brain that dealt with shame. I even knew it was cool to like drugs, all of my heroes did drugs, from Steve Jobs to Artie Lange, but for whatever reason I had always had an unusual aversion to getting fucked up.

"You want another?" - Myles

At his question I let out a sniffle and tilted my head back to regain a sense of control. Not just of my sinuses, but of our night.

"Nah I'm good man. Let's get out of here."

"You sure?"

"Yeah man. Let's roll."

"Alright then. Your loss. Let me get one more."

While I waited for him to finish up I stood there and felt the same tightness I had felt my first time trying drugs back on that boat. Though this time my balance was much easier to maintain. It had been the meeting place for the deal and it had been the circumstance. The other similarity was the high that soon ran throughout my brain. That's one thing you can't argue about with drugs, they work. One way or another, there's no escaping the effects. While I stood there for a moment annoyed with myself I soon shifted that feeling and decided that if I was going to be like this I might as well enjoy. Though my first perception of our vices was soon shared by another as a man pushed through the door and halted at the site of my friend. Killing both the moment and the high. The man looked at me, turned around, and left lightly muttering. Even with the expanding variety of communities sharing the same hobbies and vices around the world today, not many existed where our current scenario would have been viewed in a favorable light. I mean, we should have at least gone inside a stall if we were going to do this. I wasn't even sure how we had come to this place so quickly, but I guess you get around the right history and anything is possible. Normally he would have known better, but he was no longer operating under his own influence and he hadn't been for a while. Which I understood. I felt under an influence too, but my influencer was this country, this area, and as per usual I got caught up in the influence of the moment. But then, when are we not under the influence of something outside of ourselves? Under the influence of our surroundings or the voices coming at us from all sides. Or in this case, under the influence of the pleasure-seeker within. It's funny that we still use the word "high" to describe how you get when you're under the influence, because most people seem to need something from the outside for the illusion of being grounded. And part of me can be more sympathetic towards that in the drudgery of a normal day, it's the fact that we're on vacation which is confusing me. But maybe that's the thing. It doesn't matter where you are, eventually you're back looking for the next distraction. Which is perfect because life comes at you one hit at a time if you do it right. Whether it's drugs, movies, sports, or the company of others. It's all a dose of distraction. The only thing that really bothered me about this particular distraction was the instantaneous nature of the affects. It never felt earned. It was merely one focused inhalation. But earned or not I don't know that I could find a time when my time wasn't being used as an interruption to the eventuality which awaited me at the end of this life and everything I knew.

Once we got back Myles was quick to enjoy his newest purchase while inviting the others to join in. I left the room hoping they remembered to close the ground level window which faced the sidewalk and shared the same side of the hostel as the busiest street. I made my way upstairs to the terrace and to my surprise found it filled with teenagers in some sort of group. Amongst them I only saw two verifiable adults so I went their way and over the next few minutes learned that they were down here as part of some humanitarian group out of Ottawa set to help clean up inlets up and down the coast. The main guy went on to enthusiastically tell me how he had been a part of that venture for the last sixteen years. While the twenties might have proven a bit more active than I had planned, the thought of being a teenager in a hostel so far away from home would have been fairly striking to me in my teens. Come to think of it, it probably would have ruined me all together. If I had seen this type of life existing, I don't know that I could have done what I was told to do. But if I had done this first, I don't know how I would have wound up anywhere worthwhile. Though to my surprise the kids seemed content playing a series of cards and board games while the night passed them by. Eventually the guys made it upstairs and joined me along the terrace. When I asked them what they wanted to do I found out that they had not used any of the previous thirty minutes to shower or get ready.

"What the hell have you all been doing?"- Patrick

"Laying by the AC trying not to hyperventilate."

"How long you guys need before we can get moving?"

"Another thirty and we'll be all good bro."

"Aight. Imma go talk to the front desk and see if they've got any suggestions."

When I got down the stairs I saw an empty chair at the front desk so I walked outside to go see if I could find a bar somewhere close by. With each step I felt something the equator does to me every time. My body was good to go, but by 9 P.M. we had been entranced in total darkness for almost three hours and eventually the feeling of exhaustion that I had come to expect began to set in as it usually did. Regardless of the presence of anything which may be rumored to keep you awake. Since I already went to the right with Myles I went left and found an avenue leading closer to the water. As I walked I found a side street hugging the shoreline like a Caribbean Georgetown. This area had either been the most recently restored or the best preserved. I decided to scout the area out a bit and determine what food options we had available. A few blocks later I came to a spot on a corner overlooking the water with a surprisingly low number of women standing outside. In fact it was zero. Instead there was an Asian twenty-something with blonde streaks in his hair holding a menu and ushering people inside. I looked at him with hesitation and confusion before I started talking.

"Hablas Español?" - Patrick

He responded back in fluent fucking Spanish and said to come in for drinks.

"I don't normally have to ask, but where are you from?" - Patrick

"Austin, Texas."

"Right. What's your name man?"

"I'm Julian. Nice to meet ya."

From there he went on and told me his dad had come down here working for a gas company and since then had brought him down to spend each summer and time between his college semesters. When I asked him about his uniform and how he had managed to find work he was pretty straight about it.

"It's under the table. I bring people in. They pay me. Simple as that. You looking for somewhere to eat?" - Julian

"We're not really pressed on food. My friends just want a few drinks."

"Tell you what. As long as you all order a round of drinks, I'll give you a pitcher of beer for free."

"I can deal with that. Be back shortly."

I went back to gather the guys and found them on the terrace laughing at a massive sunburn on Austin's back which kinda resembled a set of bright red wings spanning from shoulder to shoulder. I got them out of the door before telling them the place I had chosen was a few blocks further than any of the other perfectly good restaurants along our route. This didn't bother them at first, but the sun had set in and I could tell they were growing impatient as we passed the 4th consecutive block of activity without slowing down to consider the options.

"Dude where the hell are we going? I see drinks, I see patios. And yet my feet are still moving." - Austin

"Dude, trust me, I found a spot with a cool view of the bay. It's only a few more blocks away. The bartender said he'll give us a deal."

"Fucking Christ Patrick. All deals have a two-block max from now on okay?"

When we made it inside we sat at the first table by the door and a cute Venezuelan waitress approached us with a basket of chips and a few plate settings. From there Julian stopped by and brought us a pitcher of unlabeled beer.

"This Pacifico?" - Patrick

"Yup. Gonna grab you guys some limes and a menu."

As he started walking away Myles chimed in with a table wide request.

"No need for menus. We'll take four margaritas and bring me the spiciest sauce you've got for these chips."

His authoritative nature showed me it was gonna be a long night of drinking and I best get prepared. The look on his face told that as they were enjoying their second round of drinks. During the consumption of which I mainly stared out the window enjoying a slim view of the bay as the lights from the newer side of the city reflected across the water. By now my system was clean of our earlier decision. Any test would have said otherwise, but my mind was back. But once it was back it led me to the feeling of guilt I got anytime I broke a self-imposed rule. I mean. Technically I only broke one rule. I was after all in Panama. But as a whole I was going against the only way I knew how to use to quit anything once I decided to. Which was through outright refusal from thereon out. Cold turkey was the only moderation I understood. And this wasn't some self-righteous decision to stay pure or anything. It was just I knew my tendency to carry on once I found an enjoyable time or anything that facilitated it. And the last thing I needed was to love something that pulled at my already wandering soul via the physical manifestation of a few small grains easily hidden between your credit card and ID. But, that fear in itself was perhaps unwarranted since my addiction was always some sort of experience. Although my only history with any powder had been through the guise of experience so it was difficult to trust myself since I knew the potential fruits of its labor. By this point of over analysis Myles looked at me and tried to bring me back around for a shot.

"You good bro? Or do you need to go to the bathroom again?"

"I'm cool man. Just enjoying my view."

"Life's in here bro. Not out there."

He may have been right, but as I looked outside I noticed a series of lights flashing as three SUVs approached slowly down the stone covered streets. When they parked the doors opened up and a group of men got out and began walking along the sidewalk in front of the restaurant. All in swift form with symmetrical fashion, but even with plenty of speed they barely made it to the other side of the street before a small crowded started forming around them. Distinctly dressed apart from the onlookers were six men in black suits with tactical fitting and guns to match. Amongst these men a 7th man stood out. One with a great head of hair and the smile of a politician. To alleviate our confusion Myles looked up and asked the waitress who it was outside. A question to which she pondered as her eyes darted outside and then widened at a sudden realization.

"Adiós míos, es el Presidente."

"Of *THIS* country?" - Patrick

"Yes!"

"Guys, let's go meet him."- Myles

The words left Myles mouth almost as quickly as he left his seat and ran out the door and into the crowd. We all followed behind and dashed out of our seats until we burst out onto the street and hurried towards the convey. Which I only now realize may have been a bit rash. I would never think to move so quickly in the eyes of the secret service. But for some reason he felt purposely accessible.

"Excuse me, Sir, Sir." - Myles

As the man continued to walk I interrupted his attempts with a less formal greeting.

"Oye Señor!"

To which he stopped and pointed his attention towards Austin and I, looking at us for a moment with a blank face and then smiling as he presented us with a polite wave.

"Are you boys Americans?"

"How could you tell?" - Wes

His face immediately darted towards my friends orange t-shirt with an outline of the United States and a heart placed in the area closest to Virginia.

"Come on over." - President

He was the definition of a politician. Charming, engaging, tall. His smile was welcoming and his hands never let up from touching someone in the greeting process.

"Welcome to Panama. How are you boys enjoying our beautiful country?" - President

"Where's the good fishing Mr. Prez? I wanna know all the secret spots." - Austin

"I'm sure we have plenty of spots if you ask along the way. Where are you boys from?" - President

"Virginia" - Myles

"Lovely state. I'll be landing in Charlottesville this time next week."

In this moment of pause between all of us the President continued to gaze on at us uncertain why we had no response. And in that moment I lost the filter which tells you you're around a world leader.

"Get the fuck outta here. No you're not."

"Wait, are you serious?"- Wes

Now with a head slanted to the side and a squinted look of curiosity, he stepped even closer to us and began to explain.

"Indeed I am. I'm moving my son back to school. He just finished a semester abroad." - President

"Too bad we're not gonna be around. Coulda shown you a good time." - Myles

At this point it seemed his security team was growing impatient from the growing size of the crowd and I figured before we were told to leave we should try to get a quick favor. More than my own surprise at meeting the President, I was most shocked at the ability of the locals to get so close to their leader. In my own time I've seen the access to our leaders dwindle, and yet here I was sharing a sidewalk with the President without any concern for this or that. As I leaned in towards him I hoped to be discrete and gave him the out with a quick back and forth in Spanish.

"I understand if you don't want to start a line, but it would mean a lot to my friends if they could get a picture."

The President agreed to my request and stood at the center of our group allowing the four of us to crowd him as his secretary took our phone to grab a picture. When he asked what all we had done and Wes used the opportunity to exert his feelings about the canal being closed earlier.

"Dude, what kinda attraction closes at four?"

"Well," he laughed, "we gotta let the people relax. You must go again in the morning." - President

"I see plenty of relaxing. Not a chance I'm going back there and wasting my gas money again." - Myles

At this point the President looked back and reached his hand up to place it on my friends shoulder, "Señor I urge you to see it, it's one of mans greatest achievements."

"If you think it's so great, get us some tickets, maybe then I'll think about going, but I wasn't impressed. I'm glad the gate was locked."

"Well, tell you what, if you go again I can have tickets waiting for you. Call it my diplomatic duties, just give your names to my secretary."

I stood there happily going along, but in disbelief at what my friend had just potentially finagled. I think the President enjoyed the bold nature of my friend. I looked at his secretary, who by now was taking out his notebook and seemed to take the President's words very seriously. As his secretary took down the last name Myles looked over at him.

"Dude. You better live up to your word or I'm gonna blast your lies all over my Twitter."

In all of my years of watching the news I'd never seen a world leader appear more thrown off than at that moment. As we all shook his hand and left I thanked him in Spanish and walked away with a curiosity about the validity of his promise as well as an overall excitement for what we had just experienced.

"Dude that was badass! We got tickets for tomorrow! Damn we shoulda complimented him on all of the special hospitality we've been shown." - Myles

With that he nudged me and shared a childish grin at his night thus far. The President didn't know it, but he had saved us from spending the rest of our night in that restaurant. Now Myles was interrupted and in the mood to get walking around the city, a mode I could get on board with. Which was good because I could see it in his eyes before the President came along, he was ready to turn those margaritas into a subscription if my man kept the chips coming. Walking back the conversation eventually got to Myles and his thoughts on how easy everything had seemed.

"If it's this easy to meet the President down here why couldn't you ever get yourself a better job down here with someone like that? You're good at talking to people. Hell all you gotta do is walk up to them apparently."

I happily ignored his question as we walked towards the entrance to Casco Viejo. Although the first hostel had been without vacancies, the desk had told the guys to return in the evening if they wished to enjoy the bar and lounge which opened to the public after ten. Once we got there I managed to feign enjoyment for a half an hour or so, but the music did not bring me back to some great days, it did not bring me back to the nights of dancing with an island girl on a Mexican beach. It only brought about a reminder of the one barrier I still had with my Spanish capabilities; communicating over the sound of loud music in a crowded bar. Done doing it, not even gonna try. And if the guys had wanted to just stand around drinking beers looking at strangers, we could do that outside. And they certainly didn't need me to do it. I figured Austin would be on the same wave as me so I looked over and got his attention with the wave of my hands in front of his face.

"You about this place?" - Patrick

"Fuck no."

"That's what I thought. You wanna walk back?"

" Yeah. Are we coming back?"

"Why?"

"Because I'm about to take off my shirt as we walk out of this bitch."

"Let's maybe hold off on that. We might stay here tomorrow."

"Gotcha. Fuck. Alright."

As we started to walk away Myles came up and grabbed my arm with an inquiry as to why our night was ending so soon.

"Where you guys going? You're not gonna stay and have some drinks?"

The twist in my face should have given him all the answer he needed. My feelings weren't any different now than they were when we were younger and I don't know why he expected they would be. Nonetheless he seemed in need of an explanation.

"Nah man we're going home." - Patrick

"Alright kill joy. Go ahead and take Austin with ya I guess."

"Bruh. This man ain't stealing me. He's saving me. We'll see ya back at our room. Go dance with Wes or something."

Once Austin and I got beyond the reaches of the speakers we paused on a slanted street as Austin lit up a cigarette and I broke the silence.

"Dude I hate that shit. You can't hear a damn thing in there. Did you tell me something happened to your hearing a while back?" - Patrick

"Yeah. I got into a little accident on the farm."

"That sucks. Both ears fucked up?"

"Nah. I still got the one that works. But both my eyes work and right now I wanna take em to the terrace and go people watch. You down?"

"Works for me."

"Cool. Bro, I still don't get how you speak so much Spanish. How did you learn that shit?"

"It was either that or don't talk to anybody, and well, we all know me, that's not an option."

Seeing him stare back at me through the cloud of a cigarette I decided to elaborate.

"I don't know dude. Just learn vocabulary and listen. You'll start to put the order together and shit like that."

"Yeah, but dude, you don't just learn random words."

"Think about it as it applies to English, if I asked you, *how are you,*

You wouldn't respond carrot, would you?"

"Bro you don't know if I'm feeling carrot or not."

"I'm just trying to make a point smart ass. Learn a few questions and a few responses and just see what happens."

"Right. Keep talkin' while we get a walkin'. I don' know about this."

His point was well made so we walked back to the hostel and posted up at a small table along the edge of the terrace over looking the main boulevard. I had always loved how we seemed to be on the same wavelengths with regards to how long we could tolerate crowds and noise. Although most of the time his tolerance shrank before mine which sometimes made for an awkward conversation as I told him I wasn't quite ready to leave. Though this time his timing had been spot on. On our way up Austin had snagged a case of beer from the room and the moment we plopped in our seats he cracked open two and placed one at each side.

"So how you liking it down here?" - Patrick

"This place is cool, but it's not the same when you can't talk to anyone."

As he sat there gulping his beer he looked off the terrace as if his eyes were staring into his world back home.

"I wonder if that's how kids feel until they learn to talk. Maybe that's why they're always fucking crying. I wanted to cry at least twice today."

"Could be. I've always wondered what a kid knows that it doesn't know."

"They know it all dude. You see all those kids here earlier? Where were those types of field trips when we were growing up?"

"Dude I have no idea. I don't think I even knew some of these places existed when I was a kid. I wouldn't have known how to get myself down here even if I had known. That's why the kids now have it so much better."

"I gotta see what to do to get my mine on some trips sponsored by groups like that."

"You'd be cool with them going away like this?"

"Not anytime too soon. But the wife and I have been talking about it lately. Figure if we get them involved in something like that now, they'll have a better idea what to do with their lives. Cuz I am not wasting my money if they're gonna start school not knowing what they're trying to do."

"I doubt you gotta worry about that. Kids have a lot more avenues to explore than we did growing up. You ever think about getting them into a foreign language or something they can use later?"

"Not really. We're not in the type of place for them to get much practice outside of the classroom. And I don't wanna confuse the younger ones."

"Well if the parents down here thought like that I woulda never had a job. Why not have them all learn and let it be their thing as siblings?"

"Ya know Pat, times like this it really shows you don't have kids. Having three kids to plot against you is already hard enough without imaging them speaking some shit I don't understand."

"Could always learn one with them."

"Oh yeah. Let me get right on that."

"You could. Get Duolingo. It's like a language learning app. Download that shit on your phone and just fuck with it for a while. You could have the kids do the same with an iPad."

"Yeah. Maybe. I don't got the time like you do man. Kids make shit busy. When they go fishing with me I spend so much time helping them hook their lines that I never get a moment to focus. I'm always being asked to do shit. I don't wanna be asked in Spanish too."

"I feel you dude. Just an idea. It doesn't take much. Sit and listen a few minutes a day. Everyone has the time to listen."

"Yeah maybe."

"Plus you have no idea how much it could help them in the future. I got more than a few thoughts about why it's good to learn another language when you're young."

"Well?"

"Okay. It exercises the mind, it creates a better world by creating a more intertwined people and it gives your kids another perspective from which to see existence. It also gives them better marketability. Word it how you want. It's just a good skill to have. And learning begets learning. Anyways, I'm beat. You gonna stay here and finish this case?"

"Yeah probably. You passin' out?"

"Yeah man. I've been ready to for a while now."

"Alright bro I'll catch ya tomorrow."

I walked down to our room and found an extra bed left folded up in the back of the room. I decided to claim that and within no time had fallen asleep. The air conditioner faded on and off throughout the night and with the help of the stairwell placed above our room I became immune to the noises of the hostel and remained asleep as the guys came back throughout the night.

Day 3: Canal Street

Casco Viejo, Panama

Despite the combination of a late night following a long day I still woke up fairly early and ready to take the opportunity of a rising sun and a room full of hungover friends to get in a few hours of exploring before everyone got moving. It was just after seven so I put on my sandals and went outside where I took a left down the alley towards the edge of Casco Viejo. When I made it to the main avenue my face was met with a beam of sunshine which stayed with me as I continued down several blocks until I came to a small plaza with a statue of Simon Bolivar, known around these parts as The Great Liberator. A title gained during his attempts to unify Latin America with the creation of a super-nation coined Gran-Colombia, a reality which never came to fruition, but a struggle which forever changed the political and social landscape of the continent. His name had followed me throughout the Caribbean and now here I was in the epicenter of his achievements. As I continued down the sidewalk I came upon a few sections of street which had been taped off during some sort of construction. At first I thought it was the early signs of modernization, but the closer I got the more it looked like an attempt at continued preservation by those hoping to hang onto the historical look which graced the region.

As I circled around the older side of town I made my way down a hill which led to the fisherman's wharf. On my walk down I found it odd to see that not even the people on their morning jogs ran in sleeveless shirts. Over the years I had done a pretty good job of handling the heat of Latin America, but the sun today was unusually uncomfortable. In my attempts to live by the code of acting as the locals do, I stopped a man in military attire and asked him his thoughts on the matter.

"Señor, hay mucho calor. Is anyone bothered if I take my shirt off while I'm walking around?"

I had hoped the sweat dripping down my forehead would have granted me a sympathetic no, but I had forgotten that I was in a relatively conservative country where the national norm was to remain properly dressed on sidewalks. In a deep voice with a misplaced Caribbean accent the man replied to me in the negative.

"Si. Es Malo. There are too many women and children walking around this time of day."

"Pues. Okay. Que tengas un buen dia."

I wonder what he would have said if I were a busty backpacker? Surely he could have found it within himself to allow me the relief of all that heat if the future relief meant a revealing to his liking. With that let down I left my shirt on but remained frustrated at my continued discomfort and his logic. Why did it matter to anyone if a shirtless person is walking around? I guess I should have expected this from the same region that once told me I had to put on a shirt before I could even cross a border. And I don't mean some official crossing, I'm talking a dirt road and an office the size of a phone booth. That type of crossing. I don't know who was crazier that day. The authorities or the ten year old shoeshiner who tried to convince me to pay him to shine my sandals while we waited to cross. The frustration of the heat was soon redirected to a frustration with myself as I walked around contemplating the events of yesterday. Surely I could not gauge my actions as detrimental considering how the night ended. I mean, I woke up the next day and all. And if nature gave me another chance then surely I could afford myself one as well. After-all it's not like I had been the most structured of individuals during most of my life as it were. I had only become a man of routine in-order to counter the areas where I was lacking in stability. That was after college, before then I just felt like I was somehow managing to get along with a fly by the seat of my pants existence placated by my ability to make it through school and society without much concern or difficulty.

I continued walking towards the water until I found myself drawn to the sounds of people scurrying through a metal gate which led me inside the local fisherman's wharf. As I followed the crowds of fishermen I was introduced to the smells of todays catch being carried through the air from a series of tiny fishing boats docked several rows deep in the surrounding bay. I was noticeably the only tourist in this area which proved to be fruitful because the cost of dining was set at prices for locals. Uncertain how their system worked I sat down at a small table and waited until a waitress came over and attempted to guide me in the direction of a few larger meals. It's not that I wasn't hungry, but a fish head seemed like an aggressive way to start the morning so I looked down at the menu to pick from a variety of smaller options. After looking further I'm not sure why I wandered in there. I wasn't usually a huge fan seafood. Especially not the commonly popular dishes of shrimp, crabs, and lobster. Which is to say most seafood. I just don't understand how we became sold on the idea of paying so much money for bottom feeders. But despite that I had wandered into a fisherman's world so I settled on a Mediterranean style ceviche and waited a few minutes until the waitress brought my food.

When my dish arrived I saw that I was going to have to down my food in violation of yet another conflict created from an observation of my past. You see, I've found it hard to see an Octopus as food after seeing a video of one escaping from its tank at an aquarium one night. Not just because it could sneak out, but because of what it was capable of once it did. In the video it got out of its tank, found its way to another, killed the fish which resided in it, and then returned back to the original tank, unnoticed by anyone other than those monitoring the cameras after a series of fish had gone missing. A video which since seen has made me come to gauge them as arguably more intelligent than some of my human counterparts. Either way I stated to eat and as I neared the bottom of the cup my phone started to buzz.

"We overslept. We gotta be out in thirty. Where are you?"

"On the way."

I paid my bill and ran up the hill back to Casco Viejo wondering the whole time if the guys had packed and showered or if they were as unprepared to leave as I was. When I got to the room I was surprised to find the guys ready and waiting so I gathered my things and headed to the front desk to settle up. While checking out I took a moment to speak with the front desk attendant and ask his advice on a few things to see along the drive to Costa Rica. On his list were a few surf spots, some secluded beaches, and a suggestion to go up to a coffee farms near Boquete. For navigation he suggested we buy a map due to the lack of phone service along the way. I asked him if they had one for sale, but he had to defer me to a stationary store a few blocks down. From that point I had already done everything I wanted to do so it didn't matter to me what we did next as far as exploring the city was concerned. Even though we didn't have to be in Costa Rica for a few days it seemed like a good idea to get going in that direction before the days got away from us. Plus if we got on the road soon enough we had the chance to be on a beach for sunset somewhere in Mid-Panama.

It's not that I didn't expect to, but I was relieved to find the car where we left it the night before. I wasn't normally one to be too concerned with the possibility of auto-theft but I had planted the seed in my mind the moment I was made aware that all rentals in Panama had special tags which indicated their rental status. Which I have to say is an ill planned idea on the part of the rental companies, but to each his own. We loaded the bags and I started the air conditioner to cool the car down while the guys ran to the store to buy a Panamanian road map. By the time they got back I had planted myself in the drivers seat and arranged everything to my liking with the AC running on high to make for a cool ride up the coast. As the doors opened Wes was the first one to enter the car and got the discussion started on our plan of attack. Or at least his hopes for it. His voice was filled with confidence, but still with a childlike presence to his hope as he looked to Myles for confirmation.

"So we're going to the canal right? I mean, if we've got tickets waiting…"

"Are you that fuckin' gullible? There's not gonna be any tickets waiting for any of us."

To which Austin interrupted.

"Well dude even if there ain't. It's the only thing I knew about this country before we came here anyway. Might as well see the damn thing."

"If you guys wanna see it then yeah we can go. I don't care. I just wanna get some food first. I'm starving."

Guess none of them got to enjoy a styrofoam cup of ceviche before noon. Hmm. I decided not to mention that to them for now. Not to avoid jealousy or even to deny them food, I just didn't want to deal with parking by the wharf if they asked me to show them where I had eaten. And if I was gonna tag along for another bite I needed to make sure it was for something a bit more filling and a bit less fishy. I was glad that we were taking time to go to the canal. This would give me a little bit more time to search for somewhere to sleep on our way up the coast. This along with the fact that I was pretty pumped to go see such an interesting human accomplishment. For all of my love of history, it's not something I had ever imagined going out of my way to see, but I was more than happy to be doing so. When we made it to the entrance of Mira Flores we pulled through a gate and came upon a surprisingly humble parking lot with space for only a few tour buses and about twenty cars. As we parked and got out we saw a long stairway leading up a steep hill lined with a metal gate which branched off on either side and served as the only fixed barrier separating onlookers from the heavily trafficked waters ahead.

As we approached the steps Wes told me how he had been trying to get into shape and asked if I wanted to race him up the stairs. Always up for an excuse to skip a few steps, I agreed to his challenge and we jetted up the stairs. It was pretty evenly matched, but we both beat Austin and Myles by a full minute or more as they took their time calmly climbing their way up. When the guys reached the top of the stairs they walked passed me as I took a moment to look ahead at a large grey building which served as the entrance for tourists visiting the canal. When I made it through the door I heard the guys already in the middle of making a hell of a first impression.

"We go to school with his son, we're just down here on spring break." - Myles

"Yeah man you ever dined with the President? You can come to dinner if you want." - Wes

"Boys, we don't just give away tickets."

"We're not joking. Just check your papers. There must be some type of list." - Myles

I looked on and saw a skeptical glare coming from the supervisor, but after opening his phone and looking at a memo he whispered something into the clerks ear which led her to begin printing off four tickets. The guard seemed as confused as I was, but our confusion stemmed from much different reasons. He was wondering who we were and I was wondering who would have expected such a busy man to remember such an unimportant encounter. We grabbed our tickets and pushed through the first set of doors where we were greeted by a security desk and a row of metal detectors. It was then that Myles realized he still had his knife on him.

"Fuck man. I'm not trying to walk back down those stairs. I'm gonna ask them if I can leave it here."

In doing so he reached around to his lower back and brandished a 5-inch hunting knife with a string attached to it. We had known a time when you could check your weapon at the door, otherwise I would have seen that as strange, but to my surprise the guard was from the same cloth. Something I found none to surprising when I reflect on my time abroad. That may have been the best part about traveling. It showed me just how similar my hometown and it's people had been to that of those around the rest of the world. Odd as it may seem, whether you consider yourself a redneck or a person from the hills you likely share more in common with the members of the slums and chavelas around the world than you think. It was that very similarity which helped me get through my first year away from the place which had raised me. The backyards and the evening cookouts had been the same as they were at home. The only difference was the food. The front yards were still filled with junked cars surrounded by uncut grass and chickens wondering through chunks of cinderblock leftover from projects never quite completed. The labels on the cases of beer may have been different, but the character in these peoples souls had been the same regardless of where the pin dropped me.

"Okay Gauchos. Enjoy the canal. Leave the knife."

Myles looked at me skeptically before he handed over the knife to the waiting hand of a man too large to fight back if he decided to keep it. And it seemed like the guards eager nature had set off a flag in his head.

Which I totally understood since the last knife of mine to end up in the hands of an officer had wound up magically lost in the court system. As we entered the main lobby we saw an audience of no more than a hundred people making their way through the four story structure which had a glass ceiling and top to bottom windows exposing the loch from every vantage point possible. In the middle of the guest services was a sign blinking which indicated that a ship was due through in about thirty-five minutes. The guys saw this and asked about sticking around to watch it pass through. It wasn't like I was likely to be back in the area for quite a while so I figured why not. A statement that I knew to have some holes historically, but still, if I didn't plan to be here before, it's unlikely I'll stumble my way here later.

As we passed through the complex the guys split off in their own directions with Myles and Austin making their way to the top floor while Wes went towards the archives in the basement level. I considered following him because I was intrigued about the written history just as much as he was, but I decided instead to go straight to the museum to try and find some visuals to go along with the story. I opted not to wait at the only elevator available and instead took the stairs around the corner up to the second floor. As I walked into the museums entrance I saw a series of rooms filled with televisions hanging above display cases filled with rock samples and mini-models of the early construction process. Most notable among all of the artifacts was a scaled down version of how they moved the rocks and debris along conveyer belts and then onto a ship where they were eventually dropped into the nearby ocean. A task originally completed by lines of people with shovels moving walls of dirt away from deepening embankments while being bombarded with mosquitos and tropical humidity. A combination which led to the early deaths of many, but the eventual discovery of the cure for Yellow Fever. One of the many problems which made it easy to understand why the French were ready to drop the project in 1902. Although one can hardly call being paid $40 million dollars dropping anything.

I made way outside and to the front of the canal where a small set of bleachers were set up to provide a view of vessels passing through the lochs as they waited for the water to be drained. I used this time to go sit in one of the chairs and take in the scenery around me. I looked on in awe at the river snaking through the mountains. Perhaps one of the only crossings we have today which is able to maintain the pure aesthetics of nature as nothing looks more natural through a jungle than the movement of water. Which it did so with such natural perfection that it appeared to have crept through over a million years of evolution. A feat none too large for the persistence of water, but back then I cannot imagine the audacity it must have taken for someone of mere human capacity to look at this same scene one-hundred and fifty years removed from our current levels of technology and think it possible to bust through to the other side. But then again the only thing more persistent than water is the persistence of people. And perhaps that's what adds to the grandiose nature of such a large project, the commitment to the time it takes, and the recognition of its' inevitable passing, with or without progress on our part. The only difference is who shall make the claim, man or nature.

Seeing this modern marvel led me down the same thought process I found myself in when I first set eyes on the monument commemorating the Wright brothers and their first flight over Kitty Hawk, North Carolina. It's interesting how certain technologies just evolve much slower than others. I would imagine humans have been digging since the beginning of man, but still it took from the beginning of time until a hundred years ago to finally dig through fifty miles of earth and connect two oceans. But with flight we had progressed much quicker once we got going. At which point we went from envying birds and their ability to soar among the heavens until one December day in 1903 where we achieved flight for the first time. Albeit for less than a mile, but nonetheless accomplished. And then in just over a hundred years we went from not being able to get our feet off of the ground to navigating *Voyager 1* beyond the reaches of our solar system while obtaining histories best photos of our formerly dubbed planet known to my generation as Pluto. Maybe the benefits of flight seemed much more obvious at first while the idea of digging didn't have the same call to urgency nor the same infinite future.

From my seat at the top of the bleachers I watched as a large freighter began its' slow approach towards the lochs. I can't imagine how cool it must be for the crew members on the ships passing through the canal. First they're surrounded by the ocean for weeks on end and then they get a brief vacation cutting through some of the greenest terrains the world has to offer. Thanks to the museum I came to find out that the canal provides their own captains to take each ship through the canal in order to provide the safest passage possible. Which is nice of them considering that it can cost up to $150,000 in tolls to journey through. But that's a small price to pay when you're saving 14 days of time and fuel. Of course they are fair in considering lower costs for smaller ships. I even found an example of a swimmer paying a six-dollar toll for his crossing.

Stretching across the loch was a metal bridge with the ability to retract to either side as ships passed through the high concrete walls which extended in both directions. As the ship approached it steered through the narrow passage and came to a halt as pipes began to dump water from the loch containing the ship to the neighboring loch until the water levels became equal and the ship could be pulled through. When the ship completed its trip through the gates closed and I watched as the loch began to slowly fill with the same precision as it had been emptied. Once we had seen a ship go through and toured the museums I felt the monument had reached its limits in the entertainment department. That feeling was shared by the guys and we all wound up in the main lobby around the same time and decided to leave. Before collecting his knife Myles ran over to a small coffee shop to grab us a few empanadas and a bottle of water to hold us over for the first part of our drive.

As we left Wes approached me with his phone and showed me several pictures he had taken of his great-great grandfathers signature and any subsequent information he found regarding his family's contribution. Perhaps seeing his family name immortalized in a friendly light would give him some relief from the pressure of being responsible for his family's legacy. One which had been branded in younger years through the opaqued perspective of a small community as they looked on at a family of adventurous souls doing as they pleased. I knew he had been excited for this part of the day and I admit that this had been better than expected, but I was more stoked that in a few hours I would finally be able to say I had piloted this road at every end of the Northern Hemisphere. You see I had been a lot of places and driven a lot of roads, but I had been drawn to the experience of driving on the Pacific Coastal Highway through the words of the early Beatnik writers and the eyes of Hollywood in the 1950's. Which is why I was so excited to tackle a part of the route they never could. For as much as I envied those lucky enough to come after and enjoy the spoils of my age, I too recognized how fortunate I was to come a few steps after a generation limited by the confines of the navigable world, and into a new time where the term 'too far' had no real meaning.

The highways here were not like those back home where one can rely on a series of signs to direct you to your next destination. Here you just gotta know where the hell you're going if you wanna get there. And despite the low volumes of traffic on the roads each town still had overpasses for pedestrians to get from one side to the other at each bus stop. I was rather impressed to see this given that it's not a luxury possessed by most modern cities. This is not to say they looked modern, they were just slightly above the quality of dolled up scaffolding, but they were convenient. We passed a few of these small crossways until we came upon one which invited us to slow down by the aroma of chicken roasting a quarter mile before we could tell which side of the street it was coming from. I knew if we could pig out right now I wouldn't need to worry about stopping again until we reached the next hostel. Which was good because it didn't look like there was much else ahead according to our maps. Just as we came up on one of those overpasses we saw a puff of smoke coming from a street vendor to the right beyond the bus stop. I slowed down and pulled our car into a parking lot which shared it's location between a gas station and the local street vendors. As we got out to stretch I looked around and saw a series of small homes spread out on the hills behind us and a series of commercial endeavors across the street.

While I waited for the others to order I looked to my left and noticed that we had been joined by a gorgeous woman in white pants, one of the harder things to ignore when I find myself with the advantage of sunglasses. When she stood next to me she met me at my shoulders which put a head of luscious black hair at eye level and wafted the scents of freshly washed lochs into the air around me. If she had taken off her glasses and revealed green eyes I might have given up the single life and my life back home at her request. But alas, all that I got was a polite hello when I threw an *'Hola'* her way. Which of course didn't go unnoticed.

"Strike out?" - Austin

"It's that hair, it does me in."

"Don't most of the girls here have hair like that…"

"Puts me in a rather difficult position."

Come to think of it. This whole place was putting me in a difficult position. I was surrounded by every familiar urge and temptation that I had been programmed to love throughout my twenties. Only one thing was lacking. My treasured solitude. I had become addicted to the freedom of choice which came from a lack of obligations beyond my own two feet. And looking around I saw all of the indicators as to how I could spend my day if I were to choose to do so. If I were alone I bet I could convince someone here to let me hang out and go to a barbecue where they would introduce me to some homemade hot sauce and then ask to see if the American had any ability to dribble a soccer ball, but that was the past. Perhaps that's what I was struggling with the most at home. The things which I had grown accustomed to enjoying were no longer around me. And here I looked down crooked streets of dust and gravel running by a schoolyard with a Virgin Mary in the middle and I saw a moment in time more familiar to me than the majority of the ones I had been experiencing since returning home last year. Everything in this moment was more familiar, the environment, the people, it all seemed more approachable than it had been years ago, but perhaps that was a sign of my confidence as it had aggregated over time with the enhancement of my Spanish speaking abilities. Despite how it sounds I held off my nostalgia long enough to order my chicken and informed the cook that she could keep the mustard-mayo concoction to herself. I was only interested in all of the hot sauce she could spare. As I placed my order I looked to the right at a flock of chickens living in a dust bowl existence while annoying a sandy grey dog searching for a place of peace for his afternoon nap. I don't think I need to ask her if that's where my meal came from.

Once I got my food I sat down and looked at the map to see what our options were for shelter tonight. I looked to see which town we could make it to before daylight had gone away. In my search I came across an area about two hours from the border. By the looks of it I figured we would have to drive until a little after sunset if we really wanted to make it that far. After the boys finished eating we got going and made our way deeper into the countryside eventually losing sight of anything vaguely resembling a city while lush mountains devoured our peripherals. As I continued to drive the guys found their own quiet places and fell asleep with their heads tilted towards the window. I drove for a while without seeing any signs of life until I came up to a flashing sign signaling me to stop and wait for oncoming traffic which had been given the green light on what had turned into a temporary one-way road. No one was ahead of me so I inherited the unfortunate position as first car in the ever growing line of locals making their way through. Which was the worst situation to be in because I had no idea of the local standards. Like what are the rules? Should I ignore the signs or should I stay put.

Eventually our sentence was lifted by a green light which came after three cars and fifteen minutes had passed by. The guys had all fallen asleep again which was good because that meant they weren't awake when I almost crashed a few miles later when traffic backed up out of nowhere. Well, it wasn't out of nowhere. There were cones for almost a mile so I barely took them seriously and they were narrowing from two lanes to one as I approached some small town. Of course I thought I had enough time to reach for Wes's iPod before I needed to stop. Which I did at precisely the same time the truck in front of me came to a halt. I swerved and hit the brakes and only missed hitting him because I took the car halfway off the road. If I had stayed the course, we would be explaining to a few people why their bumpers were bent and their tail lights no longer blinked. But luckily that did not come to pass, nor did the shit talking from the back seat that I was sure to get if it had. They could say what they wanted, but I knew what type of driver I was; an experienced one. But experience meant nothing to a person who had just been hit by two thousand pounds of steel. And even as I type this my hands sweat with anxiety at the memory of barely missing that bumper.

When we came up on the town of Santiago I decided to divert our course towards the coast so that we could sleep somewhere near a beach. In hopes of avoiding the risk of another close call I tapped Wes on his shoulder looking for help.

"Does your phone work right now" - Patrick

"What? Yeah."

"Ok, I need you to find us somewhere to stay."

"What are we near?"

"I'm not sure. Use your GPS to find something along the coast about an hour ahead."

"Okay. Here's one near Las Lajas."

"What's it look like?"

"I can't tell man. These pictures take forever. But it's on the beach and it says they have kayaks."

"Let's go for that one. Call and I'll see if we can get a room."

We called and were greeted by a peculiar accent attached to a kind voice which gave us directions to a hostel along the shore of Las Lajas. Only after we booked it did we discover that the hostel was labeled one of the most eco-friendly in the area and was sustained entirely by renewable energies. Which was great and I knew Myles would be interested, but I really wanted a warm shower, a luxury I had become keenly adapted to since returning to the United States. But down here they already looked at warm showers as a secondary luxury. So it was almost impossible to think they would bother creating a warm shower in a spot fueled by solar power. Even though there's no lack of sun. We took down the address and continued along the highway until we came to the turn-off which had been described in the directions. Just like she said, right before the white barn.

The road leading down to the beach was riddled with an unnecessary amount of curves as it followed the bends of a river leading to the ocean. When the roadway got to the shore it split off to either side with a parking lot off to the left with a sign welcoming us to the *Lajas*

Eco-Hostel. There we parked our car and walked towards an archway which opened up to a relaxing layout with four short palm trees and two hammocks with rock paths separating the outside from the front desk where a woman of extreme bust sat behind a dimly lit counter wearing a tank top and a two-day ponytail. Though if I am to be particular with my words busty was a bit of an understatement, she was the type to have back problems later in life due to the front loading nature had given her.

"Ah welcome, you must be the boys that called."

"Yes mam. And you are?"

"My name is Gloria. Get your passports ready and I'll get you your keys. Here are some towels. Breakfast is served between 7 A.M. and 10 A.M. The beds are made and I suggest you use the mosquito nets."

Just before I left I saw a basket of fruit behind the counter holding a blend of mangoes, coconuts and some other tiny fruits which decorated the basket nicely and drew attention even when there wasn't hunger.

"Is that for sale?" - Patrick

"It's all up for grabs. Take anything you like."

With that she handed me a mango and I walked off to the far side of the hostel down a dark path of smooth rocks leading to a small dormitory with four beds. I heaved my bag on the top bunk to lay my claim and noticed that I had not been followed back to the dorms. I pulled out a bottle of water from my bag and filled my right hand with a small puddle of water to splash in my face. As I held my wet palm to my forehead I contemplated calling it a night and perching up on my bunk until morning. I wanted a shower since I missed out on one this morning, but the outdoor unit didn't have any lighting, a mistake made by placing it on the side of the building instead of out front where the light could be shared. I laid there and almost passed out until I heard sounds of wind chimes dragging in the taste of salty air. A feeling which soon called me to my feet and towards the action of seeing the beach.

I left the dorms and went to grab a flashlight out of the car before heading to the beach. As I closed the trunk I began walking down a gravel road which I was told took me to the ocean. I walked with my head tilted and looked up to catch a glimpse of the night sky through the palm trees which formed a barrier between myself and the shore. When I got to the beach I saw the moving of flashing lights in the distance along the shoreline. I planted myself firmly in the sand and looked at the flat stretches of beach around me which sprawled towards the horizon to be met with an impossible darkness as far as the eye could imagine it was seeing. Amongst the breeze in my ear and the sound of waves rolling up on the beach I heard Austin's voice guiding Myles through his tackle box as they got ready to fish. A set of sounds which dragged me closer to the shore until I met their voices with my presence.

"I don't even know why I bothered paying for a room. I'm gonna be out here casting lines all night." - Austin

"Glad you like it. Dude it's crazy how dark it is here."

With that he reached up and turned on a headlamp which was tightly wrapped around his forehead. As the light beamed in my direction I lost what little night vision I had gained and squinted as he turned a knob changing the glow from a bright white to a faded blue and then light red.

"My bad bro. This thing's fucking awesome ain't it?"

"Totally. You good? I"m gonna go take a walk."

"Oh yeah. You don't gotta worry about me bro."

"Where's Myles?"

"Who knows. I think he walked up that way."

While my vision slowly came back I looked around and debated which direction to head in. Either side was equally secluded. I say secluded, but that doesn't mean the beach was abandoned. All around me groups of crabs scattered along the sand and moved inland with the crashing waves as their sharp steps darted away from a thin sheet of water which washed up and created a brief reflection of the stars above before fading back into the ocean.

"Trying to go for a walk?" - Patrick

"I'm down." - Wes

"Alright let's go towards that inlet she told us about."

As we made our way along the shore I found us shifting between moments of talking with one another and moments of pure silence as we both took in the sheer darkness all around us. The clouds were thick enough to cover what little moonlight was attempting to shine through, and the lack of city lights created an endless stretch of sand graced by the sounds of the ocean lightly breaking to our right. And then in the darkness Wes noticed something drifting in the water with a light green glow.

"Dude check out that shit glowing over there. I think it's phytoplankton. You see it?" - Wes

"Is that what that is?"

"Yeah dude. Come with me."

"That's pretty cool. Can we touch it?"

"Yeah man. It won't hurt ya. Just run your hands through the water. Can't believe you've never seen these before. Ya know, I thought you'd be all into the life down here. Honestly, when Myles told me you were gonna be the one translating for us, I thought we'd be meeting you in some tiny town down here or something."

"Nah. Little late for that type of convenience. I haven't lived down in these parts for quite a while."

"That sucks, why were you in such a hurry to leave this place?"

"A hurry? I was down here for almost ten years."

"Oh damn. I didn't realize you were gone for that long."

"Yeah. Sometimes neither did I."

"Did you know you were gonna stay so long?"

"No. I planned to go back after a year originally. But each year I found new reasons to stay and there was always some new place I needed to see next. Which ended up being something I was awful at turning down. The moment I had an invitation to go somewhere new I was more than ready to drop whatever plans I had made over the last year to return home and get things started."

"Well why didn't you up finish school then get back to teaching if you liked it that much? You'd probably be making so much money now if you had gotten a Law degree."

"I'm aware. Thanks for the reminder, but my head was in a different place then. I was just trying to take some time to see the world and explore my options. I needed to decompress."

"How was teaching supposed to help figure out more options?"

"I don't know. Maybe it wasn't. It was just something I knew I could do without feeling guilty about not being in school. It was easy to justify traveling and helping people learn English at the same time. Maybe I should have stolen some career ideas from my students."

"See that's what I'm afraid of. I don't wanna find myself doing the same shit five years from now ya know? No offense."

"Oh I get it, no offense taken, but if that's the case then I wouldn't wait too long before you start making some moves. There's nothing wrong with what you're doing right now. Unless it ain't what you wanna do, but if you know you wanna do something. Go do it. There's never any need to hesitate. Very little will have changed when you come back if things don't go well. Just make sure to check in with yourself once in a while and redirect if you need to. That's probably the biggest mistake I made, not checking in on myself."

"What was the thing that got you to finally check in then?"

"Oh, you know, this girl calling me out on my bullshit."

"A girlfriend?"

"Nah. We might have dated if I had checked in on myself a few years earlier. She was a getting her PhD and I was still hoping around the world, not exactly what she was looking for. Still went out on a few dates with me though."

"How did you meet?"

"We got set up by some people from the university. She was super sweet. I think she was studying psychology. Gave me a lot of cool books to look at. All with the same kinda *find your way* message."

At this moment the conversation reminded me of the many which had taken place as friends visited throughout the years and told me of their uncertainties and their successes as time went on. There was a mixture between the friends who thought I had found a way to do it right, and the ones you thought I was crazy. Which from some of their positions in life I'm sure that particular viewpoint was rather justified. Because their decisions were equally outside of my understanding. I saw some of them getting married. I saw kids being born. Weddings missed and funerals ignored. I saw the lives of those once my contemporaries passing before my eyes and I felt as if they were out pacing me more and more each year. Even though the destinations some of us had moved to were not places consciously sought after. And while I did not see life as some sort of race I still saw my friends as appropriate markers for where one should be going. Especially when the bachelor of all bachelors was wed and the last of my bartender friends had set down their mixing tins. Hell even the snowboarders eventually found their ways into some neat existence carved out of the lives they had chosen. It was the same type of conversation which had ultimately led to me questioning what I was doing with my life after a series of reminders brought things back which were once desires, but had somehow become forgotten dreams. Which no one around me would have known. By that point I had stopped telling people anything about my academic past or my plans because the conversation always led to them asking what I was doing next. Or it led to how awesome they thought it was that I got to do that with my time. And either way it served as a reinforcement to how I was living. Which was easy to do because I felt good about being a teacher. It was cool to know I was helping people learn and sometimes I liked to think I played a role in whatever they would do with their English one day. It was a way to reason with myself as to why I was still there at twenty-seven, although the gap between there and thirty had proven more self-critical. I think that was the first time it really came to me. Before then I have no recollection of what I was thinking. I just know that I did and I stayed doing. Luckily that only resulted in a few lost years. And by that I mean lost for me, not for those around me. Not a bad trade-off for the amount of time I got to myself. For over five years my life had been completely my own and during that time I just went along running with whatever seemed like the most interesting thing to do at the moment. Which was a convenient way to live for sure, but the enjoyment of it had led to a lack of pensive action on where the trail was going.

In my opinion the ones who did it right were the small group of my friends that moved out West and spent a few seasons riding down the mountains while making enough money in whatever ski-town they had found to keep themselves afloat while living a pretty neat existence. Those are the only kids I was ever jealous of after college. In light of no preferred option they had taken the leap and given their time away to something they knew they would enjoy. Meanwhile anytime I considered what I was going to do I usually found myself with a giant blank emerging from the thought process. Which was admittedly my fault; before college I hadn't really thought about what else I would do with my degree beyond going to grad school. So when I decided not to use it, I just viewed it as kinda useless. No more than a piece of paper to talk about. A subject which would soon find itself run into the ground beyond the formalities of a five minute conversation. With each year that passed I grew more uncertain about what I was going to do to ultimately change the course of my life which had been set after deciding to leave the United States. I knew I needed to do something beyond teaching English and fucking off in the tropics. But each time I would bring myself to consider the alternatives, a voice inside would pop in to remind me that I was enjoying myself and there was nothing wrong with that. Especially not when I was living a life free of responsibilities beyond that which stared me in the face each morning as I looked in the mirror. As we found ourselves walking in un-guided thought we came across a series of large lampposts bordering a property which caused us both to pause and realize that we had gone too far. As we retraced our steps we used the flashlights on our phones and came across some fishing gear sprawled out next to a log along the exit to the beach access. It looked like the guys had gone walking in the opposite direction and due to the darkness we had not seen their gear left behind. I stared off and didn't see flashlights or any indicators on where exactly my friends had gone. Oh well, I had a responsibility as the translator for the trip, but not as a nighttime guider of ill-advised explorations.

"I'm gonna crash. You staying up?" - Patrick

"Yeah. Think they'll mind if I sleep in one of those hammocks?"

"No, but those mosquito nets are on the bed for a reason."

As I got settled in bed the mosquito net draped over me and seeped to parts of my leg so much that I wondered how it would do me any good or if the point of the clinging was to better serve me up as a nice soft plain for a mosquito to rest on while he dines. Before I went to bed I pulled out my phone and found the WiFi to the hostel and connected long enough to type a message to Renata. I was supposed to see her in four days and I still didn't have a good idea where I would be when she arrived.

"Don't freak out. All is well, but some things have changed. We're not even in Costa Rica right now. Send me the time and flight details for your arrival and I'll meet you at the airport when you come in…"

Day 4: To Higher Grounds
Las Lajas, Panama

E ven though I tried avoiding the obligation of early mornings the majority of my adult life I still considered myself to be a morning person. Mainly because it was the only thing which had given me the ability to maintain some sort of routine when I knew the rest of my day would be given away to the wills of others. After getting out of bed and grabbing my bag I went to the front desk to see what the situation was for breakfast. There I met the same woman from the night before and she soon sold me on the $5 breakfast they had every morning. No one working there looked underfed so I felt pretty good about my odds even though the sign described it as a continental breakfast.

We started discussing what to do in the area and she pointed out a few water related activities and told me about some kayaks the hostel had for rent if we wanted. I didn't want to guess yet at what everyone wanted so I deflected the invite for the moment and asked about the origin of her accent as well as a few details about how the hostel got started. Not just the solar, but the tinier details which had been so meticulously displayed throughout the property. Everything from the bottles used to fill in the concrete walls to the two liter bottles now supporting some sort of lettuce growing in a makeshift garden out front. In response she explained how she had come from the Amalfi Coast and had been living in Panama for almost eleven years. Although she had been speaking Spanish for many years before the move. Like many relocated people I've met I couldn't understand why she had traded one paradise for another. Perhaps she preferred sandy beaches over rocky shores. Either way I'm not sure I'll ever understand anyone who transplants themselves from a previously settled environment filled with the comforts and beauty of the modern world to another. I may have always been away, but I never wanted to stay, it never felt home, it just felt homey.

While we wrapped up our conversation Wes made his way out and started doing his morning stretches from the edge of a bench next to some picnic tables. Since no one else was there to interrupt us I sat down next to him and followed his lead through a series of stretches. I had been good for many things over the years, especially personal care, but I had to admit that stretching had been neglected more than not and I was drastically trying to make that shift. When he saw me imitating his steps he looked over and owned up to a certain reality.

"Figure I might as well stay loose if I'm gonna be drunk the whole time. That's what anatomy class made me realize. Keep yourself loose and half the problems are solved before they start."

"Sounds solid."

"Yeah man. Gotta get it together again. I let myself go a bit while I was dating the ex. You know how it goes."

I appreciated his self-awareness. And his preparation to find ways not to avoid his own tendencies was largely caused by that. He had the time to think about those sides of life. We all had the time to think about more than we ever had. In many ways we had become a modernized embodiment of the Greeks who once walked in robes and practiced the teachings of the Stoics. We were so lucky. We had time to read, time to wonder, time to question the nature of why. All through the natural steps which led one to being concerned with a stabilized comfort. To know ones survival shall continue until old age takes them out. All the while expecting for that existence to include the best of eats, seats, and parties. As we sat there a young islander named Beto came out of the kitchen with two mismatched cups of coffee on white saucers and dropped them on the table in front of us. As we started to sip our coffee Austin and Myles appeared from the dorms looking haggard from a mixture of late night fishing and early morning heat. As they both sat down I reached out to ask about their first night in the wild.

"What time did y'all get back last night?"

The guys then relayed their version of what had happened after Wes and I called it a night. According to them they brought up some lobster nets which were strung up along the shore and found an unverified number of white bricks entangled in the traps. I wondered immediately why my friends hadn't taken this movie script opportunity to then slam down a kilo on the table in front of me. And luckily Wes had zero fucking problem calling them out while he started laughing.

"Ok, so where are they?"

"We had to leave them." - Myles

"Yeah we saw some lights coming our way when we were messing with them and we had to run off." - Austin

"Yeah. But we saw these guys come unload the nets and leave. Still didn't make it back in til sunrise." - Myles

"I see." - Patrick

During this Beto brought out two more coffees accompanied by a large pitcher filled with a milky liquid under a layer of chia seeds and a blended banana. I had always enjoyed how fresh the food was down here. I had missed that part. The likelihood that the food I would eat would be food from around the area and harvested around yesterday.

After eating I figured it would be a good time to see if we had a plan for the rest of the day. If we wanted we could be at the border and on our way to San Jose by mid-afternoon, but I got the idea that we were all trying to have a full day in the sun for once. A day without a timeline. We had made such great timing already that we could actually afford two or three more days in Panama if we wanted. And apparently Myles had found a thing or two to do.

"I wanna go up to this cloud forest I found. It looks pretty cool. We were gonna go to one in Costa Rica, but if they got one here we might as well do that." - Myles

Myles brought his phone over to reveal his recent discovery. On his screen I saw a picture of a yellow building surrounded by fog with what appeared to be some zip-lines loading slowly on his phone. I then scrolled through the photos in hopes of gaining a better idea of what we were going to see, but the service was so slow I could only muster up the patience to sit through the loading of four photos before giving up on any others. In those few photos I saw mountainous views and something that looked like a coffee farm which was enough to sell me on the idea.

"How far away is it?" - Patrick

"About two hours. Think they'll have rooms open? I don't wanna drive all the way up there to find out they don't."

"They'll have rooms. It doesn't look like it's on any bus routes and I doubt anyone is walking that far."

"Cool. You going down to the beach?"

"Yeah. You?"

"Shortly. I wanna find that lady and ask a few questions about their solar set up here. They must have a storage facility for all the extra energy they collect."

"I didn't see anything around here big enough for that."

"Nah dude. They don't need a ton of space. Bet they could hook that shit up and make this place into anything they wanted. I'm gonna show her how to make those showers nice and warm without it costing her a dime."

Once everyone got changed and ready we started making our way to the beach. In the daylight entrance to the beach was lined with lean-to's and hammocks surrounding fires still smoldering from the morning feast. As we walked through a row of palm-trees with white borders painted around the bottom I saw a few locals in their hammocks relaxing to the feel of the early afternoon breeze. But they lost some of their relaxation the moment they caught the glimpses of Myles and his painfully white legs which were still reflecting the sunlight. But soon enough their attention reverted back to the underbelly of palm leaves hanging above. If I could wish one skill on anyone it would be knowing how to relax as these people did in the presence of blinding paleness. When I got back to his side I looked over at him and tried to assess his state of mind.

"Are you in the mood to draw everyones attention?"

"Nope. Just hoping for a tan."

I always appreciated anyone who could be so shameless, but I still preferred to hold onto a slim piece of humility when wandering around in public. Something which just didn't apply to this guy. As the morning went on Myles and Austin used the next few hours to get some sleep in the sand seemingly unconcerned by the sun. I spent most of my time within the palm line avoiding the heat and laying around. Once we had absorbed enough sun for the day we got our stuff together and made it back to the hostel where we learned our host had left to get some supplies. Since we had no unfinished business we packed up and folded our blankets before leaving her a note thanking her for taking care of us on such short notice. As we started driving I imagined that we might see some more people, but the road was fairly empty for the next half-hour or so and I cruised along until we came across a series of roads that split off toward the mountain. Unsure what to do, I smacked Wes's feet from their resting place on the dashboard. He jolted and opened his eyes and began responding as if he had heard my concern in his sleep.

"It says straight. No. I mean right." - Wes

"What?"

"Right. We were supposed to turn right."

"Where?"

"Fuck I don't know dude. Back there, like that last turn."

I ignored his panicked directions and continued down the road towards the main town as Myles chimed in with his inquiries about our next move.

"Where are we going?"

"If we've passed the turnoff already we might as well go and get some supplies while we're close to a town."

"Cool. I need to get some cash from an ATM anyway."

When we got into town we made it to store which looked like a grocery store, but after a quick walkthrough we saw it was more for camping supplies and hardware. Before leaving I went up to a store clerk and she informed me that there was a grocery store just around the corner. As we got in the car I went to back out and Myles suddenly opened his door.

"You guys go ahead. I'm gonna use that ATM and then head over."

"Alright man, we'll be across the street."

I got into the store and immediately fell into the trance of a shopping mode induced by hunger and aromatic teasing from the bakery hidden somewhere in the back of the store. The meats looked a bit old so I went to get some eggs. They're always the easiest bet for transporting when you don't have refrigeration. Even during the warm weather I can take eggs with me from one coast to another without concern. As I finished up and made my way to the check out I was joined by Myles who had been wandering around looking for us.

"What booze you guys get?" - Myles

"Nothing yet. Was waiting on you for that."

"Okay. Lemme go grab one."

Myles returned a moment later with a big bottle of Vodka and started fumbling through his pockets. It was then that it came to Myles' attention that he had lost his wallet somewhere since leaving the store across the street.

"What do you mean you don't have it?" - Patrick

"Last time I had it was over at that ATM. I got my card out. Made a withdraw. And then put it right back in my pocket."

"Do you have the money you pulled out?"

"No. That was in the wallet."

"Of course it was."

I looked down and saw he was wearing gym shorts with one of the pockets slightly turned out. Myles didn't seem happy about it, but he was rather unbothered by the annoyance compared to what I would expect out of him.

"God damnit. Okay. Go back to the ATM. I'll get Wes and Austin to go look around the floor while I go ask if they found anything. Were you walking around the store long before you found us?"

"Nah man. Just a minute or two."

After that we spent a good twenty minutes running around and doing the same things everyone does when something is lost. First we started digging through the shopping cart and everywhere else that made sense before tracing our steps up and down the isles examining every inch of the floor. As that proved fruitless we broadened our search to a list of ever more unlikely spots and started running down isles where we had never stepped and filled with ingredients we would never buy. I walked around with a mind filling up with the important questions, like, How *could you lose such an important item doing such a routine transaction? Why would you not be especially diligent doing that shit in a foreign country?* Uncertain of any answers all I could bring myself to think was how the chances of finding it were lessening by the moment. If only he would have just let me drive him over I would have at least been with him to notice when he dropped it, but no. After all of my running around the Vodka salesgirl must have thought I was tryin to come up with ways to talk with her because I had passed by her feet three times now trying to notice anything along the floor by the liquor. If he dropped it anywhere, this would be where. I knew if he couldn't find it we would be in a tough situation since none of the banks would be able to get the ball rolling on a new card until after the weekend. And even once we did, where would they send it? We don't even know where we'll be twenty-four hours from now. Let alone three business days. With each minute that passed I saw the sun slowly fading beyond the Pacific. We would soon be heading towards a mountain destination at a time that I would call less than favorable. It was best to get up the mountain before dark for reasons of practicality as well as seeing a sunset. In a place like this the roads could be filled with anything from locals blocking the streets, herds of animals roaming, or just the general danger of sharp turns with no guardrail to make up for your lack of knowledge.

In my mind our search was over, but I couldn't be the one to make someone stop looking for their wallet. I mean I'd be pissed. Replacing my ID abroad was easily the most annoying thing I ever did as a nomad and I understood him not wanting to get to that step. As he approached me he looked fed up enough to let me know that we wouldn't be standing around much longer. When he got next to me he looked at the Vodka selections and then turned to grab a bottle of rum off the nearest shelf.

"Patrick, can you take care of this stuff and I'll have my secretary wire us some money when we get to San Jose?" - Myles

"Yeah dude I got you."

"Awesome. I'm ready to get drunk."

"So that's it? The search is over?"

"Yeah fuck it dude. Another one of my items lost to Panama."

Had I known a $20 bottle of rum could have solved this problem I would have paid for two of them an hour ago. I took the bottle from him and walked over to the register where we had left our cart after discovering his wallet was missing. Before leaving I made sure to give the cashier our information in case they found his wallet in the future. High hopes I know. But if their President is so honest, who knows what the people are like.

By the time we made it back to the turnoff the sun was sinking fast

93

and only a shred of light remained to brighten up the mountains around us. I wasn't mad that I didn't see the sunset. I've seen at least a thousand, but I wanted to see what the sunset showed me. The ride up had a small road which narrowed significantly as we got closer to the top where we were met by a light mist. Along the way there were a few   scattered homes on the side of the road, but for the most part it was a mixture of jungle and small level coffee farms with deep greens bordering the entire route. As we went through a series of sharp turns we were told by the GPS that we had reached the entrance to *El Perdido*. We pulled off and found ourselves in a tiny parking lot on the side of the mountain next to a small convenience store which was fed by the farms surrounding it on all sides. As we got out another car pulled up which let out a fair skinned girl with reddish hair who started pulling a multitude of bags from the back of her car. While the guys searched through the car I used my time to sit and change out of my wet shorts. Once changed I got out and walked up to the new traveler.

"Are you heading to *El Perdido*?"

"I am. Are you all staying there tonight?"

"That's the plan. Do you know how to get there?"

"Absolutely. You can follow me up."

As I told her yes I realized we had called earlier, but in all of the confusion we had forgotten to ever call them back and arrange a room. This would be of those situations where we just go in hoping they have pity on us and can find somewhere on the floor if need be.

"Thank you. We thought we would make it up before the sunset."

"Oh me too. And hi, My name is Emily. Nice to meet you."

"Nice to meet you too. Over there is Myles, that's Wes, and that one is Austin."

"Howdy." - Austin

"Here, lemme help you." - Patrick

"Thanks, but someone is coming down to help take my things up."

"Anywhere to go fishing around here? We're looking for some river trout." - Austin

"I don't know what that is. But there's a river over that mountain." - Emily.

"Hell yeah. I bet mountain trout gets bigger higher up." - Austin

As we stood there a short stocky man came out and Emily spoke to him in a broken but coherent version of Spanish and handed him a few dollars which he placed in his pocket. Her accent came out as Germanic as did the English she used with us. Although everyone appeared ready she stood there and delayed our departing in order to smoke a cigarette before we took the walk up. Even offering one to the man about to haul up their luggage. During the conversation which took place over the time-lapse of a slow burning menthol it was revealed that she actually worked at the hostel and was just getting back from two weeks away traveling the northern shores of South America. Further inquiry led her to reveal she had been born and raised on a sailboat the first seven years of her life. Traveling from port to port she eventually settled back in Germany where her mom enrolled her in school. Her family had never made it to the Caribbean and a younger her had promised herself that she would spend two years casually exploring once she finished school. She was now on her fifth.

After they finished their cigarettes Emily led us around the right side of the shop to a gravel path with a series of small wooden posts leading the way. As we went further we began snaking up the mountain via a series of narrow passage ways which often required us to walk single file holding our bags above our heads. If I had been doing this alone based off of directions from a printed piece of paper it's likely I would have given up and opted to do the trek when daylight returned.

"That red hair must stick out like a sore thumb here." - Patrick

"Oh yeah. They see me coming a mile away."

"At least you handle the language well enough. Did you pick it up down here?"

"Thanks. I learned enough phrases to get by until I found my way. But German is my primary language, which is great because they're probably our biggest draw outside of the Americas."

We got to the top after around fifteen minutes of exhaustive walking and saw the sprawled out campus which made up the hostel *El Perdido*. The majority of the buildings were painted yellow and had tin roofs covered in streaks of red paint. There were a few small structures resembling private homes and a stone pathway which snaked to all the important spots of a centrally located building that appeared to have the front desk and a lit up outdoor lobby. Half way down the path and off to the right was a cage. A pair of eyes gleamed from the back of the cage, going without a blink.

"What's in there?" - Patrick

"Oh that's Rocky. He's our pet Kinkajou. Let's take a break. I need to check his water while I'm here." - Emily

As we stood there and caught our breathe she walked towards the front of a cage made of wooden blanks and chicken wire.

"What the hell is that? Never seen something like that." - Wes

"Well he's a bit like a monkey if they mixed it with a raccoon. They call them honey bears around here." - Emily

"That's confusing. What does he eat?" - Wes

"Mainly fruits. Never actually seen him eat honey." - Emily

"Is he friendly?" - Patrick

"Yeah. You should come see him later." - Emily

"Why's he in a cage? He dangerous?" - Myles

"He's injured. We found him on the ground a few weeks ago. We had to make this cage on pretty short notice if you can't tell." - Emily

"Well you managed to get a legit door on the front. I say that's pretty good for short notice." - Myles

"Can we pet him?" - Patrick

"Yes, but first we gotta get you situated." - Emily

The next few minutes she went into tour mode and spoke to us with the practiced cadence of a broken record. She had given this story and this tour a thousand times by now and it showed in her delivery which mimicked a stage performer hitting their cues as she explained the locations to the kitchen and laundry room. She then introduced us to her counterpart, an Austrian named Amelia who was spending her summer working at the front desk and giving tours of the jungle. The two of them seemed like permanent fixtures latching to impermanence. Soon to be added to the list of the many expats who never returned home. An idea which I understood in part. To the people down here the problems of daily life are not nearly the same as they are for the people in the swings of normal society. Here if someone can get their hands on food, sex, shelter, and sand then there's not much reason to think about abandoning ship.

After we found our rooms and dropped off our belongings Wes and I walked up the stairs and turned onto a path which broke off towards the guest house we passed on our way in. Along the path were a few benches and hammocks which provided a perfect place to sit and see an uninterrupted view of the night sky hovering above the canopy off to our sides. I was so happy to finally be up here in the mountains. I could finally fucking relax and not stress about what trouble the guys could bring their way. And no matter what trouble they brought, at least this high up I could see it coming. It was perhaps the oldest known type of security to have an uninterrupted view between you and your horizon. And here we were with more than 4,000 feet between us and the lower terraces of the world.

This place reminded me of a time in existence that few can recall from recent memory. A time when you weren't accessible to everyone 24/7. A day when you were allowed to tell others you'd call them later.

Nowadays I've been forced to see it as a great luxury to grant myself the time away from technology and from the obligations raining upon me as a result of my perpetual accessibility. And I know the advancements are great, but aren't they infringements as well? When eminent domain takes over, it does so for the purpose of the collective, but there is always the unseen which is infringed upon, and in this case it is the domain of our privacy. Not privacy in the sense that someone is watching, but in the sense that someone is *always* watching, or for that matter always able of watch. For it is capability which is just as threatening as execution. All in all this place was perfect for our group because it was a place which catered to a reckless style of living and did not call for much discretion among its members. While we sat there Myles came by and dropped off a bottle as he put his hands on my shoulder.

"You finally drinking with me tonight?" - Myles

"Just leave the bottle. I'll be sure to use it." - Patrick

"Wes, make sure this mother fucker actually drinks. He always says he does, but I've never seen him drunk." - Myles

"There you go again. Sorry I don't get twisted and start falling over myself."

"Maybe you would if you actually took more than a shot."

At this Wes started laughing and butted into the conversation.

"What is he talking about?"

"He's just exaggerating. I've been drunk with him plenty of times when we were younger. Hell I've drank with you probably more than anyone else who knows me."

From behind the growing glow of a freshly puffed cigarette Myles looked back at Wes and gave him some instruction.

"Here Wes, I'm leaving you the bottle. Just make sure he actually swallows it."

"I'll make sure he does."

In his assertions he was half-right. I hadn't gotten drunk with him often over the years, but that wasn't for the sake of exclusion, it went for pretty much the case for anyone who knew me. This time not for a lack of experimenting, I just never enjoyed drinking regardless of what level of drunk we were going for. Which didn't match well his style because he was one of those guys who could just sit and have a few beers with anyone. Using the bonds of alcohol to tighten friendships and loosen inhibitions. Which in fairness aligned with how the majority of society viewed it, but for myself it just didn't flow with the same ease. It just turned me into a clumsier version of myself with a morning of headache and regret. Which is one of the reasons I had liked being down here on my own. I never had to refuse more than once. But with friends from home the need for refusal was constant. As we sat there I wiggled around and tried to find comfort on a bench as Wes relaxed in a mesh hammock to my side. Once we got started he didn't waste any time before reaching down to open up the bottle and take a few generous gulps.

"Next time we gotta bring some gummies." - Wes

"Why?"

"Myles is great when he's high, he laughs for a while and then just passes out. He just refuses to smoke."

"I feel that. The actual smoke in my lungs part is my least favorite part of the process, but ironically I can't do gummy bears either, I'll never stop eating them. You about ready to head up?"

"I guess. What time you think people will start partying?"

"Not sure, I see some people on the porch already, but it still looks pretty low key."

"Well let's get on fixin' that."

After taking another swig he extended the open end towards me and asked if I wanted a hit. Wes and I sat there passing the bottle back and forth as we saw the deck above begin to fill up with people rotating in from their temporary hiding spots to grab a beer and see what all the noise was about. By now Austin and Myles had taken over the playlist and were entertaining the crowds with a range of music chosen from his phone. They didn't act any different than I remembered growing up. With them you got what you got. No affront or fake faces. Just pure unhindered nature. A rarity among people these days. At least the versions we see in public.

While Wes continued to sip his rum I sat there thinking about how happy I was to have had our plans so messed up. A part of me would have loved to have stayed in some luxurious treehouse, but this was the type of place I would rather be in at the end of the day. And it was the type of place most travelers with a preference for more inclusive accommodations would never see. Which for some reason gave me a bit of happiness to consider as I took another gulp from the bottle. I don't know why it mattered to me. Perhaps I hated hearing the tales of those people who would look at me in the city and say, *"Oh what? You lived where? Oh my God it's so lovely there."* And then proceed to tell me about some small ex-pat village or an all inclusive resort where they had stayed for a week back in college. After which I always nodded and worked my way out of the conversation as soon as possible, knowing I had seen a different view that the region had to offer. It wasn't that they didn't want that view. At least I don't think so. It seemed more like they didn't wanna go through the journey. That was the part of my story where they always seemed to fall off. The parts where the conditions became far from convenient. The same people who needed the constant comforts of the modern would were the types of people who would never make it up here. They wouldn't leave the capital. They would't hitch a ride on some bus up some mountain. And they would never hike up a trail carrying all of their own bags. And for that reason, they would never understand why we did it or just how great this was. This all coming from someone who still finds it questionable to do an ultra-marathon.

Then again, maybe my thoughts were such because I could never afford to be otherwise. Perhaps I was only ever a traveler of meager means because I was a man of those same means. If the entry to my existence had been different I can't assure I wouldn't have ended up doing just the same. I could only hope that in such a situation my curious nature would have taken over before I became one of the many consumed by the need to mark off every country they could in as short a time as possible. Don't get me wrong, I had my own checklist and I admired anyones willingness and desire to travel. I hope by now at least that much is clear, but I despised the necessity to do so under any guise of certainty. After which most would claim they knew what it was like to 'rough it' with the best of them. And I'll be fair, this didn't apply to all of those who had grown up with the luck of being born within the current eras most favored borders. There were plenty of people I knew who grew up wearing turtle necks and polos that had trekked up the side of mountains and washed their clothes on a washboard in the middle of Africa just like the locals. But my most recent encounters had begun to embitter me with those who had an inability to vacate whatever overpriced city they had come from for longer than it took to get a selfie at the cities top ten views. And I just never wanted to be one of those people constantly making another footprint in the guestbook of a nation while only leaving with a snapshot and a shot glass. To see the canal and not be curious about the minds who built it would be just as absurd as walking down the trail of tears in a pair of cushioned loafers and claiming you understand the struggle. It could never mean the same. And though I shout at myself and others I argue internally about this because in the end things only matter to us to the extent that we are able to define them with our own associative meanings to whatever it is we are considering. And maybe the journey to see it all was meaning enough for some. Maybe the goal was as simple as a dog marking its territory on every corner it passes without quite getting why. And who am I to judge what satisfies their goals when interpreting their environment? After all I was as big a fan as any of the freedom to wonder while I wander, and sometimes it's important to just absorb, but still I suggest taking a look at who does what and where they do it before you travel. The world you want exists. It's only a matter of finding it. Don't just take in a view. Have it explained to you. And even if we must ultimately reach the state of one refusing to get outside of our comfort zone, we should still try to learn something about the places we visit. I always try to ask myself, what did I do worth while on my trip? Did I eat with a local? Did I learn how to make something, or how they make something? What knowledge am I bringing back? Few remember a day when travel was based off the necessity to bring back something essential from lands far away, whether that be lessons or goods remains revolving. And as the bottle emptied, it felt like I had a bit of both in my hands.

When we left our spot we went up the hill to join the party, but as I stepped inside Myles pulled me aside and invited me to go down to our room for a quick sample of his leftovers. At first I felt a little iffy about the offer, but I had taken plenty of time to sit with my feelings from before and realized that I had not since had the desire to participate and therefore figured why not. In that sense, I was admittedly lucky. Not everyone could do that. Too many use to over use. But isn't that the case with anything that works? When we were finished we reunited with the growing group of people in the party. As we entered a room of people dancing I found myself taken over with energy and the urge to walk so I went out to the porch where I could escape the noise and pace around a bit. This lasted a few songs until a series of people interrupted my silence on their way to the first of many smoke breaks.

After a while I gave up on alone time and found myself talking with a girl in a black sundress with sort of a gypsy inspired look. She had the *travel the world forever* type of vibe. I heard her speaking with some people around me earlier and was able to figure out that she spoke Arabic before she mentioned her nationality. It wasn't too hard, she used the word *habibi* and that was that. She introduced herself as Cadira and told me that while Canadian by birth, her parents were Egyptian and Uruguayan, a blend only possible by the integrated state of existence which had taken place over the last few generations. Perhaps a blend even more rare than the exporting of hops. When I finally started going through the few phrases I could remember I quickly revealed my lack of depth beyond a few simple formalities. A curse of both the time it had been since I used it and the linguistic distances between our two dialects.

Which was to be expected, they may all speak Arabic, but the versions of it vary greatly from region to region, and the North African dialect had enough French woven into it to get a confused look from any outsider. It was the unifying words for 'my love' like *habibi,* and the most universal of sayings for 'no more' like *hallas,* which held them all under the same canopy known as the Levantine.

"So how do you know Arabic?" - Cadira

"I spent some time living in Morocco. I didn't really pick up a ton of Arabic though. I can just say enough to get myself a cup of coffee and maybe ask for directions to the next town. Elementary shit."

"Well you're doing better than most. Where are you from?"

"Nowhere you would know. A small town in Virginia a few hours outside of Washington D.C."

"That's even more surprising. The Americans I've met never knew other languages."

"Well I probably woulda been one of those if I hadn't lived outside of the states for long enough to need to."

Truth be told I wasn't surprised that she was suspicious of my background. People were usually hesitant to believe I was an American once they knew I could speak more than one language. That and the accent always throws them off. Which I was fortunate to have inherited from a blend of diverse accents teaching me over the years without any interference from a non-native. Though I'm sure my love of Spanish cinema and foreign films as a whole had helped just as much. That and the encouraging reality of all that became accessible to me once I learned another language.

"So what made you pick Spanish?"

"A combination somewhere between necessity and proximity. Those are the only reasons anyone learns a second language in the first place. That and falling in love."

"So true. Lemme see if I remember, *Eísai ómorfi.*"

"What's that?"

"It's Greek for *you're so pretty.* Picked it up in Mykonos. Well. I guess the more accurate thing to say would be it picked me up."

Our conversation was fueled by competition and a flow of liquor streaming through both of us which led to some bold statements on my part when I found out she was trilingual by birth, one of the few things which ever made me jealous.

"That's awesome. I'm trying to get to at least five when it's all said and done." - Patrick

"And how many do you speak already?"

"Well only two fluently. But the others are coming together pretty well. Just gotta get over the hump."

"If you've not mastered at least three by now you're already too far behind. Five is a lot. I think you gotta learn a few before you're eighteen to make that possible."

"That's not true."

"Yes it is. I wouldn't know three if I wasn't raised with them."

"You don't think so?"

"Nope. I actually failed French in high school. So just out of curiosity, which other languages are you trying to learn?"

"French for sure. Obviously Arabic. And for the last one, maybe Russian. Maybe German. See which one comes up. For now the others will give me some interesting places to travel for the next few decades."

"Why those in particular?"

"They're the top second languages of some of the more obscure places I want to see."

"You don't need to speak the language to visit somewhere."

"Oh I know. But it's more than just visiting. There are places I wanna visit and then there are places I wanna chill. If I wanna chill there, then it's likely I'm gonna wanna go back over the years. The languages of those places are the ones I wanna pick up."

"Interesting. Do you have people to practice with?"

"Eh more or less."

"If you don't have diverse versions of each, it's gonna be hard to get them down. And not everyone speaks a second language. What are you gonna do about those people?"

"The same thing I'll do with Japanese or Amharic. Find someone who speaks those for me. Or keep my mouth shut."

"Don't think you could learn them?"

"If I had the time and could go live there it'd be cool to try. Especially those two. I find them fascinating, but they're a lot to take on if I'm not gonna use them on the regular. At most I would learn a few things here and there for the essential shit like bathrooms and exits."

"Japanese isn't that obscure. There's over 100 million people there. I went to Tokyo. It was wild."

"Yeah, but it's not like I'm gonna use it outside of Japan."

"True, well even if you stick to just the basics I still think five is too much for one person. Might as well try to learn every instrument and make your own symphony."

"It's not the same."

"Oh it is. I bet all of that talk and you don't even play an instrument do you?"

"Nope. Sure don't."

"Then you may understand a lot of words. But if you don't understand the language of music then you don't understand language."

As her tone changed from curiosity to disbelief I couldn't properly articulate the issue from feeling, but I knew I didn't agree with her on sheer principle. Faith belongs with one's owns abilities before it belongs anywhere else. Plus I had met people who had done similar things and I would join them in that achievement. Trilingual neighbors and polyglot teachers somehow still teaching middle school to name a few. Unfortunately I was too drunk to convey the thoughts in my mind in coherent enough a manner to make any sense to her. And even if I could it still bothered me that someone thought something was too difficult or too time consuming to consider perusing. I mean, it was only a few ways to say a few words, it's not like I was revising *Grey's Anatomy*. The book not the show. Plus, what could be more important than understanding the structure of language? After all, it was the only way I knew how to truly understand another culture. And it was of the upmost importance as a means of making it around the world without the blinders of confusion that can come with a lack of understanding those around you. Or for that matter a means of understanding how those around you even communicate with themselves. Because once you can speak in a new language you begin to notice the shifts in how you use the words you use with yourself; and once one can master the conversation between their own two ears everything else seems simple. Though at first I had just used it as a way to get around. When I was away it wasn't like I could develop longterm relationships. Instead I focused my time on learning enough to explore on my own and got by with a few conversations along the way. And look where it had gotten me. A few degrees from the equator, in an argument with some feisty half-Egyptian. All while making me realize how much I had missed this life and the environments in provided.

As we continued to go back and forth I started sensing a conflict rising amongst the characters around me. One moment she was talking to me and then the next it seemed like she was looking over my shoulder interpreting a lengthy message. One which turned out to be from her boyfriend attempting to pull her back into their circle of travelers. She had spent too much laughing as she called me and my ambitions impossible. I think it was the loose hand behind her cigarette and the smile in her laughter that drew the outside attention. With a brief pause she told me she would be right back and went off to talk with the man motioning from beyond my sight. Standing there alone I attempted to keep my attention away from the situation as the two started to argue back and forth. Granted he was overreacting, but I couldn't blame him for his current mood. We were cornered off on the balcony and to a drunk guy who had never met me it probably appeared a lot worse than it really was and she had done nothing to calm his concerns. Nor did it look like she had any interest in doing so by how quickly she brushed him off at his closing remarks. And despite what I may have said earlier about enjoying the ways of flirtation, I wasn't doing that this time. I promise. I was just arguing capabilities and enjoying someone who could engage in a fun exchange. Though I gotta admit I understand what it feels like to hear anyone talking to your girlfriend in a foreign tongue, hell that might be the most human of all insecurities, the attention of someone we love being stolen away by something we can't understand. Perhaps in the end it was the smile she gave me in remembrance of some suave Greek charming his way into her heart which made him uncomfortable.

Of course I could see the lack of focus in her eyes and knew it was the combination of liquids which were leading the majority of her decisions tonight. As she went back to talking with me I saw her boyfriend walk off and head towards their dorm noticeably displeased. She then went on to tell me about their relationship and their plans to backpack through South America over the next few months. His name was Kellen and he had an 80's grunge look and a nomadic vibe, one of the many traits he shared with Cadira. They had met on the road and only started dating in the last few weeks when an intersection of decisions had turned into a relationship. Easy now to see how they had wound up together, perhaps even more understandable that he was concerned about her running off, he barely knew her. And they both came off as people incapable of being anchored, and that's saying quite a bit coming from myself, but I wish them the best of luck. Then again, I could be wrong. If you met a girl on the go and you really wanted to know how a life with her would be, all you gotta do is travel together for a while. Truth be told I was a bit envious they were getting the chance to try. Something about a romance on the road always appealed to me.

When Cadira went off to find her boyfriend I joined Wes and a circle of German students who were explaining how their school systems worked and told us we were likely to meet plenty more Europeans who were taking advantage of their extended holiday by backpacking for the month through the region. While talking with them I became reminded of how at home I had felt my first time coming to a hostel. It had given me a feeling of home similar to that of a frat house with a weekly rotation of brothers. The first time that I found a group of people gathering from different parts of the globe it had shown me how so many differing courses could lead to the same destination. Here we were all living in the environmental consequence of a shared decision to come here tonight. Made by some weeks ago and others earlier this morning, but one way or another we had all wound up under the same roof. As the others faded back inside I stayed on the porch and found a spot to sit on the railing. As I sat there enjoying a few moments of shut-eye Myles came through the door and offered me a quick pick me up.

"Come on man. It'll stop the hangover before it even starts."

"Nah man I'm good."

"Whatever dude. It'll be in the room if you want any."

"Much appreciated."

"Anytime. You got a $20? I need something to roll up."

"Yeah dude. There's one in the top of my bag."

He wasn't wrong, but I was already facing enough difficulty not falling over and I didn't need to send my body into another cycle of adrenaline surged intoxication just yet. When Myles left I looked down from the balcony and saw him going straight to our room to tap into what was assumably a dwindling supply of cocaine. He knew better than to offer it to anyone around us other than myself and perhaps that was his strategy at pretending to share, to offer it to the person least likely to take it. In a lot of ways I understood where he was in this moment, I had been there before, but instead of intoxication being a thing which came to him, it had become something which he sought after. As I thought about it, maybe for him the drugs were an escape away from a life where he felt invincible. He was a Goliath among men and perhaps his search for escape had required much higher doses than the world of the normally functioning could offer. Something one would need to cope with as much as one copes with mortality. And what other choice did he have? He lived in a world where a man could be self-medicated by odorless grains and maintain an existence free of judgement as long as he kept himself free of scents or signs.

I barely saw him for the rest of the night once he inherited the friendship of a British backpacker with the only oxford cut collar I'd seen this far above sea level and a particularly runny nose. Our one interaction involved him offering me a line while he waited for the pack of cigarettes to make it his way. An easy pass to take when offered by a stranger too well dressed for the situation. From here it looked like

Myles had something that someone in his life needed to address. But the problem was, it wasn't in anyones interest to call him out no matter he did. Especially not as long as he was providing. Which I guess is the curse you get when you're the boss. There was a day where that person could have been me, but I had lost the authority that I once had with him. And as far as sobering up I would feel a bit like a hypocrite to say anything to him. Nor was I sure why life was always about getting the monkey off your back. Some of us need a monkey to let us out of our cage and show us it's okay to play around once in a while. Although Myles was not a man who needed any monkey to release his wild side. Nor did he need an audience. He had helped shown me my own monkey existed, but luckily my door to that world was without a lock on either side.

By 3 A.M. a series of Irish goodbyes had thinned out the party by more than half and those left trying to keep up with the drinking power of my friends were failing hard. I could see they wouldn't stop anytime soon which told me that we were unlikely to make a morning bus unless one of us went out of the way to do so. At that I seized a lull in the music and tried to plant our favor into the minds of our hosts and the guys chimed in with the right amount of charm needed to create a verbal contract for tomorrows lodging. As I left the party I walked out the front door and made my way up a series of paths which brought me out by the cage where they kept Rocky. Inside I saw him latched to a set of branches in the back so I shined my cell-phone to see if I could bait him over, but all I saw was the reflection of two glowing eyes and a head bobbing around curiously. The gate was locked, but I had seen our host plant the keys on a slab of concrete above the door so I reached up and brought down a set of rusty keys attached to a keychain made of thin rope and what I'm pretty sure was the rung off a shower curtain. When I opened the cage he slowly made his way towards the front and then stopped in his tracks a few feet from me. I tried to make any pleasant sound I could think of to get him closer, but he seemed apprehensive to get in arms reach of a stranger. I looked around the cage for some food, but I didn't see any containers. Knowing he would be more receptive to a treat I ran down to the kitchen and started to raid the fridge looking for some fruit to attract my new friend. On the bottom shelf I found a full bag of tiny oranges so I took two, which seemed like just enough to go unnoticed and closed the fridge. When I got back to the cage I was stopped in my tracks by the sight of the door being pushed open a few inches with Rocky edging his way through.

"Fuck. No no no. Stay there."

I put my foot down to block the door and lowered my hands to reveal one of the tiny oranges as I crouched down hoping to keep him from going by. As he got closer he crept very cat like and brushed himself along my leg as he circled me. When he got close enough I looped my forearm under his belly and picked him up without any resistance. He was clearly used to the scent of humans and even clung to me as I tried to put him down once I had him far enough. Once I eased him back to the ground I skirted backwards and closed the door relieved that my mistake had not turned into some long chase for an animal I couldn't catch and probably wouldn't have been able to see. As I went down the stairs I noticed a series of hammocks on the far reaches of the deck which caused me to change my route and find the one with the best view. As I settled in I felt bursts of moist air being pushed up from the canopy below and the temperature continued to drop over the next hour as I tossed about. Pulling both sides of the hammock close to my shoulders I locked in the heat and looked up at the night sky comfortable with the certainty of a good view in the morning and a breeze to rock me to sleep.

Day 5: In the Clouds of El Perdido
Boquete, Panama

To say that I woke up this morning would imply I actually got some sleep, but if I am to be honest that's not how the translator in me would interpret the few hours I spent on high alert from the nonstop gusts of cold wind which shot their way up the mountain and into my hammock all night. Surges which caused me to twitch and reawaken at least every twenty minutes. Upon opening my eyes from this half conscious cryo-chamber I felt the soft collapse of my hoodie blocking whatever view I may have been granted as the warmth from my breathe continued to mend the cotton to my nose. As I shewed away the hood of my sweater my pupils were quickly dilated by a myriad sight of bright colors scribbled across the sky which had been beamed into the atmosphere by a vibrant pink sun slowly peaking over the chalky silhouette of Volcano Baru. The last time I woke up in the mountains overlooking something so beautiful it was with my former favorite distraction, now I sat in a hammock cold, alone, and annoyed. Oh how life changes.

Though still feeling all of the adjectives previously mentioned I was still somewhat grateful to have somehow woken up without a hangover. Something I quickly attributed to the recovery benefits I have heard attached to cryotherapy. I mean if three minutes is all that's prescribed then I can't imagine how good last night was for me. Cold had become my favorite high. Probably because it had been available so rarely over the last few years. Or perhaps I didn't go to enough places where the cold was cold enough to speak of. Harder still as those places seem to be dwindling. Of course this train of thought and moment of planetary concern was taken off track when I tried getting up and was struck with the same uneasy feeling I could associate with anytime I had gone beyond the ten drinks needed to get it going. In my state of confusion and queasiness I decided I needed to walk it off a bit and at the very least be out of sight if I needed to throw up. In hopes of avoiding that situation I got moving and made my way to the first set of bathrooms which I found halfway down a hallway alongside the lower dorms. Unfortunately there were only two occupied stalls and both had open bottoms so I decided to make the trek to a set of bathrooms overlooking the side of the property. When I made it there I saw a few cleaning buckets outside of the doors and heard some chattering coming from behind the closed stalls. Existence is a splendidly shared inconvenience sometimes. We all get to play, but we all have to play together. Now if only we could all agree on the same schedule.

When I left the restroom I decided to take some time to walk off that queasy feeling and came across a sign which advertised a maze built out of a sculpted garden and decorative rocks, a sort of art on display in an elaborate mixture that gave an amazing view as it led you away from the hostel. From the top right of the maze you could see the full expanse of the yellow buildings which made up the property surrounded by deep greens on all sides which dropped to a canopy below where a massive valley sat between a ridge of mountains snaking along each side. The volcano was still unexposed, but the far off gleam of the Pacific Ocean could now be seen being fed by the many inlets running along the coast. As I looked around I couldn't help but sit there with the overarching curiosity of how they got any of this shit up here. The path last night was so narrow in some parts that I could not have walked shoulder to shoulder with someone, let alone carry up a dryer.

I needed to wake up so I decided to go search for some coffee. The moment called for at least two cups, but I'd be happy with anything I could find. I walked back and approached the front desk to find Emily sitting hunched over in her chair attempting to keep her eyes open as a grey hoodie hid the few times she did let them close.

"Good morning. Feeling okay?" - Emily

"I feel like I should be asking you."

"I'm feeling pretty rough right now, but I'll live. It's my first day working in over two weeks."

"Yeah you'll survive."

"And what about you?"

"About as awake as I'm gonna be. Just a bit queasy."

"Have you eaten anything yet?"

"No. But I could use some toast if you got some."

"How about some coffee too?"

"You read my mind."

She gave a kind smile through her glassy eyes and went up the ladder behind her desk to a loft above where all the supplies were kept.

"Hey. Can you grab some eggs too? I don't wanna go all the way to my car right now."

"Of course. It's two for a dollar."

"I can live with that."

When she made it back down she handed me a few eggs and turned on a pot of coffee. I went and put the eggs in a bag in the fridge and then returned to the top of the stairs where I sat rocking back and forth as the aroma of locally sourced coffee filled the air around me. Once brewed she poured us both a cup and brought out some little Swiss cookies she kept for such occasions. They were more like sweetened crackers than anything, but they were the perfect thing to help settle my stomach at the time. Normally I would be in a hurry to get going with the first part of my day, but today it felt like a big enough accomplishment just to be awake. After my cup of caffeine I sat and watched as the world around me brightened up and those not affected by the night before began moving around the stairwells and lavatories to my side. As I sat there I heard some noises coming from below the deck and soon became curious as to what was going on beneath me. I stood up and started to stumble my way around the side of the building where I came across two kids crouching down under the deck peering over a tall batch of grass. This wasn't the type of place I expected to be seeing kids and I wasn't feeling in the best shape to be dealing with them or anyone else at the moment so I tried to walk away and almost made it until one of them turned around and started to wave me over in that unignorably excited way that only a child can.

"Señor! Señor! Come here! Look what we found."

As I walked towards them I guessed they were both somewhere around six to seven years of age and at first glance I thought they might even be twins. Approaching the two I realized I could not walk under the deck with the same ease as them so I ducked my head and scooted along as I found myself staring at what had gotten the boys so excited. Curled up in front of us was a snake with black, white, and red stripes lining its back.

"What kind is it?"

They both looked up at me for some sort of adult confirmation, but I had no clue. Over the last few years I had not taken the care to learn about snakes and thus far I'd been happy to avoid them and their homes.

"Uh I don't know, but why don't you all stand back over here a bit more. Has it moved since you got here?

"No. We trapped it. Wait here! I'll go get my dad. He'll know what type it is!"

While the two of us waited there the snake decided it had had enough of our inferior blockade and slithered through the grass just barely missing our feet. When the other kid finally returned he had a man with him in his forties wearing a blue t-shirt and sporting a pair of thick rimmed glasses on a well aging face.

"This is our dad! Tell him about the snake." - Kid

"Well sir. My favorite thing to tell you is that it's no longer here."

"Good. Any idea what kind it was?"

"Not a clue."

"What did it look like?"

"A few stripes. Different colors. Black."

"Hmm. Probably just a coral. Nothing to worry about. Probably safe to get down on my knees a bit hand help them look don't you think?"

I stood there as their dad joined a feigned search for their missing creature. They seemed so grown and casual about this whole thing like it was just a normal day searching for some snake in the mountains of Panama, your typical six-year old stuff. By where I was on the shared timeline of life I dwarfed them in experience, but theirs compounded would soon surpass me. Growing up I had done all of the exploring that I could for the environments where I was placed. The woods in the day, and the cornfields at night, but once I was introduced to the world of driving my existence changed completely. Who would these kids be behind the wheel and how could I ever compete with such an expansive view on the world once they got going?

"These guys seem to handle the travel well. Been on the road long?"

"Only two weeks now."

"Only? That's impressive with kids."

"Yeah. Ya know, we wanted to wait for a trip like this until they could walk and remember everything. Most importantly walk. We practically had to carry them up that trail to get here."

"That doesn't sound fun. What made you all come all the way up here?"

"Well my wife and I have always been into birdwatching and this region has some of the best. And I'm glad the kids are into the animals, but I wish they'd stop finding snakes. I keep telling them to look up in the trees not down on the ground."

The father went on to explain how he and his wife planned to see all of Italy next summer with the kids at their side. Since the snakes were no longer around I soon said my goodbyes and went back up to the kitchen to make some toast. My first view inside revealed a tightly packed room with a mixture of useful appliances and ample cabinet spaces flooded with the partially used ingredients of previous travelers. There were already multiple people working on their own dishes without interruption of one another. Luckily they had two stove tops and a double sink so it was a prime room for group cooking. I squeezed my way over to some empty counter space and started to crack my eggs into a bowl I found stacked in the corner. As in nature predators on the hunt do not interfere with the lives of other predators equally engaged and those cooking eggs do not bother those cooking the bacon. And somehow this dynamic worked as we all tried to hover around each others culinary progress. While cooking I saw the Canadian boyfriend from the night before. I knew we were likely to be in close quarters if the rain continued so I sent a few words his way hoping to smooth things over. After all, I may have been guilty of commanding her attention via good conversation, but I had done nothing worth feeling offended over. Hostels were the closest thing that the road had to NYC, but they didn't provide the same anonymity and therefore I would be best to say something and clear the air.

"Hey man. You're Kellen right?" - Patrick

He looked at me with a noticeable hesitation my greeting.

"Yeah. That's me. Whats up?"

"I'm Patrick. Nice to meet you. You're going down to Colombia I hear?"

"Yeah…In a few days. Why?"

"Your girl mentioned you all might go to the coast. There's a place you've gotta try if you get to Santa Marta, *Hambrita Lolita*, great food. And here's the name of a hostel we stayed in."

"Thanks man…I'll definitely give the food a shot, but I think we're gonna be camping most of the time."

"Oh that's awesome. Going to Tayrona?"

"Never heard of it. You'd have to ask Cadira. She's got the whole thing planned out somewhere."

"Well in case I don't see her why don't you take this. And check it out. It's a really dope park a few hours up the coast from Cartagena."

I handed him a piece of paper which he shoved in his pocket before retreating back to his cigarette and eggs. I took no offense and decided that I had done enough diplomacy for one morning and got going from there. As I left I looked back and saw the two kids from before with all of their bags strapped to their tiny bodies. Then I noticed one of the kids had a tiny guitar about the size of a ukulele.

"Is Amelia around? I wanna play her a song I wrote for her."

"You write songs?" - Emily

"Sure do. I'm gonna be a singer. Is she around?"

"No. I'm sorry, but she's still asleep. I don't think she's feeling well."

When I saw this I felt a little bad because the only reason she was not awake was that we had kept her up drinking all night. And I could remember days of being a hopelessly young kid trying to gain the right impression of an older woman. Even though I had never learned guitar to do it.

"Daddy can we put the song on YouTube? I wanna send it to Amelia when she wakes up!"

His dad patted him on the back and assured him they would get a video sent to the hostel once they returned home. I didn't hesitate to think that video will eventually make its way here via the internet. I didn't see a lot of giving up qualities in that little guy. When the kids left I sat and ate my food until Emily came to discuss our housing situation for the next night. We were welcome to stay, but we were going to have a more communal dorm since our current room was reserved for tonight. It was now after twelve and it made sense for everyone to get moving a bit either way. When I finished my food I headed down the stairs and to the right of the hostel where a simple barrier of PVC piping and some rebar separated me from the steep drop below. The steps were double the width of normal stairs and forced you to either stretch your stride or to take two small steps on each. Going down I was a bit uncomfortable to think that I had done this in absolute darkness the night before. When I made it to the room I opened the door and found Austin folding his clothes while the other two remained passed out in their cubbies.

"Hey guys we gotta move to another room."- Patrick

From inside the top cubby a voice projected,

"We're up. What's the plan for today?" - Wes

"Let's get fucked up and go fishing." - Austin

"Sounds good to me. Patrick, you go with Austin down to our car. We need a few things from his suitcase. And while you're gone we'll move everything into the new rooms. You know where they're putting us yet?" - Myles

"Nah man just talk with the front desk about that."

I was at first a little puzzled to see the guys were in a go-mode from the moment they opened their eyes, but their bodies were moving with slower reaction than their minds seemed to want.

"Pat you got the keys?" - Austin

"They're in my pocket."

"Cool. I'll be ready in just a minute to grab a coffee."

After his coffee Austin and I made the walk to the bottom down a path which was much more manageable during daylight and without the weight of our luggage. This time I was able to appreciate the entrance to a farm off to our right before the paths emptied us onto the road. The fence was wooden and simple with metallic cross bars closing below an arch which held the skull of a longhorn much like you'd expect to see at the entrance of a ranch in Texas. What an out of place relic. Beyond the fence I saw the signs of livestock leading to a series of hills covered in coffee trees. Beyond the plants nothing was visible amongst the thick clouds, not even the bright yellow paint from our mountain hideaway. We got to the car and I opened the trunk to help Austin find some small fishing lures as he started to dig through a bag stowed away under the front seat.

"Hey, look at this stuff we got." - Austin

He handed me a bag with a texture similar to that of a tea bag, but this one covered my entire palm and was filled with a fine green powder.

"Where did you get this?"

"Those guys at the beach in Peligrada. They were putting in their drink. I just need some honey or something as sweetener. Here smell it."

"No thanks. What's this shit called?"

"I don't know. It's supposed to mellow you out. Some type of ground up mushroom."

"Dude I'm not drinking some shit you got from some strangers."

"You ate their oranges without being suspicious."

"Fair point."

"Dude they were all doing it and they seemed to be having themselves a good old time. Hell it's probably why Myles lost his wallet."

"What do you mean?"

"I don't know. Just saying. It's possible. He took a big swig of it before we left the beach the other day."

"Makes sense why he didn't make such a big deal of the whole thing. Did they say how long it lasts?"

"The guy showed me four fingers. So I'm guessing four to five hours. Maybe days? Who the fuck knows. I just know it works."

"So that'll be like a week the way my body works. No thanks. You guys have fun though."

As we walked into the store he continued to pitch me on his idea and explained how he determined $40 as a good price for his purchase made in secrecy. It wasn't logic I cared to explain, but now we had it. Inside the store a mixture of convenience store and restaurant occupied the front half of the building, while the back held a series of partially stocked shelves and a counter with an ancient cash register and a few boxes of gum. Behind the counter was a little girl tall enough to reach the register, but too shy to inquire if we needed anything. Upon noticing us a woman came from behind curtains separating the store from a small room. By this time Austin had found all the ingredients he needed for our special tea and even picked up a few extra fruits.

"Algo mas?" - Little Girl

"Do you have any fish bait?" - Patrick

At this question the kid paused and looked around uncertain where to direct me. The woman then stepped into tell us about an old man named Angelo who lived down the hill and could help us with anything we needed to know about the area. From there Austin and I made our way across the street and down a gravel driveway which led to an old farm house where a water-well built in stone sat with a bucket dangling from a thick brown rope attached to a wooden frame. To my left was a pig in a kennel with some roosters clucking about in the cages behind him. A large pond graced the back of the property which reached beyond the edge of the fog. In front of the house an old man was putting some fruit on a stack of boxes to take to the market. The man, curious at the arrival of two guests, left his stack with a few yellow fruits in hand and approached us with an offering.

"Hola. What can I do for you guys."

"We're staying up at *El Peridido* and we're looking for some suggestions on good fishing spots. The lady up the hill told us you may have a few things to say about all that."

At this point the pig put his hooves over the fence and indicated with a series of grunts and snorts that he wanted to take part. He's roamed these hills plenty so why shouldn't he be included? I've always wondered how many secrets of the forest have become forever buried with the morning bacon and eggs. If anyone knows where the best fungus can be found, it's gotta be him. The old man went along to tell us of a few spots where we could find fish along the mountain and encouraged us to wait until we made it to the streams to pick our own worms. Once he had told us all he could it was time for us to move on and get our plan in order. I didn't have my notebook with me in that moment and the man was speaking so much that I only jotted down a few general directions regarding which parts of the mountain we should be walking down.

The clouds were coming in even heavier and the smell of rain loomed in the air as we made our way back up the hill. I was less than thrilled at the thought of a long hike without the proper shoes, but I had done this to myself and I had to remember that on any other day back home I would be thrilled to say yes to climbing up the side of a mountain compared to anything else I was likely to be doing. Austin and I reached the dorms to find the guys ready and waiting outside of our room.

"We doing this hike or what?" - Wes

"Only if Myles got the hot water ready." - Austin

As we walked into to the room Myles brought out a small thermos of hot water with a few coffee cups ready to be filled. We took the cups out to balcony and sat down as our feet dangled above the canopy spreading down the mountain. I peered down and happily noticed that most of my powder was still sitting at the bottom of the glass. I remembered a doctor who once told me the only difference between poison and medicine was the dosage so I stirred up the water just enough to draw some to the surface before taking a small sip. And happily so as this is the type of ready environment I had been waiting for since we got here. Not to mention I could afford to give up my night without the concerns of later obligations, lightening the load of letting go. After my sip I sat the rest of the cup down on the railing by the door and started to walk off the balcony.

"Who's carrying the backpack?" - Myles

"I got it man. Give 'er here." - Austin

"Wes. Drink your fucking tea." - Myles

"Nah I'm good."

"Alright fine. Austin, split his cup with me."

"Myles. Don't do that…Here, just gimme that."

As Myles and Austin got situated in their ponchos Wes handed his cup over to me with a set of instructions.

"Here man. Just hold this and pour it out as we go along."

"You don't want any?"

"If I'm gonna be fucked up I wanna be relaxing somewhere. Not fucking hiking like these lunatics."

We started to walk away from the property and followed the directions to the entrance of the property where we turned up a path of stones until the official path ended and we were met with a light incline of exposed roots and clay. The clouds above us had created a mist, but it had yet to turn into rainfall. Either way I was having a tough time with my right sandal. The tongue was starting to pull was from the bottom each time I landed in the mud and I knew soon enough it was likely to fall off. Though this still didn't take away from the joy I was experiencing being surrounded by the jungle again. I had always enjoyed my time in the wild. It was this type of mind clearing environment which I had used to clear my head after scrambling to get myself away from the situation in Bocas. After walking a little over ten minutes I noticed that Myles and Austin were nowhere to be seen.

"Hey. Wait a minute. Let's chill." - Patrick

"Where are the guys?"

"I don't know. We can relax a bit."

With a series of heavy breaths he responded slowly.

"Okay man. How you feeling?"

"My feet are soaked, but I did that to myself."

We waited for the guys and got consumed by the sights around us as a heightened sense of colors trickled into my eyes. The greens were more neon and the reds sharper. Soon the forest around us became monotone with the sound of raindrops hitting giant leaves on their slow journey through the canopy. The haze from the fog was cluttered with a stream of tiny rainbows along the water droplets as they passed briefly through the streams of light in the mist. There were no birds or bugs to see or hear as they had all hidden themselves in any crevice they could find on the trees around us. Stand there I began to notice patches of rich green moss facing me along a row of trees to the side of our trail. The moss back home tells me how to tell direction and if the same holds true here then we were moving north. We stood around long enough to catch our breathes and take in the sights before our two friends appeared from the fog below.

"How is the guy in sandals beating everyone in a pair of hiking boots?" - Patrick

"We're in no hurry bro." - Myles

"You fuckin' better be. The rain's gonna pick up soon so you need to move it if you're going to get back before sunset."

"Why do you think we brought lights? We're night fishing bro."

"I didn't come along to do anything in the dark."

"Well, you came along so I guess you did."

I glanced over at Wes and saw he felt the same as I did on the matter. I did not join this hike to fish in the dark and there was no language I could speak which would help us find our way through this fog in the dark. So they could do all that on their own if they pleased. I signed up for a few things, but up and down a mountainside at night in the rain just wasn't one of them and I was not going to volunteer or be coerced. When we got towards to the top I could no longer see clearly in any direction beyond a few steps ahead. All around was a blinding glow coming from the sun attempting to pierce through the clouds above us. While Wes sat there slowing his breath I stood there and looked over at a thin layer of water picking up pace as it ran down an already muddy trail.

"Alright man. You ready to head back?" - Patrick

"Yeah man I'm good." - Wes

"You guys really aren't gonna come along?" - Myles

"Nah man. I don't wanna deal with this in the dark." - Patrick

"Suit yourself. Save us some sides for this dinner we're about to ball out with."

"Will do."

With that they both stepped into the fog and within a few seconds were completely out of sight once more. As I watched their silhouettes disappear I looked over at Wes who was now crouching down catching his breath.

"How you feeling?" - Patrick

"A little thirsty, but I'll live. You good?"

"Yeah man I'm good whenever."

"Do you feel that tea at all?"

"I don't think it did anything."

"Me either dude. Myles might have cooked it too long."

"Oh well, guess it's for the better. This hike is way more intense than I thought it would be. And these fucking roots suck. Though I was hoping for the visuals of them to be a bit more intense."

"Dude it's your fault for being barefoot."

"I may not have brought hiking boots, but I didn't choose for my sandals to break either. I'm honestly ready to head back whenever. If I keep walking with that strap slipping out of place I'm gonna break my ankle."

We sat down on the driest spots we could find and rested for a bit until starting our way back down. On the way down my sandal was beginning to give on all sides with the center tie becoming increasingly loose at the completion of each step. I wasn't about to break my ankle this high up so I took them off and placed them into the space between my belt and pants to keep them secure.

"You're not gonna keep your shoes on?" - Wes

"Well it's either dirty feet or a rolled ankle."

From there we continued walking and by the time we reached the bottom it was an outright downpour all around us. When I finally saw the glimmer of lights from the hostel I picked up my pace and rushed for cover from the buckets of water emptying themselves onto the ground around me. We ran to the porch and I found a few towels on a shelf off to the side of the picnic table. As I started drying off I walked down the stairs and went into the room to grab a new shirt. While changing I noticed my cup of tea from earlier still sitting on the ledge, slowly filling with heavy drops of rain. In a rare moment of ease I decided to double-down and picked up the cup, throwing the contents back without hesitation, instantly relieving my thirst. This time I was filled with the inspiration to watch the rain from the comfort of one of the hammocks to end out my evening. Unfortunately, I soon found out I was late to the universal inspiration on that one and had to come up with another way to wait out the rain until someone vacated one of the hammocks. I figured one of them would get tired of dealing with the rain and wind combo soon enough so I moved into the common room to wait them out. Entering I saw scattered groups of travelers all around me, each going through different stages of drying and recounting their days. Off to the right a few guys were playing cards and charging phones with one of the few outlets available. In the center was a table of friends playing board games and off to the left were three girls in an open circle leaning up against a set of beanbags. To my side I saw Wes on his phone trying to update a family member about his recent trip to the canal. He had something he did not wish to keep inside anymore and it showed through the efforts he took to make his phone call work. Watching him struggle to catch the signal made me think of a time before the world had been wrapped in a digital blanket. A time I was glad to experience, though I recognized how much it had benefited to bring us all into the same rooms even when we couldn't get into the same timezones. Something I found especially necessary having grown up in a post-Cold War world with parents and a society reminding me of the dangers abroad every time I would mention crossing a border. Later seeing the countering experience would often show me that those at home and abroad lacked in few similarities beyond language. For it was as much a divider as it was a link.

Much like Wes I needed to get some talking out of my system. Either that or I needed to be on the move. I peered out the window considering whether or not to just go for another walk, but the rain was dropping in buckets and I could no longer entertain myself comfortably in the bounds of nature. It was time instead to find a character of the human world to speak with. For years my eyes had tried to seek out the most interesting person in the room based off of the clues they carried. Especially during the days I was fumbling my way through conversation and knew it was important to start with a good one because I was likely to sit there for a while. Although I must admit that at times I caught myself seeking interesting people based off of the first impression of an exceptional shell only to find that I had been led astray by misguided signals. At least up here I knew I was surrounded by people interesting enough to have ended up huddled here hiding from the rain in a room four thousand feet above the sea.

As I sampled the faces around me I noticed a girl in a maroon hoodie sitting against a faded blue beanbag. She had American features in her style, but she possessed a sharpness in her face which indicated she was from lands even colder than my Celtic ancestors. There was a sharpness to her jawline which made me struggle to pinpoint her age or point of origin. It was exotic, but in the most subtle of ways. On the front of her hoodie was an eagle with outstretched talons and a few random letters sprawling across the top. With a broad wingspan ending in delicate hands she sat clenching her knees as perfectly tanned legs extended down to striped ankle high socks tucked into a pair of bright white Chuck-Taylors. In the aforementioned position she sat rocking as she forced her lips together in a battle of nods at the remarks of two equally puzzling girls on either side of her. To her right a blonde with light eyes and a shorter figure leaned in speaking to her as her left side was consumed with the words of a young black girl who also defied my outdated understandings with a series of words uttered in a very Nordic cadence. I could not hear much clearly, not that it would have made a difference, but I at least had an inference as to their original launching pad into the world. Which sometimes is all you need to find your hello. As her two friends left I saw a look of relief land on her face. I decided that if there was ever a more relatable opening, I did not know it.

"Looks like I'm not the only one ready to start doing vacations alone." - Patrick

She grinned at me as her cheeks pushed up a guilty smile which went all the way up to a set of light hazel eyes that created a glistening capstone to her beautifully structured face. Eyes which peered into a sometimes unkind world from the view of a very kind soul. One that seemed to take in more of the world at once than others. Both in meaning and breadth.

"It's not that. I just don't wanna think about going to see the coffee farm until it stops raining and it's all they wanna talk about."

"They're trying to go tonight?"

"No, not now. They wanna go tomorrow, but I don't wanna walk in the mud to start my day either ya know?"

"I get that."

"Plus I need a day to get some work done. I didn't get anything finished on the bus like I wanted to. I'm sorry, I'm done complaining, I promise."

With that she extended her hand and met me with a delicate shake of our palms, "Hi, I'm Almeré."

"Neat name. Nice to meet you. I'm Patrick. Where you coming from?"

"Stockholm originally. And you?"

"Well I meant like traveling from, but I'm from the States. That your school on your shirt there?"

"Yeah."

"That's not Swedish though is it? It's look the same, but not."

"You're right it's not. Good eye. It's actually Dutch. I go to school in Amsterdam."

"Nice. What do you study there?"

"I'm about to enter dental school."

"And you have the time to be out backpacking? How wonderfully European of you."

"Well. I stay working on the go."

Next to her was a tiny blue backpack with thin straps and a few torn patches woven along a canvas bottom outlined in red stitching. Looking at it I became curious. Always a fan of the perfect travel bag I inquired about where it came from.

"I wonder which of us has the oldest backpack. Yours doesn't look that worn, but it sure seems more decorated."

"Yeah. I've put it through a lot lately. Most of these badges are new. And I had a lot of time to put them while I was in New York."

"How did you like the city?"

"We didn't get to leave the airport. Our layover was only a few hours. Seems crowded though. I just walked around and tried to stretch my legs."

"Bummer. Was that your only time in the States?"

"Yeah. Closest I've been otherwise was in the Caribbean. I hope to do a proper trip through the US sometime soon though."

"You gotta get on that. It's a great place to cruise around. I'm assuming you can drive?"

"Absolutely, but I rather take a bike. And I know! I've heard. I can't decide which to do first. I wanna see some of your bigger places like New York City, but I really wanna go to Zion Park or something near the Grand Canyon. We don't have anything like that back home."

"Yeah, it's not the type of terrain I think of when I think of your part of the world."

"You've been to Sweden?"

"Sadly not. Been close to your school, never your hometown."

"Where were you?"

"Belgium. Antwerp specifically."

"You were that close and you didn't make it to Amsterdam? What kind of tourist are you?"

"I mean, I wanted to, but I only had one full day to myself and I was broke as fuck. College was not friendly to my bank account."

"How long were you in Europe?"

"Just under two weeks."

"That can add up fast on a college budget."

"Oh I know. I think I had $6 left when I got back. Like a week before rent was due. Totally worth it though. I highly suggest traveling broke a few times. Even if you have to pretend. It'll teach you all you need to know. But looking back, I woulda gone to Amsterdam if I would have known I wouldn't have been back by now. There's so much to see. Never expected to be back in Panama before returning to Europe."

"You've been all over the place it seems. When were you here?"

"Few years back, but I didn't even see this side of the country then. I was mainly on these islands the entire time."

"Do you mean Bocas?"

"Yeah I do. How did you know?"

This got her to start telling me about her recent trip to the same cluster of islands I had chosen years before. Her innocence showed for the first time as she spoke of the island and didn't once mention the crazy night scene or the bar built around a sunken ship. It was odd enough just to hear her talk about a place that I knew to once be nothing short of nefarious. We had both experienced the same place from vastly different points of view and expectations. And by her testimony it seemed that we had managed to miss out on how it used to be. Like *Howl's Castle* moving in the night the smugglers had probably relocated their hiding spots and would never again grant us access to their layers. I decided not to start with the extreme and tell her about my time down there beyond a few formalities of good weather and tropical compliments. I didn't know her well enough to get into those details. Not in less time than I would have to explain in the writing of this book.

"So what brings you down here again?" - Almeré

"I'm translating for some guys on a fishing trip."

"Where are they from?"

"Same place as me. Virginia."

"Must be a drag to work while they're having fun."

"It's not like it's much work. It's just some talking here and there. And looking over my shoulder a bit more than I would like."

"That's unfortunate. How long have you been working as a translator?"

"Five or six days now. I guess a week if you count our day at the airport."

"Pardon me?"

"Yeah. I guess I'm doing this as a job, but it's all kinda new. And yet all the same. I used to teach English. So in a lot of ways it's basically the same thing."

"How is that even close to the same thing? Isn't the point of translating that they don't have to learn the words and *YOU* do the talking?"

"Yeah, but it's like the constant first day of class where they're asking about something while giving me zero context for it. Same with these guys. They'll ask me for a word and then just walk away. And that's the same as when you start teaching kids. They're always asking you for the word they need in the moment."

"I never thought about it like that. Where did you teach?"

"Other than a few months in Marrakesh I floated between the Central and South American worlds."

"That's so cool. I've gotten to travel a lot, but I've never lived anywhere abroad longer than a few weeks."

"I recommend it if you get the chance. It's such a cool experience to live in another country long enough to develop your routine."

"Oh I bet! It could really help me with some other things I wanna do in life too. I thought about that a lot when I started my backpacking trip last month. Here. Lemme show you where I've been!"

I leaned in as she started giving me a tour of her last few weeks via a series of albums on her iPhone. I was lucky to have plenty of old photos to show her myself, but hers had a wider variety of exotic places than I did on all of my old devices combined. As I sat next to her it was impossible not to notice a subtle floral scent coming off of her clothing which made her presence even more inviting than her charm had. I've never been good with the names of perfumes. I just know I can't catch that one on the wind without turning around since that night. In talking with her I learned she had a ton of insight on the world, while at times still possessing a naivety that only thins over time. She was in many ways the entire package, representing every end of the spectrum of intrigue. I had only seen a few before. And there's always something sobering about them as there was with her. Despite the fact that I was far from sober. Though even that seems hard to claim at this moment. She had drawn in my focus in such a way that my mind was free of any of the distractions set in motion by the substances still absorbing into my body through the slow process of digestion. I had felt it kick-in sure, but she slowly winning the battle of substance vs. substance. After scrolling through her most recent photos I came across a series of shots where she was posing with some kids near an elephant. All of them had bright smiles and clenched toothbrushes in their fists, excluding the elephant who held some bamboo leaves circled up in his trunk.

"What was going on here?"

"Oh these are the kids who got their braces off that day. We all thought it would be cool to get a picture that morning."

"What were you doing there?"

"I was volunteering at a hospital with this group trying to bring better dental hygiene to the region."

"Where was this?"

"Thailand."

"You had to travel to the other side of the world to find suitable volunteer work?"

"No, but a friend of mine moved there with her husband a few years back to start a hospital and I figured it would be a good excuse to visit. Her posting was the perfect way to get in some practice and test out what I'm studying."

"If you're going to be a dentist I guess it can't hurt to prep early. What got you interested in being a dentist anyhow? Someone in the family a dentist?"

"Not that I know of. I just knew I wanted a job I could no matter where I was in the world. And what's more universal than a smile?"

"Fair point."

"Exactly. How about your teeth? How are they looking?"

Widening my grin I exposed my canines and showed her the end result of a long arduous youth spent wearing braces.

"See! Even you had braces!"

"Seems your plan appears solid. Excited to graduate and get started?"

"I guess. I don't plan to do it for a while."

"What do you mean? Gonna take a year off and travel?"

"No. I don't know how long I'll take actually. Whenever I decide I'm ready."

"You're just gonna learn to be a dentist and then not...?

"The inside of the mouth isn't going to change right?"

"Uh. I guess not."

"Exactly. I can do it any time I want. So why not try a few things first? I have an internship and I think it's going to lead to a job. He'll see."

"Who?"

"My dad. He thinks I'm still in Thailand. I knew this trip would get him off my back. He doesn't really get the artist thing."

"Most parents don't. What kinda art do you do?"

"Mainly sketches. I'm planning to make a book out of my ones from my retreat. That's what I've been hoping to get done since I started this trip. Maybe one day I'll do a section of the book from each part of the world with some type of volunteer thing. It's been on my mind constantly. I just need to sort out the stories to put underneath the portraits. And finish my sketches."

"Is this for a class or something?"

"No. Not at all. I did all of these portraits and sketches of the kids smiling after getting their teeth cleaned. Wanna see? I've been getting my portfolio together since I left Thailand. If you want to be an artist you gotta have a portfolio. Here look. How can you see those faces and not wanna help kids smile?"

In talking she brought out a camel brown notebook twice as large as the average hand and started flipping through the pages until she paused on one with a series of blurbs attached to a sketch which covered half of the page. Truth be told. Her pictures were great. Next to each one was a small snapshot of the kid. Sometimes in a portrait pose of their own. Other times standing next to Almeré with a toothbrush and a grin. And though my opinion on styles and strokes can only be credited to go so far, each one of her drawings captured something unique in the kids face. Each one lit up the page and showed great detail. I couldn't tell which was more important to her, the art of drawing or the art of understanding the subject of her art. Either way it was obvious she had skill. Each drawing captured something different, even though they were all portraits. I would never be the artist she was. It wasn't about the skill of drawing. I saw someone who had the same focused that I loved, the same kinda thirst for life, and the same vibrance I hoped to put into the world.

"I notice you put little stories under the sketches?"

"Yeah. I write too."

"Well what do you write? Other than these blurbs in a language I don't understand."

"Stuff."

"Don't make this like pulling teeth. What have you written? Ever been published?"

"Just things for the paper at my school so far, but I start an internship at a museum downtown when I get back."

"You're going to do that while working at the paper AND going to dental school? I applaud you. I think."

"No no. I'm ambitious, not crazy. I won't be at the paper next semester. The editor and I just don't see eye to eye on enough of my projects. I only really stay because I'm trying to get any experience I can before school ends. And it was a lot of fun my first year. I got to report on art shows and new exhibits when I first started, but there's only so much of that happening each week. Might as well work at a museum directly. I know it won't be as much variety, but I should get the chance to meet some other people in the art world if I'm at the same place long enough."

"You like art, you ever thought of photography? Seem to have an eye for those types of things."

"Not really. I like something about the art coming right from my fingertips. Here, check out this one."

As she started to explain her art I looked at her wondering where would I be now if I had been as thought out as her at the same age. Or if I had been so practiced in something I found to be as enjoyable as she found drawing. I could see it in her. A human with potential and intention can not long be ignored by the world; and she was overflowing with both. The only thing she possessed more of than those attributes was talent. Something which I realized after scrolling through her notebook a bit more. As it has been said before, quality is indefinable and undeniable all while being indescribable, so I shall spare the details and layers of justifications describing her drawings. Of course talent when applied to art is often a result of what happens when we chase our interests more than our curiosities. And this girl looked like someone who had done that from the beginning. The only flaw I saw was the youthful syndromes of wanting to do everything at the same time; something which when calmed can take a person anywhere, but it sounded like she was managing to do it all already so who the fuck was I to say anything about that? It's different when someone says, I want to do something, compared to when they say, I *am* doing. And it only took the last hour staring into her eyes to see that I was peering into a soul taking their life very seriously, even if they appeared not to be taking life itself seriously. I dare say her feelings to link the serious with the artistic were a benefit of the life she saw in her second city. Though I would usually never speak on somewhere I have never been, as I reader I can be certain it's a place with a history strong in both the arts and in business. Had I come from a place with a more artistic vibe perhaps I would have felt the same ease with my own expressions at an earlier age. Perhaps I could have been more honest with the world about the life I was trying to live once I was in it and allowed myself to enjoy it for a while without the guilt of a looming *what's the back-up plan?* I used to answer people all the time by saying I was doing a final year of teaching here or there, at times impressing people close to forty who were at the mid-life crisis stage of life looking for change. Meanwhile I saw people who were younger than me, like twenty year olds who had wild direction in their lives and I couldn't understand how I had grown up so void. Why had my curious mind never settled on one thing? It's not as if I went without going back-and-forth with myself. It wasn't just the voice of my friends who got inside of me, I was always asking myself what the plan was long before the days of people telling me that I had to drop it all and find my passion. All the while knowing I wasn't looking for my passion as much as I was looking for a path. To me passion was something meant to be embodied in all that you did, not some hill you stood on only after figuring out how to make money with what you loved to do. The idea of finding my passion seemed ridiculous. Snowboarding and walking through the woods all day was my passion. Purpose seemed to matter more.

"Those are really good. And I love your notebook."

"Yeah it's quality leather. Do you have a notebook?"

"Always. Got two for this trip."

"Me too. I got a new one just for Thailand. Only thing that sucks is I lost this pen my grandma gave me for graduation."

"Damn. Was it one of those fancy ones?"

"The fanciest. It was this really cool experience where I got to go to this shop and test a few out until I found the right one. I should have known better than to take it with me to the beach. Oh well. At least I still have my notebook."

"Had it long?"

"Oh yeah. Well not this one, but I've always had them. I started keeping them as a kid. I love looking back at them now. Sometimes it's like reading from the mind of an entirely different person."

"Oh I bet. That's great you can write and sketch. I wish I had the talent for both. I can't draw for shit."

"I'm sure you could if you tried."

"I doubt it. I'm not really that artistic."

"That's not true. There are plenty of types of art. Language is an art. Your voice is the instrument."

"Okay, well none of the other arts ever came as naturally."

"That's not natural either. You had to practice first. Start by drawing what you know. Have you ever tried to draw yourself?"

"Like do a portrait? No. Never given it the thought."

"Okay well here. Let's start with something simple. Try to draw your eyebrows. I've got a mirror in my bag you can use."

"What? Why my eyebrows?"

"It'll be a lot easier to draw the rest of your face if we know the emotion we're drawing around. And the landscape around your eyes needs to start with the brows. Here, just take this page and try to sketch what you see in the mirror. I'll help."

Sitting there I watched as she laid the book on my lap, leaned in, and started drawing a series of arcs as one would associate with the top of an eyebrow. Watching her instruction I continued to be struck with the oddity of the thought that I could be learning so much from someone so far behind me in life, at least far as time was concerned.

"The most important thing is to make sure the proportions are right. Remember, the face is broken down into three levels. Think of it like three squares and keep the eyebrows close to the eyes for a calm expression."

Having nothing more to say than, "Okay." I stared back at her as she kept her head buried in the flows of a sketch, making no sense from the angles of which I was viewing. For a moment I looked on embracing the luck of the moment I was in. I loved watching creation in real time. Whether it be a sketch, a new melody on a piano, or the coupling of just the write series of words, it was all some sort of creation. And here I was in the presence of a renaissance girl, the type of person capable of making those around her unstoppable literally by proximity. Too focused on her hand and thoughts surrounding the creativity circulating inside of it I hadn't noticed when she looked back up at me.

"See what I'm saying?"

"Yeah. I think. Sure."

"Okay now you try."

In her instructions she took control of my hand and began guiding me through the motions until I had completed enough of a rendition of my eyebrow for the teacher inside of her to feel satisfied. Though the artist within me was less than pleased. After that I started tracing over the arch in a series of strokes until she grabbed my hand and stopped me from ruining our work any further. From both a birds eye view and the perspective of the one experiencing I would say we were instantly comfortable with each other. Or that is to say she was beyond comfortable with me. Which said a lot, because as I had known it, a man may find it easy to fall into the inviting embrace of a pretty woman, but a woman is far less likely to be entranced by the same waves. Though she may be the one of the two most hoping to just fall into the moment as it is. It's a trait of the romantic. One that carries over from our views of love into anything else we see or care to feel. And at that moment all I could feel was her hand taking control of mine and a tingle of warmth and electricity which seemed to transfer from her fingertips to mine as lighting bouncing from one cloud to another. For as long as someone like this stayed on the road the combination of her good looks and charisma would make her the dying fantasy of many men. Most of whom would never realize they could never get her. And even fewer that would ever understand why. Though even I couldn't be sure if it was just the circumstances of being placed under the same rain riddled roof which had kept her in my presence for so long. All of the coincidences of the moment spoke to a part of me which had always imagined that I would find some adventurous partner drifting throughout the world on my journeys abroad. Despite feeling like I had missed out on much of what I thought I was going to get in my twenties I had seen that there's a certain experience of love on the road that I think we all wish we knew which makes it possible at any time. Something that comes from that timeless feeling of seeming more exciting on the road than at home.

"No no. Slow down. You've gotta give your eyes time to catch up with what you're doing. Use some patience. It just takes time." - Almeré

"Did you study art at some time or is this skill one of self cultivation?"

"It's always been a thing of mine. That's why it's going to be so hard to leave Amsterdam when I do one day. The museums are so great there. I love going to them for inspiration when I need it. Hopefully I can absorb plenty of that at the new job."

As she tightened her clasp around the top of my hand her fingers began to interlock with mine and whether by accident or by chemistry our hands moved in a unison guided by the force of her artistic intentions. While I let my hand flow with hers I traced my eyes up her wrist and towards her face a few times admiring the focus in her actions. The artist within her gleamed through a lightly cracked smile which spread satisfied by that which she was creating. Around this time her friends returned and placed themselves at our side causing a pause in our progress both artistic and personal. Looking up my eyes were met by a towering blonde with a particularly lean face projecting a message of suspicion in Swedish as Almeré looked on and then shook her head. I can only imagine that the girl had asked her if she wanted to be saved from the conversation with a stranger since the interaction was too short to reiterate their request for tomorrow's trip to the coffee farm.

"Attempting a rescue?" - Patrick

"Huh?"

"Nothing. Friends from home?"

"Yeah. They said that dinner is ready. You hungry?"

"I can always eat."

"Then let's go grab some food. I'm starving."

The jungle and this conversation had served their roles as sobering agents, but that didn't stop me from swiftly departing from our conversation when the dinner bell rang. I would finally be able to give sobriety one final nail in the coffin with some food for the night as we all moved out of the room and onto the deck where an array of food had been sprawled across the picnic table with a stack of plates and silverware off to the side. On the first plate was a blend of hummus followed up by a salad and some fresh pita bread. I never thought to ask them how they had such authentic food this far up, but I hand't done that in any situation where I saw unexpected foods in unexpected places. Hummus in Panama and lasagna in Colombia, who would have thought. As a crowd formed around the two tables a woman from Montreal took control of the collective ear with her stories surrounding a road trip she took through the U.S. as a teenager somewhere in the early eighties. This caught my interest because it had been a Canadian many years before who made me realize how much I had underutilized the traveling capabilities of America. We had begun talking about the cities along the I-95 corridor and the next thing I knew she was connecting dots to parts of the country I had never been to and could name places to eat in each city. Which kinda embarrassed me at the time because I was a seasoned driver. As I sat and ate my hummus thoughts surrounding the conversation I had with my new friend came to me and I realized that in the entire two hour exchange I had not once mentioned my job working in hotels or anything regarding my life in the district. I had not given her any information about the last few months of my life. I don't even think she knew what I did for work back home. But why would I, it wasn't the part which mattered to me and my story. Sitting there my thoughts were interrupted by the sight of Myles and Austin making their way down the stairs towards the common area. As Myles passed by me in a soaked hoodie I looked on with sympathy, but soon redirected it towards Austin as I noticed a body dripping with water and no shirt in sight.

"You all better have saved me some dinner." - Myles

I guess any mellow mood inducing drugs had now left his system. With that comment Myles sat down and grabbed a big plate of food as Amelia nudged me from the next table.

"Your friends should rest. That ones got a bad case of the Panamanian Flu." - Amelia

"The Panamanian Flu?" - Patrick

She gave me a look and put her finger up to her nose to block one nostril. I looked side to side and pretended not to know what she was talking about. I wanted to break the silence so I went for the most obvious question.

"Did you all at least catch anything?" - Patrick

"No. We couldn't see shit." - Austin

"What about your fancy lights?"

"In that fuckin rain? Hell no. We woulda needed a team of fucking spotlights."

Once dinner was done those who did not go to sleep made their way back into the lounge where the groups had consolidated with the largest portion playing a game of Spades. Before going back inside I walked over to the hammock which was now drenched in rain and looked to see if I could find a neck pillow which had given me comfort the night before. Sadly no luck. When I returned to the lounge I saw Almeré doodling in a sketchbook, uninvolved in the game of trivia taking place at the table of friends next to her. When she saw me she waived me over to fill an empty seat in the beanbag next to her. When I sat down she pointed over at Wes who was now hugging the edge of the room trying to balance Wi-Fi signal with warmth.

"Is that your friend? Tell him to join us. I think my friends could use another spades player." - Almeré

"Nah. He's got his headphones in, I'm not gonna bother him. I think he got a movie downloaded on his phone for tonight."

"Who watches a movie on vacation?"

"Well we all got our own worlds we escape to once in a while."

"I guess. I just never think to bring a movie. I think the only time we did that was when my family went with our dad to Cuba. That's the only time I can remember traveling with movies to watch at the hotel."

"What were you doing in Cuba?"

"My dad had a business trip down there."

"Beautiful place isn't it?"

"From what I remember. You've been?"

"Yeah I was actually thinking about it earlier. Mountains here kinda reminded me of it."

"Oh I bet. I think of Havana all the time. But all we really got to see was the hotel."

"Can't say I saw the city either. Other than the hour it took us to drive out of it."

"You didn't want to stay around and explore?"

"Wasn't my call. The girl I was with wanted to get us to some spots she knew along the coast. As soon as we got to the city we rented a jeep from some connection she had and took off."

"Was she from the island?"

"Yeah."

"Oh nice. Did you meet her family and all of that?"

"Nah, we didn't get the chance. We were only there for a few days and we kinda packed in a lot of plans for that short of a time."

"Yeah, but still. You don't travel all that way and not meet her family. At least a lunch or something. She was your girlfriend right?"

"I guess that's what you could call her. We never really got around to calling it anything. Even if you're right I wasn't gonna argue. I had a beautiful woman offering to show me around hidden beaches all day. What could I be mad about?"

"I guess so."

"It's cool really. I didn't expect to meet them that time. We had just started hanging out and they had a lot of catching up to do if we did. And even under ideal conditions I think our age difference still would have gotten to them. I don't think she wanted to deal with that whole ordeal on a quick getaway. Seemed like the point of that trip was much the opposite."

"Oh, how much older was she?"

"Well I had just turned twenty-three and she was thirty."

"Oh. How did you all meet each other then?"

"She was the head of the ESL school I taught at down in Veracruz, Mexico."

"Teacher dating the principal? Didn't know they allowed that."

"I imagine they don't, but we didn't go around advertising it."

"Was it hard keep the other teachers from finding out?"

"More annoying than anything. You have to catch yourself a lot. I just wish we could have acted more normal outside of the school."

"Why? Was she uptight about being affectionate in public? I hate that."

"No it was a little more complicated than that."

"How so?"

At her question I paused and got quieter than she had seen me in our entire conversation. A rarity with which she took suspicion. Rolling my eyes and looking away I eased into an answer.

"Well, let's say she was freshly single when we met."

"How freshly are you talking…?"

"More than I would have preferred. She had been engaged earlier in the year before we met. "

"OK wow, no wonder she didn't want you to meet her family."

"Yeah. She told me she didn't want them to know she was dating so soon. Well I don't know that I would call us dating. I'm separated from it enough to come to terms with being the rebound, or a fun escape, whatever you wanna call it."

"So what happened? Did they get back together?"

"That's probably where it was going. I can't really be sure."

"You don't know?"

"No. I only know what it looked like towards the end. That's when her phone started blowing up randomly and she would always walk away to take the call."

"That doesn't mean anything."

"Eh. Maybe not, but it certainly looked like that. She was always taking me out of town, always avoiding certain spots, you know, the usual things people do when they're balancing two existences."

"Did you stop seeing her when you noticed all of that?"

"No. I was conflicted, but I wasn't *THAT* conflicted. Plus you can't get but so mad when you're in that type of situation."

"But why *be* in that situation? And how could you keep seeing her after you knew that?"

"I don't *know* anything. I'm just telling you what I saw."

"Well you said you all ended, so they must have gotten back together right?"

"No, and it doesn't matter. I wasn't sitting there thinking I was going to marry this girl. She was having fun with me and I was having fun with her. Once I looked at it like that it didn't matter."

"You never wanted to know though? I would feel guilty if they were still a thing…"

"Maybe, but whatever feelings of guilt I was supposed to have went away when I thought about why they broke up. From what she said, he had a ton of *amantes* scattered around the place. That's Spanish for *'lovers'*. He was a pilot of some kind and from what she told me his flights weren't always for work."

"That doesn't make it okay."

"You seem kinda shocked by the world for someone who has seen so much of it. I'm sorry, that was rude. Look, it's a sad reality, but this is the type of shit that happens sometimes. I didn't mean to *'date'* her. I knew it was a bad idea, I'm not a fucking idiot. I just thought it would be a fun date or two and it just got out of hand. That's all that ever happens. And I know I'm supposed to feel bad, but what was I supposed to do? I mean, it was gonna be somebody. And at the end of the day, she was really cool. It was easy to be friends, flirts, and everything between. I don't know what else to say. She was hanging out with me all of the time so I figured she was over him or using me to get over him."

"Do you ever talk to her anymore?"

"Uh no. That's not an option."

"Why not? Did it end badly?"

"You could say that."

With her hands now up at her face she looked at me with eyes widening by the moment.

"Well what happened? I'm sorry, you don't have to tell me."

"Nah it's cool, but you gotta promise not to get all sad for me."

"I can't promise I won't get sad, that's not how sadness works…"

Noticing the blank expression on my face she quickly corrected.

"Okay fine! I promise. Now tell me what happened to you two."

As I sat there I took in a deep breath and got back in touch with a reality I had not often brought up, though I had not gone very long without thinking of it.

"Nothing happened to *us*, something happened to *her*. She uh. She died in an accident a few weeks after we got back from our trip. I uh. Yeah. That's how that situation ended…There was no break up, no final conversation. It was just over. Us, her life, all of it."

When I finished speaking Almeré sat looking at me, uncertain what to say next. A reaction I had become used to and one which had led me to keeping that story to myself for the most part. That and the overall nature of the topic made it so I rarely got a chance to speak on the subject, but as always I found it rather liberating when speaking with someone who had no vested interest in my future.

"I uh…I'm sorry, I just don't know what to say."

"It's okay."

"Well, what happened? How did she…"

"They said she was on her way home from school and a car hit her while she was crossing the street."

"That's…that's just awful. You must have been devastated."

"Yeah….that's one of the words I remember."

"We don't have to talk about it if you don't want to."

"No it's cool. I'm good now. I mean, not good, but we can talk about it all you want."

"I don't know what to ask. I don't know what I can ask."

"Ask whatever you want."

"Okay, well, how did you find out she died?"

"Like everyone else did, on the announcements at school."

"Oh my God are you serious? No one called you?"

"Who would call me? Who would think to call me? I wasn't a part of her life like that."

"Yeah, but she must have told her girlfriends about you?"

"Doesn't seem like it. I don't how known my existence was among her friends. And I wasn't gonna find out which ones did the hard way."

"I uh. How did you handle the funeral?"

"I didn't go."

"What? Why not?"

"I don't know, I felt stupid. Plus it was in Cuba. That was hard enough to get to the first time. There was all this passport shit I had to do as an American."

"Stupid why? You two worked together."

"Yeah, that's all well and good, but I wasn't taking the gamble on enough people being that stupid. I have no idea what kinda stuff her fiancé was involved in, but I saw a picture of him once and his suit looked expensive as fuck, like glossy in that way that says *don't fuck with me*. So yeah. I figured it best to avoid any mention of my name and hers in the same sentence."

"Do you think anyone suspected anything?"

"I doubt it. We had eased up on seeing each other a lot after that trip to Cuba. Other than school I had no other connections to her life. Probably why seeing me made the most sense for her. Who knows."

Pausing for a moment I let her eyes dart back and forth before speaking again, "Look, it's cool if you don't know what to say. I know it doesn't make sense to you, took me forever to make sense of it."

"I can only imagine. How did you manage to deal with everything being all alone? Did you stay the rest of the year?"

"Well it would have looked weird if I left out of nowhere."

"Where did you decide to go?"

"I took a teaching job in North Africa the following semester."

"Why so far away?"

"Seemed like a nice idea to go somewhere where people wouldn't think to mention her. And I needed some time away from the environments that made me think of her ya know?"

"You didn't wanna go home after something like that?"

"What good would that have done?"

"I don't know. Just seems awful to go and be alone as a way to deal with anything so sad."

"Maybe in your world. I rather be alone than be around people reminding me that I should be down about something."

Looking down with a bit of hesitation she defended her position with a rare blend of sarcasm and sympathy, "I guess we're not all as good at handling those things on our own."

"I didn't say I was good at it. I just found a way that works for me. As far as I'm concerned bad is bad. The degree doesn't really make a difference when it comes to stuff like that. Which I don't know I woulda thought before all of this. So it's not like I didn't pull a little bit of good from the whole thing where I could."

"How could you pull anything good from something like that?"

"Well listen, everything is relative, and comparatively speaking, nothing is likely to ever suck or confuse me as much as life did in the months after she died. If I was able to handle that then I figured I could handle anything the world decides to throw at me. Also, it taught me not to hang onto bad emotions too long and not to relive bad times over and over in my head. That lesson was worth its' weight in gold. And above all else, I enjoyed my time with her. She was really cool."

"Hang on? What are you a robot? No one goes right back to happy anytime soon after something like that. Things like that take time."

"Well needing time is a whole other argument. For now let's stick to happy. Happy isn't a state of being that anyone can expect to occupy for infinitum. It's just a feeling. And a feeling isn't the same thing as love. We just think of it that way. Love is more of a way to live. Also, you don't get to decide how your endings in life go. I'm not saying any of it was good. I just know it taught me not to let a bad experience rob me of appreciating everything else around me. Because honestly I'm mad when I think about how I let that situation rob me of so much mental space when I was in Morocco. I could have done so much more while I was in that area of the world if I had just gotten outside of my own head."

"I think maybe you're being too hard on yourself. Time is only wasted if you don't learn something."

"I agree. It's not like I didn't handled it well, but it's not like I was doing great. I definitely wasn't myself. I wanted to get away, but that also wasn't the time to reintroduce myself to the world back home, that's why I picked a new spot in a new type of culture. Sucks. I barely went out or interacted with the locals the way I had everywhere else. It's why my Arabic isn't nearly as good as my Spanish. I wasn't social. The whole time I was just going through the motions. And for what? Because I was sad? I lived with it long enough to know I didn't bury it away, but I shoulda let that go way sooner than I did. I didn't even make it to Spain and I was practically a boat ride away. That still pisses me off."

"I think other people would call that normal."

"Perhaps. But it was also debilitating for someone trying to get the most out of his time abroad."

"Well maybe what you needed was time to yourself."

"I suppose."

"Well there. You got what you needed."

"Maybe. I'm just mad I wasn't me for a while."

"Well, no better way to learn who you are."

"True."

Continuing to talk, she brushed off a series of invitations by the last of her departing friends and we found our moving along until we were both sitting in an empty room somewhere after 3 A.M. Shortly after she caught herself losing track while telling a story about her time at sea and decided it was time for bed. Saying goodbye she gave a firm hug with the clenching of her fingertips landing in my back as a goodbye before heading off to bed. Ya know, on the road you get to meet a lot of people. And often the curse of this lifestyle is once in a while there is that person that you wish you could see for as many tomorrows as possible. Those are the people who are impossible not to fall in love with, and even with all logic and understanding for the fleeting nature of the very moment I was in, I couldn't help but succumb to that power. I'd never seen so much potential in one person before, and there was something so alluring that I couldn't help but hope I got to be around it again. Even if only to see the outcome of all the roads her ambitions were on. She was the reminder of a spark I once had with another individual who became very special to me. Someone who taught me that I should not waste my time hoping for butterflies when I could experience someone who would strike me with lightning. Which had been something forgotten for too long now. And for that reason I was glad to have met her, as much now as I was then. Sometimes the world puts that person there, not to take the place of the person who previously occupied it, but to remind us of a space that still exists. And as we left the room I walked with a mind clearer and quieter than it had been in a while. It was like that feeling after a long night of sleep. I knew she would become like the many beautiful sights and spectacular places I had visited over the years. A memory of a moment and the aura around it forever locked as a place in my mind which I wish could be visited again in a future realer than memories.

After brushing my teeth I walked to the dorms and found my way up a stack of bunk beds via a ladder meant to help anyone attempting to scale the three layers of mattresses they had managed to stack. Once at the top I wedged myself in amongst my friends and pulled at a piece of blanket big enough to cover up my legs and remained sardined there for the rest of the night.

Day 6: A Bus Over The Border
Boquete, Panama

I was the first one to pull myself out of the hypnotically deep sleep caused by the steady drip of an early morning rain which trickled ever so softly on the tin roof above us throughout the first hours of our new day. After a quick rub of the eyes and a rezoning of the brain I rescued myself from this hypnosis and scooted my way around the others until I got myself situated on the ladder ready to climb down. About half-way down my journey a hand reached out from the second tier of bunks and grabbed my arm gently. As I followed the wrist to the body attached I heard Almeré's soft voice projecting from a light blue sleeping bag.

"Morning Pat. Do you know what time it is?"

The surprise of seeing her caused me to hesitate a moment as I hovered on the middle of the ladder with her hand still bracing my arm.

"Around eight I think... I'm going to get some breakfast."

I finished my trip down the ladder and made my way outside where I stood on the balcony accompanied by a light mist dampening the ground around me as the offending clouds drifted slowly through the property. At first glance it did not look like the days weather was going to be any different from where we left off yesterday. That is perhaps one of the downsides to mountainous regions, there is always some sort of climate happening around them. From there I ran up to the kitchen where I found an assortment of early morning chefs crowding the stovetop. I joined the mess and found a small burner to cook my eggs on before taking my meal into the common room. It wasn't so much a room as it was a series of picnic tables covered by a tin roof, but it was the perfect place to enjoy your meal. As I started eating I couldn't help but overhear the Canadian woman from last night frantic on the phone attempting to gain some understanding with whoever was on the other end of her call.

"You'll be WHERE in 30 minutes? DONDE?"

"Excuse me, Lemme help ya out here. May I see the phone?"

At my request she handed me an old *Nokia* and tried to inform me that the man on the other end was trying to find them in-order to return their luggage, lost at the airport days before.

"*Hola señor. Si si. Estamos cerca de la tienda. Sí claro. Estás lejos? Ok bueno.*" - Patrick

From there I returned the phone and informed her that their stuff would be down the hill in around thirty minutes.

"Thank you so much! Our luggage has been lost for over a week and the airline finally got our bag to some guy that offered to have his brother bring up it to us." - Canadian

"Anywhere else that might sound strange. Well glad to help. Where you all going after this?"

"We're gonna stick around here and visit some of the coffee farms. Then it's up the road to Guatemala."

"What you doing there?"

"We're off to see the ruins in Tikal. Can you believe we've been to Cancun twice and still not seen any of the Mayan ruins? I told my husband we couldn't miss it this time."

"Well, good deal. You won't be disappointed."

As I distanced myself and finished up my food I continued to sit for a while after my meal and take in the view provided by the landscapes around us. After enough time admiring I got up and went to grab my clothes from the dryer. As I passed through the lobby I stopped and heard Emily asking Myles if we were going to be staying for another night. To which he replied that we were planning on heading out today, but that he was sorry to leave.

"I'm sure you're glad to see us go." - Myles

"Are you kidding? You guys were the most fun people we've seen in months! You all are welcome back anytime." - Emily

"I'll be sure to take you up on that." - Myles

"I'll be back before they will." - Patrick

"Damn right you will. I wanna get outta here." - Myles

"Alright. Then what do you suggest we do with our day?" - Patrick

"I don't care as long as we get out of here. This rain shit is depressing. Told you, I came here to escape the seasonal depression, not make it worse." - Myles

"Are you gonna see the waterfall first?" - Emily

"Why go to a waterfall if I am already wet?" - Myles

"What did you expect? Look where you're at. This is the fucking jungle. It's wet. Always." - Patrick

"I wanted to see clouds. I didn't expect to sleep in them." - Myles

"So where do you wanna go?"

"Well where can we go?"

"Our options are pretty limited. We can go to a beach or we can take the car back and catch the bus to San Jose and get ourselves situated from there."

"How long is the ride to Costa Rica?"

"Probably an hour or so to the border. But it's gonna take the entire day to get us up to San Jose."

"What about going up to go to those islands?"

"That's a lot of backtracking man. The girls at the front desk told me the road going across the mountain has been closed off for a few months now. So unless we want to backtrack like six hours we're out of luck. And keep in mind. If we go do the island thing we still gotta make it back around here to return the car off and do all of that in enough time to get Austin to the airport in a few days."

"Damnit. I don't wanna spend the whole day driving again."

"Whether we do it now or we do it later, we're gonna have to do it. So just tell me what to go get ready for."

The guys looked like they were all worn from a number of factors; the long days drive, the lack of sleep, the drinking, the cocaine, the hike. At this point they all needed a few more hours of sleep and a few more hours of abstinence to skip out on the headaches currently invading their minds.

"Maybe what you could use is some time to sleep and once we're in San Jose maybe we can get a car and head to the coast." - Patrick

"True. I wouldn't mind sleeping and I'll do anything to get out of Panama. I still can't believe there's only one place in that entire country to rent a car. How long did you say this ride is gonna be?" - Myles

"Depends on how many stops the driver decides to make."

"What do you mean decides?"

"Sometimes they pull off for a while or run errands."

"Fuck. So we need to get our shit together and get on the first bus outta here."

"Unless we wanna do an overnight bus and spend the day up here."

"Fuck that. Let's get moving."

Even though he seemed annoyed at the trip, I couldn't help but be excited. It would be a great way to see the surroundings and gain the chance for an occasional nap. But I guess that was my perspective as at the driver. If I were in the backseat this whole time I might feel different. And if these guys thought the time was an issue, they should see what it's like when you're looking at out the window and can't see anything except for a steep drop into a canopy. After going from Santa Cruz to La Paz all other bus rides seemed far less daunting than I ever knew they could be. And at least this highway would be one with a consistent two-way road.

While the guys gathered their things I spent a few moments enjoying the sight of a double rainbow which was slowly forming to the North. I couldn't believe I was leaving without doing any of the cool shit they had to offer here. Not that hiking wasn't enough, but this place had so much on their little cork boards. I saw stuff about horse riding, waterfalls, and hikes up to the volcano. None of which I would get to do. Though I had gotten to meet some good people. One in particular which I hoped to say goodbye to before leaving. As I stood there gazing off at the conditions perfecting for the newly formed set of rainbows I caught the guys making their way up the stairs below me. As they turned the corner and entered the main floor I threw on my backpack and moved slowly across the deck and into the dining area. Walking with them I looked around hoping to spot Almeré somewhere to say goodbye, but with a quick scan my eyes couldn't find any of her group. In what I'm sure appeared to be sudden and scurried I faked a quick trip to the bathroom where I ran into the dorm room and saw all of her things neatly folded next to a rolled up sleeping bag in her cubby. *Damn.* At that I pulled out my notebook and wrote down my information and looked for a place to leave it amongst her things. Uncertain what was hers and what wasn't I decided to run by the front desk and drop it with Emily as we left. After doing so I threw my stuff in my bag and caught up to the guys who were now about a third of the way down the hill. Approaching I took notice of how beat up they all looked. Myles the most obviously haggard looking of them all. His body had been worn sick from the weather and his own daily inputs, though those may not have contributed nearly as much as the clouds. We had gone from subzero temperatures, to the equator, and now found ourselves leaving a damp jungle high in the mountains. I guess it's fair to say our bodies hadn't decided what reaction to give our changing environment. And though I normally lean more in the favor of the adage that you don't control the world around you, only your reactions to it, no matter how clear my mind gets my sinuses never seem to cooperate with the philosophy. By the time we got down the mountain we had about thirty-five minutes to return the car before noon and get ourselves onto the bus which was also scheduled to leave around the same time as our car was due back. Since we had a fair amount of luggage we decided to leave the guys with our bags so they could grab our tickets while we returned the car.

"Okay so you guys get the tickets. We'll be right back." - Patrick

"Now how the fuck are we gonna do that? Who else here knows the word for ticket? Wes? Did you write it down when Patrick gave us our Spanish lesson this morning?" - Austin

"Nope." - Wes

"It's *boleto. Bo-Le'-Toe.*" - Patrick

"Right." - Austin

As they both stared at me for a moment I gave in and undid my seatbelt.

"Fuck. Alright, I'll be right back. Myles start wiping down the car while I find this booth." - Patrick

"Got it." - Myles

As I went off Myles launched into cleaning mode and brought out a pack of baby wipes to add a sparkle to the car once everything had been removed. When I arrived at the ticket booth I found a plate glass window with AC flooding out of the bottom crack, but with no one behind the desk to sell me a ticket. This had always been one aspect of a more relaxed lifestyle where I had to accept the trade off that came from operating in this region. That's the problem, when you need stuff done, when the paperwork actually must get finished, it's painfully noticeable how there's not a lot of care put into some peoples schedules here. And that creates an atmosphere where it's common for someone to abandon their post to watch an afternoon soccer match leaving a sign to tell you they'll be back in thirty. I ran around looking for a solution, but was met with no luck until I found a guy who told me the clerk would be back any minute. We were running too low on time so I ran back to the car and showed Austin where the ticket booth was so that he could buy the tickets while we were gone. Even checking the prices to put the exact amount of money in his hand for the transaction. From there I grabbed a few essentials out of my bag and drove off with Myles towards the rental office. We tried to use the GPS to guide us, but each time we thought we were going the right way we would end up approaching a one-way street where we needed to make a right, but could only take a left. Or the road would split off and I would panic and end up following it the wrong way. All of this was made even more difficult by the fact that Myles had no ability to read Spanish and therefore spent more time trying to pronounce the names of upcoming turns than actually telling me where to turn.

When we found the rental office we pulled up to the front and waited a few minutes before a clerk returned from across the street where he had gone to grab a cup of coffee. Like I said before, there are no specific hours of operation here. When he began his inspection he started taking down a few notes about the car and revealed to us that we were going to be losing some of our deposit because he had found a series of dents on the side of the car which had gone unmarked on the emailed version of our lease. When it came time to give a rebuttal Myles couldn't find the original papers we had signed so we were forced to argue with the guy until we came to the agreement to part with $200 from our deposit. I knew we were getting robbed, but I had no way to prove it and we were already running out of time to make our bus and I wanted no part in staying here all day. Not that every town doesn't have some potential, but I couldn't imagine what we would do all day without a car.

As we got out of the rental office we hailed a cab and made it back to the station with five minutes to find our friends and the bus. As I had not heard otherwise I assumed the guys had taken care of the tickets and our bags in our absence so we ran over the loading station and started looking for buses departing to San Jose. The guys were nowhere to be seen but as we ran along the side of the buses I heard a yell from one of the windows which told me to stop. As I ran around the other side I was met by Wes exiting the bus with our tickets in his hand. We gave them to the driver and walked inside where we saw Austin in the back row sitting next to all of our things. Normally when I took a bus I was a fan of sitting in the front row so I could get a more elevated view of my surroundings, but today I was not in the mood to talk with a stranger for the next ten hours. Which is the tradeoff you make when you're seated next to a gabby bus driver. The bus had not been sold out from the border so I moved to the empty row in front of us and took a seat next to the window as I placed my bag in the seat to my right.

A few minutes after getting settled I closed my eyes as the bus pulled us away from the station and onto the final stretch of Panamanian highway we would see on this trip. The ride continued as did my rest until our momentum stalled and I opened my eyes to see a long line of cars crawling towards what looked like the border. While that line made steady progress our bus and two others were directed to pull off to the right where a series of officers stood waiting to search all incoming buses inside and out. Most of my border crossings had taken place at airport counters around the world, but I still remembered the more personal nature of crossing by via land. They see you coming, how you arrive, and what crowd you're with. Standing there the whole thing felt like this weird grey area where each side clearly wanted to pass along their own and not have to deal with the other side coming along, but that's most modern borders.

When the bus stopped we were told to exit with all of our belongings. As we got out we were ushered into a line which had formed towards the entrance of a small building where a series of teller-style windows separated us from a room filled with silver desks and customs agents. At the bottom of each piece of plated glass was a small crack just large enough for voices to enter and cool air to escape. From that crack we were called one by one to approach with our papers. At the desk we encountered agents alerting us that we must have our passports ready to be stamped on our way out. I had gone through this before, but last time I had not given any notice when I left. To no surprise we were asked to step aside for a moment as security wanted to take a closer look at our things. I doubted they were actually worried, but the agents looked curious to go through the *BAZOOKA* case laying on their desk, as did the majority of those in line behind us. As we complied we followed them into a room and were greeted by a series of stainless steel tables and a few customs agents with latex gloves. Shortly after we were joined by a man in an army uniform with a clipboard in his hand. I couldn't see what was on it beyond the vague uncertainty of what looked like four squares with faces on them. Leaning in he made his intentions clear to the other guards and they moved in our direction. Taking us into another room we were told to stand up against a wall as a set of German Shepards buried their noses in our pockets. While being molested by their snouts we looked on as the customs agents took apart our luggage, at one point asking us to assess the value of our items. As he inquired I looked knowing they were holding over $5,000 in fishing equipment, but it seemed unwise to volunteer that information until I knew where those secrets would be written.

"Around $500. Is there problem?" - Patrick

With no response given in return he went back to his business as we looked on. Once the dogs had finished with us they were then taken into the room with our luggage where they were given a full display of our belongings. Still uncertain what to say, I glanced at my friends, all of whom looked more annoyed than concerned.

"Don't know what you guys are looking for bro. I'm a Christian. Ain't nothing out of order in those bags." - Myles

"Shut up dude." - Wes

With a shrug and a smile he looked back at Wes giving a wink. Seeming to understand his English, the man of highest rank tucked his clipboard away and directed his attention at the wall where we stood. After a few minutes of explaining what had brought us to Panama, we were met with a set of suspicious eyes uncertain what to do with our answers. He never brought up the topic of drugs. He never mentioned anyone getting into our car, and he never let me on as to why we were on their list that day, but this time we were lucky. Myles had finished anything we had the night before and the rain had washed off any residue from the exposed parts of our bags. Even our clothes were too wet to hold any odors beyond that of the jungle. Looking back at his clipboard and then up again, he cocked his jaw to the left and spoke in a deep perfect English, this time with his eyes staring deeply into mine.

"No boys. Sorry for the interruption. Better go catch your bus."

As they nudged us out of the room we quickly shoved our stuff back into our bags and moved towards the line to enter Costa Rica. Somehow with our exit stamps approved, thanking us for our time in PANAMA. Once we showed our passports again we were allowed to go stand by our bus while they finished searching it.

"What's up with the bus?" - Myles

"Looks like they're doing another run through, but we should be able to load up in a few minutes." - Patrick

"What the fuck? They didn't search us good enough already? I can take off my pants if I need to, but it's too hot to be standing out here like this."

"Dude. Just chill."

"Come on Pattyboy. Aren't you happy I already did all of my cocaine? Them guys aren't gonna find anything. Fuckin' bitches."

"Trust me dude. I'm just as glad as you are."

As I waited to board the bus I walked around for a few minutes and tried to forget what had just happened. As far as my mind needed to be concerned, we were out of trouble and soon enough, out of Panama too. On my walk I spotted an indigenous woman selling some small items which were said to be handcrafted by the members of her locally residing tribe. I glanced at a distance with a feeling of regret as I knew I could not take any of her trinkets with me at this moment, but I paused for a moment to admire her unique appearance as she passed by me. Seeing her created a feeling of nostalgia from my brief encounters with a diminishing portion of the world which still resided in the jungles around us. I knew beyond the horizon of these borders a set of people have remained isolated from the outside and only recently began to feel the tampering of those in the civilized world. Not just here in Costa Rica, but anywhere where the originals have been violently tossed into the new way of things after so many years practicing an isolated existence. A type of existence more easily maintained in the days before air-travel and free-trade globalized all it could. While it was once the norm to remain together with those from your point of origin, now that idea has become yet another piece of the mosaic crumbling through the sand dunes of time.

Once we were allowed to reload I returned to my seat and decided it was time to text an old friend who I had recently seen running around somewhere in Central America. Throughout my life I had done an admittedly poor job with keeping up with people from back home. But for a few fellow travelers I've met along the way I did a bit better job at maintaining the relationship. Of course this was always easier with someone who expected so much less. Which is why I had become friends with nurses, teachers, and all of the other people living abnormal schedules throughout the world. Despite not being much of a drinker I had also become friends with many bartenders and knew them to be a nomads best friend, both for connections and for conversation.

Even though we were a generation able to travel anywhere at any time I had learned frequent travelers went without many people they were able to say they went back with. This held true with the exception of a French girl I met lifeguarding one summer at my friends apartment complex in Myrtle Beach back in college. We met one of my last nights there, but we hit it off so well that over the years we managed to keep in touch as we both hoped around the globe. She traveled a lot so every once in a while we would meet up in the same country or schedule to be on the same bus for a few hours. And there was that time we worked together for a few weeks at a beachside bar when we both got stuck waiting on visas. Last I had spoken to her she was going between Nicaragua and Costa Rica, but that was almost a year ago.

I had long since started categorizing people in my phone based on their country or nearest city, trying to remember when and where to hit up who. Time to see if she was still anywhere next to her name.We also shared in one other very common aspect in life. Something which had actually served as our bonding agent from the beginning. Our love of bread. Say what you want about bread in regards to it's current position on the social chopping block, but bread has always been a necessary addition to whatever I was cooking. And few people knew bread better than the French. Though I know the Germans will argue they're the best, but when don't they. When we first met she was still pretty rusty with her English and it was one of the few times I regretted not picking up French when I had the chance earlier in life. Though it was probably our inability to completely understand each other which made the conversation go so long. With each thing she tried to explain she followed with a string of over the top gestures and caused me to laugh more than a few times. I remember the wildest thing she told me was about how she had gotten a job her first week as a server without even knowing how to read the menu. I don't know how she did that. It took me a week to understand, *Apaga la Luz!* I kept thinking they wanted me to pay the light bill, not turn them off.

"Did I see you're in Costa Rica or are those pictures as out of date as my last address for you?" - Patrick

146

"HEY! Yeah, I'm here riding out my final year in the area."
"Final year? Believe it when I see it. Where exactly are you?"
"I guess you would know if I had an updated address for you."
"I know. I've been MIA. Sorry."
"It's cool. I get it. I'm working at a hostel in San Jose. Whats up?"
"Long story, but I'm on a bus and I just crossed the border into Costa Rica.
Do you have any rooms available for tonight?"
"Of course! How long are you here?"
"One more week. I've got three people with me. That too many?"
"Not at all! I'll hold you a room."
"Awesome. Send me the info and I should by there by 9 P.M."

As our conversation ended I got to thinking about how although we had not spent nearly as much time together I still felt like I knew Matilda better in some ways than I did those I was traveling with. Despite there being some of the most obvious things which she didn't know about me and I the simplest things I probably didn't know about her. Forget simple. Sometimes even the basic stuff. She didn't even know I wasn't teaching anymore. Sometimes I felt bad about not touching base more often with everyone in my life, but I wasn't always good at keeping every side of my life updated with the others and I never know who cared about anything beyond their anchored images of my past and the version of me they knew. And by the time her and I started crossing paths again I had already become accustomed to momentary friendships. Growing up and throughout college my house had always been an environment with a steady flow of people at all hours. Endless streams of roommates and that in and out nature of characters in my life made the idea of transient friendships completely reasonable, and the ability to adjust to those new people in a moments notice was what had made me so amicable to the life I fell into. And I couldn't be more grateful for that. I know this serves as quite the contradiction to how much I like being alone, but I always believed the relationship between those two sides of myself to be just as important as the sides which aligned.

About two hours up the road we stopped at a roadside market with a small cafeteria where the driver told us we had a thirty minute break to eat and stretch our legs. I drank a bottle of water and held back from downing a few others because I knew my childlike bladder would come to haunt me in due time if I did. While I walked around the guys went off to find some food from the cafeteria style set of vendors taking up a small building next to the bus stop. As I stood there scoping out our stop off I saw a man off in the distance who made me wish we had been able to cross the border with our own vehicle and control pace of our own journey. Behind him a sign reading, *HANDMADE HAMMOCKS*, drew sense to what he was doing with all of that rope at his side. Sadly I wouldn't have enough time to run across and check it out if I planned to eat. A shame though, because my friends would be up to go talk to him too. They knew just as much as anyone else that the coolest places were those little spots you found on the side of some backroad. Whether it be some little restaurant run by a local family or a shopped filled with items made by a local artisan. No where else will you have a better time than when you find the woman willing to give you a tour of the castle her family has watched over for six generations. Or when you find the local with the sourdough bread grown from a culture started by her late grandfather after the war. But for the moment, the only world I needed consisted of a few scoops of rice and hopefully some fresh chicken. Which of course I was able to find before making my way to a table in the middle where the guys had taken their findings.

"This is perfect. A few more pieces of yuca and I'm good to nap for the rest of this ride. Patrick how far you think we are?" - Myles

"I think we're about one more nap from being where we're trying to go." - Patrick

"Fuck you. I'll ask the bus driver." - Myles

"We'll be there before ten. Just chill. I already got us a spot to stay."

"They got a pool?" - Austin

"I only know we've got a bed for the night."

"Party in San Jose. Hell yeah boys." - Myles

When we were done eating we took one more bathroom break and got out to stretch a bit before getting back on the bus. I had promised myself to finish at least one book on this trip so when we loaded up I turned on *Zorba the Greek*, the story of an old man and his life exploring the Greek Isles. Only then did I notice the missing earbud from my headphones, the one remained slightly in my ear, while the cord from the other dangled down at my chest, lending the beginnings of the story to the outside world. Just before taking my head away from the windows and hiding it inside of my hoodie I saw a sign for the city of Jaco and made a note to remember its' location and distance from San Jose. It looked like a large enough city along the coast to visit later, and from this point forward I had nothing planned. I looked down at my phone and the ETA said 9:13 P.M.

Over the next few hours I faded in and out of sleep as my attention was split between a dreamscape and the subtle British accent of the narrator explaining Zorba and all his adventures. I only started to open my eyes as the darkness allowing for such sleep was broken up by the shadows of streetlights passing over as we entered the city. When I was here before I was not able to explore San Jose beyond a quick come and go, but it was nice to see some of the improvements which had taken place. Although generally speaking it was the same unfinished project as before. A few construction sites had finally been completed, but the same sense of urgency did not exist here as it did in the city-clustered North East of my own country. It's almost like the people here don't care, but why should they? It's nice enough. And nice enough is all you need when the climate floats at a year round eighty with more pleasantry than inconvenience. The bus continued crawling as we navigated through narrowing streets and flashing red lights until we made it to the regional bus station. When it finally came to a halt we waited for the doors to open as Myles summoned an Uber. I got out and stood in the parking lot stretching a bit as Myles came out with his phone up in the air waving in frustration.

"Fucking fuck!" - Myles

"What's wrong?" - Patrick

"The card I cancelled is the one I use for my Uber."

With that he looked around hoping for a savior.

"Are you serious? None of you have Uber? Austin?"

"No dude. I have a Subaru. I drive that mother fucker everywhere."

"Patrick?" - Myles

"I'm with Austin on that one." - Patrick

"Guess we're walking." - Wes

Now the same bags which had been overweight for the plane needed to be carried twenty minutes across town. Oh how I hate to be right. I saw the guys carrying a look of discouragement on their faces as they glanced down at their overweight bag.

"So I'll take it half way and you take it the rest of the way. That work for you Austin?" - Myles

"I say we rock, paper, scissors it. Loser carries."

"You really wanna risk having to carry it the whole way? I'm not gonna help you when I see you struggling as I enjoy my stroll through town."

"All or nothing."

"Ok. On 1.2.3..."

They both shot out their hands and made the signs of a scissor and a piece of paper. With Myles on the losing end.

"Totally worth it."

Myles took a deep breathe and hiked the bag up over his shoulder and grunted with his effort to balance it between his head and finger tips as we all began walking.

"Just point me in the direction." - Myles

"We've gotta go out that gate there and then head up that street to the main drag. From there it looks like a 20 minutes walk." - Patrick

Over the next twenty minutes we only saw one other person on an opposing corner as we cut through a few neighborhoods. Which was somewhat concerning because this part of town didn't look abandoned, but the people were nowhere to be found. Odd, considering it was still before midnight. As we neared the address we came upon a city square with plaques and monuments on one end and a police station sitting at the other.

"Guess that means no partying tonight boys. Oh well." - Myles

"Fuck that. Invite em' over. Beers on me." - Austin

"After that fucking walk I don't want any beers. I just wanna find a fucking bed you rock paper cheating mother fucker." - Myles

Exhausted from the walk the guys dropped their bags as we approached the entrance which sat caddy corner from the furthest end of the court square. I stood at the gate and sent Matilda a text as I pushed a button next to the call box. When we were buzzed up I opened the door and held it for the guys as they walked in and up the stairs to the foyer of the hostel. At the front desk sat a Costa Rican twenty-something and my long unseen friend Matilda. Her hair was shorter than I had ever seen, somewhere between the ears and neck. Her honey brown eyes lit up and a smile was drawn on her milky face as she jumped out of her seat and hurled herself around the edge of the front desk where she greeted me with a firm hug and an accent still as thick as the day we first met.

"Patrick! Oh my god it's so good to see you! I can't believe you're here." - Matilda

When I felt her hug I was filled with the warm feeling of a friendship spent far from one another.

"So nice to see you! Here. Meet my friends." - Patrick

"Pleasure. The kitchen is still serving dinner if you all are hungry."

"I like you already. Hi, I'm Austin." - Austin

"Nice to meet you. I got you a dorm for four and all the coffee you could want." - Matilda

"Awesome. Coffee later. Food now. What food you got?" - Myles

"There should be some pizza on the counter outside. Help yourselves and I'll go get your keys." - Matilda

The guys went towards the counter as I went on with Matilda while she guided me on a walk through the hostel. Once we passed through the lounge we were led to an open courtyard with a pool at it's center. To the back was an open air kitchen with a few bar stools. To the left was a line of hammocks beside a bar stocked with two freezers of beer. To the right were a maze of hallways which led to the dorms and a few private rooms. All around picnic tables made for plentiful seating, but for the most part the guests occupied their own corners of the courtyard in groups of two or three scattered throughout. This is usually only the case in hostels of hub cities or along borders where people are more likely in a position of transit and only staying for the night. Even during the brief days when I had the money for nicer hotels with higher views, I still preferred spots like this where I could get to know people around a fire among the city lights.

When we got situated I sat across from Matilda and appreciated the rarity of being face to face with her after all this time. Ironically in an environment similar to the one we met in all those years back. Since that day our relationship was maintained through a series of emails by two people who had a mild understanding of the others language, but an absolute interest in how the other lived. Something I'm sure both of us could tell by the translated wordings of our messages back and forth.

"Nice to finally be in the same city again." - Patrick

"I know. It's so good to see you! It's been far too long. How's your trip going?" - Matilda

"Good so far. Loving this weather."

"You think this is warm? I need it to warm up so I can get some good dives in before I leave."

"Leave? How long you been here?"

"Since May. So almost a year."

"Where you going next?"

This had become one the most consistent questions between the two of us. And in some ways the answer was the basis of our friendship during a time when the only thing we could ever update each other on was our locations. That was it. Anything after that was just a matter of extending the fantasy. But for two travelers in constant motion it was hard enough to keep track of the pin-balling of life in your own circles, let alone in the circles of others. That's why it was always more likely for people to label us ex-pats instead of nomads, for it's easier to consider someone forever gone than forever roaming.

"Back to France."

"Heading home for a change?"

"I go home all the time. I just never stay long. You should know. I've invited you there plenty of times."

"I know. I know. I promise I'll get there soon."

"Well now you have no other choice if you want to see me. I'm gonna be there around the clock after this year."

"Really now?"

"Yeah. You remember me telling you about my grandmothers old farm?"

"The one with the horses and all those trails?"

"Yeah that one. Well, I've been fixing it up over the last couple of summers and it's almost ready for me to live there full time. The barn at least."

"Tired of sharing your kitchen with strangers?"

"Pretty soon that's gonna be the least of what I share."

"What do you mean?"

"What I mean is I plan to turn the barn into a hostel pretty soon and eventually I am going to arrange some stuff for people to do when they come and stay."

"I like the idea. Especially if you've got the space. How long you been planning that?"

"A few years now. It just took a while before I got into the actual moving on the plans. Once I did things got moving pretty quickly. I forgot how much I love working with my hands. I even built a little spot for a bird sanctuary."

"Oh that's cool."

"Yeah. It wasn't that hard. I just had to get a few of the right plants and set them up. It's way more of a science than I knew."

"I have no doubt about that. So birds and horses? You've got a fair amount of space I imagine? Never mind. That's a stupid question. I mean it must be big. You have fucking horses after all."

"Well it's actually way more space than I need. Especially now. Most of the horses are gone."

"Oh really? They're gone?"

"Yeah. Most of them went to my aunt Lanette. We're down to just two Percheron's. You know, those big bulky horses? It's okay though. Those giants are enough to feed for now. But yeah, now I gotta decide how I'm gonna split up the stables. It's too open right now."

"What are you thinking you're gonna do?"

"Still debating. After all of this time away I do like the idea of a place with private rooms, but dorms would give me a better chance at attracting groups. I need to figure out a few more things about what I'm trying to build first. I already have the simple stuff."

"I feel that."

"Yeah. I'll show you some pictures later when I get my laptop. Love to hear your thoughts on what did to the entrance. Do you want another smoke?"

"No, I'm good. So, what brought all of this about?"

"It just feels like time to show people my side of the world for a change. And it'll help make visiting my hometown a bit more affordable for some of the people I've met down here. Southern France is just too expensive these days."

"That's all well and good, but you're gonna miss it down here. I promise. You're gonna get antsy eventually."

"I'm sure I will after a while. But I always end up running back to the same kinds of spots no matter what city I'm in. It's like I'm always changing my location, but I've never really changed my environment."

"Kinda fell under the temptation to keep going to the same party?"

"I guess you could say that. It was all the same. No matter where I went. I wasn't me. I was just my routine. Day after day."

"Well if it's what you like why change it?"

"I'm not changing anything. But if I'm gonna keep doing that I might as well put all of those things in my own place. And that's what I plan to do. I'm gonna make my home my favorite place in every way possible. It was nice to see the world but, I am who I am. And right now I'm someone who misses home."

"Fair enough."

"Yeah. You know. I always thought I wanted to do something like that down here. I always said I would start importing stuff from France and open my own little store of favorites. But I just didn't do it. Home kept calling, but I never pulled through on that. I hope you come check it out. Really. Try and find a post teaching near me. You could come work on the farm on the weekends. I'll give ya a bunk anytime you need."

"No can do."

"Why's that?"

"Well for one I stopped teaching last year."

"No way? Why didn't you say anything?"

"I wasn't avoiding it. It just hadn't come up."

"So what are you up to now?"

"Working at a hotel oddly enough."

"You? Doing what? You're a people person, but you're not a *people* person."

"I know. I'm doing account management stuff."

"Yup. That doesn't sound like you."

"I don't know what to tell you."

"Then what are you doing? If you're gonna do that why don't you come take my place here when I leave? I'm sure they would hire you. It's just as good. If not better."

"Can't do that. I've spent too much time down here and I'll   never sit still long enough to do anything I need to get done if I do."

"Yeah I've never known you to be good at staying in one place. Pot calling the kettle black on that one though. What kind of thing are you looking for next? You can't just stay somewhere you don't belong."

"And therein lies the problem. I have no clue."

"Is there anything you've not done yet that you wanna do?"

"That's sort of a never-ending answer. But it's not like there's anything I walk around thinking about everyday. Plenty of places I wanna visit, but that's not what I'm trying to solve."

"No. I could have guessed that one. Well if one of the things you're looking to try is construction come my way. I need all the help I can get. I'll give you my address before you go. I promise it won't be changing again anytime soon!"

"I'll consider it."

"You better. What was it you went to school for? I know you've told me, but I can't remember."

"No worries. I'm sure I barely talked about it. I studied Political Science. Which was basically meant to keep myself informed and networking before going to grad school."

"Oh. So why the hotels? Did you want to be done teaching or were you just trying to get back to the states?"

"Neither answer in particular."

"Then why leave?"

"It just felt like I was falling behind from where I should be by now."

"And where was that?"

"I don't know. Adulting and all of that stuff. Kinda hard to feel serious about myself when all I did was play for ten years. I figured I should get myself a stable job and stay in the same city to change things up for a while. And yeah I guess it's easier to do that in my own country. But it wasn't about returning home or anything like that. It was just easier to do it there."

"Ever thought about going back to school?"

"Nah. I'd be starting over in the dark. I'm tired of that."

"Thought about quitting your job and finding work translating or teaching on the side?"

"Not really, I feel like that would be a huge backpedal from what I'm trying to do."

"Knowing what you don't want to do is just as important as knowing what you do want to do. Perhaps you're ahead of the game. Why not go and try a few new things and see what else you don't like. You could take a class in some new field and see what happens. It's no different than you learning French. Anything you wanna do is just about learning the lingo. You gotta talk the talk. You know all about that."

"True."

"And look at me. I don't really know what I'm doing with a horse stable. But I'll figure it out. And until then I'll get the right people around me and just learn the talk."

"So what happens after that?"

"What do you mean?

"Is that gonna be it? Just work on the property forever?

"Duh. That's the point. They're gonna burry me there. That's my home. I'm still going to travel, it's just not gonna be the focus of my life anymore."

I didn't know what to say. Perhaps she had found her perfect blend between labor and love. For that, I felt happy for my friend. What else could anyone want other than an existence that they never wished to retire from? If it worked, it sounded like a dream. A dream of a day where one could find a pursuit so worthy of one's own persistence that they never felt the want to retire from its duties. That sounded like the only feeling worthy of sacrificing my life away to obtain. The only other friend to even express something similar in the realities of his own life was a buddy in the military who kept stressing to me how I coulda been well on my way to retirement by the time he saw me at 28. Which was true, but I never wanted to want to retire. There was no joy in that thought for me. Not to say there was joy in that thought for him either. He didn't seem in any hurry to quit. Unfortunately so, there are few vocations in which one can work forever. There are some in which even those who enjoy their work are forced out by the burdens and misconceptions of old age.

Though I can't with honesty say I had done much to do anything about realizing that thought on my own beyond a fantasy here and there. Not since taking that swing at making a documentary with Myles. I had only participated in passive defiance by choosing a future which allowed for an annual switch up as long as I was okay with the move being lateral. And in doing so I had sold myself short and perhaps at times been a bit too stagnant. Something for which I felt more than guilty about, but I guess from where I stood at the time, it seemed far more logical to do something I knew to be enjoyable than to do anything that I thought I might actually feel stuck in. It's not as if I was ever lost per se. That's perhaps the largest misconception about some of us constant travelers. Or at least about myself. I wasn't lost. I just knew what I didn't want to do. And that was enough reason not to return and not to do anything else. I didn't see my job or my life as an anchor, but instead a device which could move me through the existence I was hoping to live. What made me return was just a sinking reality that I had to do something, otherwise become one of the forever lost. Which is how I was starting to look from the outside. I was already at a big enough risk of being deemed one of those you should never hire. My resume after college had done little to impress my way into a new life. It was one thing to have a gap, it was another to be seen jumping back and forth between instabilities. And when in deep reflection a part of me always wonders if I'll ever get over the urge of exploring all existences possible.

Even though she was right, in all of my uncertainty I still had this urge to find a way to live my life on the go as much as possible. Especially after the resurgence of feelings resulting from being on the road this last week. That's the only thing I was certain I enjoyed. It added to the adventure and created a goal for each day. One to move along the next spot until we'd reached our destination. Although in life the destination is not always as easy to see as the clear ending of a two-week trip where boarding passes are readied and spirits are lifted. No, sometimes those destinations are stop-offs meant to give us a rest for the next leg of our ever expanding existence. And ever expanding was how I imagined mine. As well as how I envisioned the future each time I gave it some true thought. It's why I loved the allure of a new place no matter where it was. A new environment throws us into a state of altered thinking and becomes a drug of its own after a while. You're so engaged with the world around you that a forced focus starts to take over. When you're somewhere new something is always slightly undiscovered. And there's always somewhere new to discover. Though if that type of future was my end game, I would likely never see the finish line. And if it were one I was ever going to pursue I needed to focus my search on a different way of life than I had been used to, but with the same mobility. As our varied conversation and slow game of catch up went on we eventually fell victim to the curses of energy and became zombies yearning more for sleep than further conversation. When we came to terms with this we parted ways and took ourselves to our respective rooms. Once situated I starred at the bunk above me and slowly fell asleep to the light hum of a city unconcerned about the morning to come.

Day 7: As He Saw It
San Jose, Costa Rica

I pretended to sleep through the roar of five trains passing through the city before I finally gave in and started moving this morning. The noises were easy to ignore at first through the help of my pillow wrapped around my face, but once they combined with the honking of horns and the beeping of buses I knew my state of delusion could no longer be maintained. Once I accepted this and left the room I went to the pool to soak up some sun while I tried to make the reality of being awake meet with the feeling. And that kept me still for about another hour or so until a shadow hovering over my lounge chair started speaking in my direction.

"Morning bro. Want some breakfast? My treat. Here have some coffee." - Myles

I squinted a bit and stretched my arms out to draw in a deep breath before responding.

"Don't you mean your tab?" - Patrick

"No. My treat. I picked up a few $20's this morning. I walked by you earlier but you was sleepin' like a baby."

"Nice. Should we see if everyone else wants to go?"

"Nah, we'll feed 'em later."

"How long you been up?"

"I been up a while bro. I already fixed the shower this morning."

"What?

"The shower head. The one they had was shit so I went to a hardware store and bought one and put it in for em. Go check it out."

"Oh shit. That's fucking awesome."

"Yeah dude. Tell your girl thanks for hooking us up."

At that we left and walked towards the city center where a variety of government buildings, museums, and schools sat clustered amongst a few apartment complexes rising twenty stories or so into the air. A few blocks into our walk Myles noticed a little bakery on a corner with the sign *Maria's Panaderia* hanging out front. Wrapping around both sides of the building was a mural depicting a jaguar perusing the jungle floor with the occasional piece of broken concrete disrupting his prowl and the surrounding floral scenery. As we walked inside we approached a counter where a stack of individually wrapped cookies sat next to an espresso machine and an old school cash register. I started feeling the cookies for softness when a lady interrupted the first stage of my purchasing process.

"Hola. How may I help you?" - Maria

"Hola. Well what do you recommend?" - Patrick

"Are you looking for a pastry or bread?" - Maria

"We're open to whatever you suggest. Actually, can I try that one there. The yellowish bread." - Patrick

"Sure. I'll give you a few samples." - Maria

She reached in the case and broke off a sliver for the two of us to try. One which resembled cornbread and the other which had more of a rustic look to it. I tried the one resembling cornbread first. And I kid you not, it was then, and remains to this day, to be one of the best breads I've ever tried. It was a special type of *pan de elote* with just a bit more sweetness than how they make it in the states. Basically a croissant and cornbread combined.

"Dude, you gotta try this." - Patrick

When he took the bread from my hand he started scarfing it down and lost a few crumbs to his beard which would later be donated to the floor.

"Now that there is some damn good bread." - Myles

"Maybe the best cornbread I've ever had. Who's the cook?" - Patrick

"My mother." - Maria

"Dude, she said her mom makes it." - Patrick

"Ask her how she makes it feel like this." - Myles

"Is there any chance you could tell us what her trick is? It's so soft."

"I wish I could, but I don't know her recipe."

"Well when does she make her drops?"

"About once a week. Usually on Mondays."

"Mam this bread would be perfect to cook with my grandma. I thought it would be cool to bring her a recipe back from my travels that we could make when I see her again. Any chance you could help?"

"Well I could always call her and see what she says."

As she called her mother Myles and I looked at each other somewhat surprised at what was taking place. I mean, there's a certain level of hospitality that just goes beyond anything you'd expect. And we were from the South, the place synonymous with hospitality.

"Hola Mami! I have a few men here that wanna know if you would mind sharing your recipe to our special pan de elote?…No mama. They're just boys from America. They're not from *Carmen's*. No, I'm sure. Here you can talk to one of them."

At this point she held her hand over the receiver and whispered,

"You'll have to forgive her. Those people at *Carmen's* are always trying to copy her recipes. They've been at each other for years." - Maria

"Yo I'll fuck em up if I have to. Just point me the way." - Myles

"Calm yourself. Our victory today will be the bread." - Patrick

While she continued to talk I placed my notebook on the counter and Maria turned it towards herself and grabbed the pen from my hand without any hesitation. One of the few things I would ever take umbrage with, but in this case she had earned carte-blanche due to the specific nature of her all important mission. From there she leaned into the counter and began writing a series of instructions which covered the pocket-sized page under her palm. As she did this I stood back and covered my other ear to better understand the aged accent which began speaking softly from the other end of the call.

"Hola Hijo. I hope you and your abuela enjoy my bread, but you must promise not to give this recipe to any other bakers okay?" - Madre de Maria.

"I promise mam'. Not a soul." - Patrick

"Okay Hijo. Now tell my daughter I will talk with her later. I've got a lot of baking left to do. Mucho Gusto. Que tengas un buen dia."

"Tambien Señora. Thank you very much!" - Patrick

Myles looked pleased with the exchange as we walked out.

"Way to fuckin go!" - Myles

"Hell yeah man. I can't believe that actually worked."

We downed what little bread we had bought as we moved along and ended up gifting the final crumbs to some birds who were busy harassing a dog on the street corner.

"So what now? Should go get that car before it gets late?" - Patrick

"Yeah let's take care of that. Then we can get out of the city and to the beach before the day is lost."

"Sounds good."

I had yet to address this problem beyond my mind, but I knew since Myles didn't have a credit card anymore then the responsibility of renting the car would likely fall on me since I was the one most suited to do the driving. At least now with the position as primary driver I had earned something beyond obligatory complacency in the decisions to be made. We got back to the hostel and I went upstairs to consult the concierge about her thoughts on some good towns to visit along the Pacific. She took my map and said she would circle a few spots while I was gone. From there I went with Myles and waited outside until a cab came to take us to the airport. When we got there we found their figures far less extreme than that of the rental companies in Panama, but they were still asking more than we would have paid anywhere else.

"Hey man you're gonna have to sign for this rental. They're not gonna let me without my license." - Myles

"Am I going to be the only one on the insurance?"

"Yeah it looks like it. The guys are back at the hostel so unless we wanna bring them back here to scan their ID's it's gonna be all you."

"Then you're the only one cool to drive other than me. Deal?"

Back home I wouldn't have given much thought to someone else driving. At least not if they had a license, but here I couldn't risk the results of going through a roadblock with an unregistered driver. Or at least I didn't wanna pay for the inconvenience should it come up. This same type of situation is what had essentially led to me being the one in charge of the driving growing up, and by default the one not drinking. Aside from that there was always something else going on. Whether it was work or school. I never got to allow myself much of the down time present in the youths of those I grew up with. Which of course was made up for every day after graduation, but even in my first few years on the go I kept mostly to myself and stayed out of bars to avoid any situations or misunderstandings that could get me caught off guard while traveling alone uncertain what I was saying and who I was saying it to.

When we got back to the hostel we found the boys sitting around talking with a few of the workers by the pool. Wes had spent some time talking with them and had come up with a few ideas for where we should go. The best of which was a hostel in a town called Jaco where they had a surfer friendly hostel with rentals and lessons.

"Myles you ever surfed?" - Patrick

"Yeah. Sucked."- Myles

"You sucked or it sucked?" - Patrick

"It sucked. It was freezing." - Myles

"Where were you surfing?" - Patrick

"In California. I think Santa Barbara. Hard to remember, it was on that road trip I took with my dirt bike." - Myles

"Okay well that's why it was cold. You were in fucking Cali. It won't be like that here." - Patrick

"I'm down to take some surfing lessons." - Wes

"If you say so." - Myles

"So we're good to go?" - Patrick

"Yeah. Let's get our shit and head out." - Myles

As the boys were getting their stuff together I went to find Matilda and say goodbye. She had mentioned the night before that she might take a few days and go up North, so I wasn't certain to see her again when we returned for our departure.

"Well I might not be around, but I'll make sure they take care of you if I'm gone." - Matilda

"Okay great. And Matilda, you need to try this shop around the corner. It's a different bread than you're used to, but ask for their pan de elote. It deserves its own postcard."

"Do you have time to go with me before you leave?"

"I wish I could but we've gotta get going. I'll take you if we stay here again on our way out. Either way you should go. It's just up the road. It's called *Maria's Panaderia*. Tell them you know the crazy Americans."

"Oh! I think I know that place. I'll go first thing tomorrow."

From there we said our goodbyes and I left to find the guys in the lobby gathering the last of their things.

"You guys ready?"

"Can we eat something on our way out?" - Myles

"You're still hungry?"

"Dude I'm starving."

"Alright. There's a few spots up that I spotted last night. Let's go check them out."

Once we packed up the car we drove up the street to a restaurant with a tiny menu and a heavy selection of seafood lining each page. They might have had the best hot sauce in San Jose. And while I was glad to have made that discovery I really didn't feel like eating. And I couldn't understand how Myles still wanted any food after all of the bread we ate on our walk around the city. When we finally got back on the road it was already noon. On the drive down Wes called to find us a hostel and became part of a little mix-up which ultimately worked out in our favor.

"Hi we would like 4 rooms. Yeah yeah, whatever works. Uh yeah. Tom? Yeah that's me. Ok thanks, we'll be there soon."

When he hung up he looked over at us with a big smile and began to reveal the results of his conversation.

"Hey guys. We got a dorm all to ourselves, but I think they gave us someone else's room. If they ask, my name is Tom."

When the highway met with the coast an hour later we turned left and continued another thirty miles or so until we got to the town of Jaco. There we found a small cluster of maybe two-thousand people resting along a mountain graced cove about an hour north of the Panamanian border. When we turned off the main road we were dumped onto a side road where the speed-limit dropped and the number of bicyclers doubled. At the end of the road we pulled in at the edge of a gravel parking lot with a large sign advertising surf board rentals for $10 a day at *Hostel Nadar por Nada*. We parked in their gravel lot and went around the edge of a large concrete wall beyond a few sets of storage sheds until we came to a large desk where check-in took place.

The bottom level of the four story hostel had a small lobby with a bar, billiards, and a series of tables which opened up to a pool on the backside. The layers between were filled with a combination of dormitories and private rooms, with one floor being split by a two room kitchen. At the very top was an open balcony with some chairs, hammocks, and a small bar to be used as overflow on the busier nights. Behind the hostel sat a series of bungalows which belonged to those willing to pay a bit extra for the privacy and convenience of their own jacuzzi. When they asked our names the girls continued our check-in process uninterrupted by the discrepancy in our passports compared to the names they had on the reservation. As the girls checked us in they gave us the breakdown of the area and the rules of the hostel. One in particular caught me off guard when she pointed to the bottom of the list at an underlined sentence which emphasized the strict forbidding of prostitutes in the hostel.

"And watch yourself if you got out in the town. They'll take your wallet if you're not paying attention."

To which another chimed in.

"Yeah. If you're looking for girls it's best to find one already staying here at the hostel."

From there they told us a series of stories about prostitutes robbing their clients and informed us the local police were not known to do much about it. In fact, if what she said was true, they were benefactors to the entire situation. As we gathered our things I walked around the bottom level and to the edge of the bar where I saw two girls sitting at the pool with their feet dangling in the water. My current perspective only gave me a profile view, but with that preview of the guests they housed I had no problem with her suggestion if the opportunity were to present itself. Standing there I ordered some blend of juices and took a look at their menu. I wasn't really that hungry, but overall it looked like a great spot for us to stay and the food looked good enough to keep us from venturing out unless we really wanted to. When I finished my drink I went upstairs and found the door to our room propped open with a steady breeze going through the studio style bedroom and the guys all sitting out on the patio. A bed had been situated in each corner of the room with only one remaining open. As I started unpacking Austin and Myles started scoping out the vacant lots which made up the space between us and the next structure about 100 yards away.

"Hey man I wanna get a better looking at something. I'm gonna take this cigarette upstairs. You coming?" - Myles

"Yeah man. Gimme a minute." - Wes

While Myles and Austin went upstairs I stayed behind with Wes and rotated between sitting outside and unpacking for the next hour or so until we realized that our counterparts were in no hurry to get back. By now the moon was near full and exposed enough of the beach for anyone to feel safe walking alone. Which is just what I was about to go do when Wes beckoned me to join him upstairs.

"Hey man let's go check out the rooftop and see what they're doing first."

"Alright man. Wanna go down to the beach after?"

"Yeah dude for sure."

As we got to the rooftop I saw Myles sitting at a bar next to an old man wearing a beat up Yankees cap with a fish hook wedged in the bill. Next to this potbellied man sat a skinny guy in his twenties and the same two girls who I had seen at the pool earlier. Towards the edge of the roof were the only other guests sitting in a set of lounge chairs facing the ocean.

"There you are! Patrick! Help me talk to this guy. He must know where the good spots are. You see the size of that fishing hook in his hat?" - Myles

"Alright. Anything in particular you wanna know?"

"Just where to go bro. I don't need any advice on how to fish."

"Gotcha. Hola Señor. How goes it?" - Patrick

"Bien Papi, Como estas?"

"Estoy bien señor. Me Llamo Patricio."

"Mucho Gusto. Soy Omar."

"Question for ya. Where do they stock this river? My friends are looking to do some fishing."

"Well nature does her stocking somewhere up in the mountains."

"Can my friends fish along the inlets down by the beach and still find some luck you think?"

"I wouldn't recommend that. Crocodiles are pretty rampant along the coast."

"Really? We haven't seen any."

"Oh trust me. Start casting some lines and you will."

As the man fed me a bit more information about where to go and what to do I relayed it to Myles and he decided that despite the warning it would be best to try an inlet on the other side of Jaco tomorrow. From there he and Austin left to go get their stuff ready for the morning.

"If your friends want to go fishing in the morning we could split all of the boat fees. We wanted to go snorkeling while we're here and Omar says he has a boat we can all take." - Two girls

"I don't know if that's a great idea." - Patrick

"And we don't go fishing with strangers." - Wes

"We're not strangers." - Gabi

"What else do we would call you?" - Patrick

"Well you could start with our names. I'm Gabi. And this is Karina." - Gabi

"Well nice to meet you. My friends call me Patrick. And this is Wes. He's not shy, he just doesn't speak much Spanish." - Patrick

Karina spoke a fair amount of English so by the natural order of things Wes took a seat next to her as I turned my attention towards Gabi. Conversation soon revealed they were both residents of San Jose and had come to the coast to hang out for a few nights. The longer we talked the more I got the feeling that Karina was taking a liking to Wes, but the language barrier was making it too difficult for either of them to catch each others subtleties. On the other hand I had no doubts about my increased favor with Gabi as she was undeniably flirtatious. Although it was hard to tell how influenced she was by the half-empty case of Pacifico bottles sitting at their feet and how much of it was my attempts at charm. Whether this or that it didn't matter because about an hour into talking Wes seemed to have struck a chord with Karina who soon took Gabi's attention away for a moment of whispers and then delivered a message meant for the group that I then relayed to Wes.

"Do you all wanna go back to our bungalow?"

"The ones outback?"

"Yeah. You guys wanna come hang out? We have some wine."

"Wes these girls want us to go down to their bungalow."

"I think that sounds like a great idea." - Wes

"Okay. Vamos." - Patrick

From there we got up and the two of us followed the sound of their sandals down the stairs until we had conquered all three floors and snaked through the lobby towards the back door. On our way down we passed by the mid-level kitchen where we saw Austin standing at a table adding some ice to a few drinks which looked freshly brewed. He tipped his hand to us as we walked by and toasted a shot in our direction. When we got to their bungalow we sat outside talking for a few minutes. Though in retrospect we should have just gone straight inside because somewhere between seeing Austin in the kitchen and arriving at their bungalow Myles had been alerted of our movement. Which I realized the moment I spotted him walking in our direction. When he made it to me he grabbed my arm and attempted to pull me away.

"Come on man. Let's get out of here."

"What the fuck are you doing?"

"Dude. Look at them. They're hookers just like the front desk warned us about. Let's get outta here."

"Why are you doing this to me right now? These girls are not hookers. And they're not bothering you. So please return the favor."

"Dude. Don't be under that spell. I know it was them I saw earlier."

"I have no doubt about what you may have seen earlier. But these girls are not the ones you saw."

At this he shrugged me off and reached in for Wes.

"Come on Wes. There's plenty of nice girls at the bar."

"Dude. Go the fuck away." - Wes

"What's wrong guys? You really can't tell the difference between a nice girl and a girl who wants you because you're buyin?" - Myles

"Dude. You think the front desk would let them rent them a spot after what they said? Come on. Just go to sleep."

"Is this how you lost my stuff last time? You trade my camera and all of that money for some sex? I won't be mad at ya I just wanna know."

"Please fucking quit. I'm not in the mood for this."

In a drunken haze he stared at me trying rationalize his mindset with every side he had laid his eyes on. But I knew that landscape to be a place he used to piece together enough parts to believe whatever version he was choosing to see at the moment. Even the most absurd of realities can do that to us from time to time and when through narrow enough eyes the result can be compounded to seem infallible to the viewer. Although there was a look of certainty that almost instilled doubt in my own mind and made me wonder if he knew something I didn't. But I had no reason to believe they were as he said. They hadn't asked me for any money or even insinuated that might be the case. Though the words of Charlie Sheen taught me we wouldn't have to pay them to fuck us, we'd just have to pay them to leave. And while that loophole and Myles' paranoia had me thinking of all of the possibilities I soon saw that we weren't going to need to pay anyone to leave.

"I'm not letting you guys pay for this. Especially you Wes. Come on let's leave these hookers to find some other guys to hustle." - Myles

At this point Karina stood up from her seat and got in between Myles and I.

"Would you please stop saying that. We are not hookers. And we are standing right in front of you." - Karina

"I'm sorry. I'll get him outta here." - Patrick

"I ain't going nowhere. If you wanna fuck them you're gonna have to do it with me sitting out here. Don't worry. I'll make sure their backup doesn't come shank you." - Myles

"Dude. Get the fuck outta here."- Patrick

"You guys will thank me in the morning when your dicks don't fall off." - Myles

"You're such a fucking asshole." - Wes

"They're going to rob you just like the girl at the front desk warned us." - Myles

"Chicos. Chicos. Vete por favor." - Karina

"Come on guys lets go." - Patrick

"God damnit Myles." - Wes

"Don't you worry boys, we'll find you two some nice girls soon enough." - Myles

"Adios chicas." - Patrick

As I walked away I exchanged an annoyed glance with Wes at the anti-climatic nature of our night and looked behind me to see Karina in the middle of explaining everything to a confused looking Gabi. Neither of us said anything as we trailed behind Myles stumbling his way back to the room one heavy breath at a time. We could have kept arguing with him sure, but there was no point in trying to regain the night and make our way back. I knew he wouldn't let that happen as long as we were in eyesight. Not without being less than worth the reward at the end of the headache.

When we made it to our room I sifted through my bag and found my headphones as Myles sequestered himself to the patio to devour a few more cigarettes. With some music playing I tried to relax a bit before falling off to sleep, but I couldn't get it out of my head. If tonight was how he thought of me then what did that say about how he thought of me when I was away. I knew it didn't really matter since we're only ever updating people on the last version of us they knew anyway. Although I wasn't sure that either one of us was doing a great job at coping with who the other had become. And not even become, just who we were seeing at the time. Whichever version it was.

Day 8: The Cove of Jaco
Jaco, Costa Rica

When I woke up I laid around for a good twenty minutes or so before getting up and starting my day. The sun was brightening up our room without directly hitting us so between that and the breeze coming off the deck it made for a pretty comfortable place to lounge around. When I finally got up I couldn't find my sandals anywhere. I looked around, but eventually I realized they weren't anywhere in the room. In need of something to wear I walked out to the patio and slipped into Austin's shoes which were drying underneath a series of bathing suits which had fallen off the railings during the night. It was amazing how quickly our clothes had accumulated in just two nights. After I got situated I brushed my teeth and ran upstairs where I found the setting much quieter than the night before. After walking around and not finding my sandals I went downstairs where I saw the world slowly prepping for the day ahead. Early morning travelers waited to check out of their rooms while the ambitious few ate their eggs at one of the colorful tables spread around the three-sided bar. I left the building and went down the alleyway towards the beach when a right turn put me toe to toe with Karina and Gabi. To my surprise they seemed unbothered by our last interaction.

"Glad we ran into you. I think we found your sandals on our porch." - Gabi

"That's good news. Do you mind if I come grab them after I get back from the beach?" - Patrick

"Of course. We're here all day."

"Awesome. I won't be long."

I went and walked around the beach and tried to figure out what, if anything, I was going to do about the situation from last night. I've found Myles usually lets the topic go the next day as opposed to putting himself in a position to be openly judged by one of the few people willing to call him out on his shit. The best I could hope for was that he would wake up with a brief headache and a shorter memory. When I got back to the hostel I shot Gabi a text and started in the direction of their bungalows. When I got there she had my sandals at her feet as the two of them sat on the front porch drinking some orange juice. As I approached I wanted to take the chance to scope out the porch and room to do a day light search and make sure Myles wasn't onto something with his accusations, but I didn't really know what would give it away? Don't all women travel with at least three pairs of high heels?

"Ladies I'm so sorry about my friend last night. I hope we didn't ruin your evening." - Patrick

"It's okay. Not your fault." - Karina

"Yeah. If you end up in San Jose without your friends feel free to give us a call on your return."

"That'll probably have to wait until the next trip. Do you mind if I use your bathroom real quick?"

"No, go ahead."

I feigned my trip to the bathroom and then said my goodbyes before heading upstairs. As I walked in the room I heard a set of conversations happening on the porch.

"Where's Patrick?" - Wes

"Who knows. Probably out talking with all the townspeople he can find." - Myles

"Oh look there he is." - Austin

"Sup?" - Patrick

"I'm trying to figure out which direction to head in. Did those hookers tell you anything useful?" - Austin

I gave a slight pause in my response as I decided to react by moving forward.

"Why don't we hit up that guy about that boat? He's probably your best bet for finding anything."

"I'm a fucking fisherman bro, I'll catch em' no matter where I go. But I'm not going on no dudes boat. I rather try my luck up the river. Myles! You coming with me? I'm gonna go get some iguanas for bait?"

"You're not gonna catch an iguana dude."

"Don't cast your shade in my direction."

"I'm just being real. They're fast as fuck. I've seen one outrun a dog and then wait it out at the bottom of a pool."

"Whatever dude. Myles you coming?"

"Yeah bro. Gimme a second." - Myles

"Come on man take a hit."

"Really? You have to press him?"

At this Austin cocked his head to the side and glared at Myles.

"Myles ain't hip brah. He's old school. He doesn't smoke."

"Don't need to fucking get high dude. Beer. There ain't nothing more natural than beer," taking a sip he grinned and looked back at Austin, "I'm cool not being a stoner."

This was probably the area of life the two disagreed upon most. He thought as I did. The whole view was fucked. If you have one glass of wine nobody calls you a wino. But one drag of a joint and you're a stoner. Or at least that's how it used to be.

The sky was perfectly clear so I decided to leave the clothes for another time and walked up to the rooftop to find a hammock for my afternoon use. Once I got up there I discovered I was able to look over the side of the building and into the adjacent yard where the grass grew more than waste high and a few palm trees harbored iguanas who would occasionally come down and grab some food before shooting back to a well picked hiding spot amongst the brush. The rooftop was uncrowded as most seafaring people were at the shore learning to surf. The beach would be pretty awesome right now, but I needed to save my skin for some sun hours just a little bit later in the afternoon. Before finding a spot to chill I looked down and saw the guys trying to be stealthy as they walked through the grass lot next to the hostel. My vantage point revealed a few iguanas only meters ahead of my friends, but with the height of this grass they were unlikely to spot what was around them until they had made too much noise and scared them off. I was lucky enough to witness the first failed attempt to spear an iguana which avoided the stick and then climbed up a palm tree with more speed than a snake into a hole. When the sun started getting to me I ran downstairs for a glass of water and found myself greeted by a small crowd of people surrounding a tiramisu cake with smoke rising from the freshly silenced dessert and the final tunes of a birthday melody being sung.

"Who's birthday did I miss?" - Patrick

"That would be mine." - Birthday lady

In front of me stood a dark slender woman who turned with her hand extended out to greet anyone willing to tell her happy birthday. As I accepted a smooth palm with fingers graced in a lavender coat clasped my hand firmly and repeated the motions of shaking until we had made it through our introduction. Looking at her I was confused. Even for someone as well traveled as myself, she seemed difficult to pin down. She was exotic in the way a person is when their genes have spent a few centuries hiking up and down the Silk Roads. Exotic not just in looks, but in dress too. Along with her deeply toned skin and perfectly painted nails she wore a yellow sundress which hovered just above the top of her matching toes and was offset by a pair of bright white sandals. All calling attention to either side of her you decided to focus on.

"And to whom am I wishing a Happy Birthday?"

"I go by Denali. And you are?"

"My friends call me Patrick. How old are you turning today?"

"I'm turning twenty-one for the 20th time now for anyone who is try-ing to keep track."

"You don't look it."

"Didn't think I did."

"Strictly here for birthday celebrations?"

"Yup. Told myself I wasn't spending another birthday in the cold."

"You don't look like someone from the cold."

"Oh I am. I live outside of Berlin."

"Okay. So let me be real for a moment birthday lady. When I look at you nothing exactly screams German or even *Germanesque* if you will... Care to fill me in?"

"What's wrong Mr. Traveler? You can't guess where I'm from?"

"Well, if you had a Spanish accent I'd start taking some shots, but your look ain't my expertise. Give me a clue."

"Why do you care?"

"I've always been fascinated at what blend of worldly circumstances leads to the creation of a particular human, in this case you. Call it cultural curiosity I guess."

"Clues won't help here. I'm originally from Nepal, but I've been gone from there so long that if people ask me where I'm really from I usually save time by saying the UK."

"Alright, so that explains the accent."

"Sure does. And you? American I assume?"

"I guess my look is a bit easier to decipher?"

"Just a bit. And you all do have a tendency to chat up strangers."

"Never been more guilty in my life. So Nepal? What's the food like there? Any chance to hostel will get a sample? Believe it or not I'm finally getting tired of arroz con pollo."

With a light laugh and a sway of her finger she let me down with a bit of self-deprecation.

"Not a chance. You're looking at the worst cook that country ever made."

"You don't have a favorite dish you can make?"

"No. I'm too busy for that. And we have so many great places to try in the city. I've been spoiled by life in a metropolitan. I usually eat out or order in the few nights I'm ever actually home."

"Oh well. I'm usually the chef in my house anyway."

"Well I was just about to take up my duties as bartender. Care to stay around for a shot?"

"Not usually how I start the day, but okay."

"Me either, but last year my gift to myself was to stop being boring. And so far that decision has made my life far more interesting."

"Ironic. My last promise to myself was to start being more

responsible."

"And how is that going?"

"Eh. I'll keep you posted."

"Well Mr. Responsible at least have a shot before you go."

Not wanting to argue and not quite ready to leave I stood there and indulged my new friend while she ordered a round for us as well as two guests standing at her side. As we stood there waiting for our shots I was pushed into her by a passerby and my hand landed smack in the middle of a plate she had been keeping at her side with what was left from her first serving of tiramisu.

"I'm sorry…"

"Don't worry. Here's a fork, don't let it go to waste."

I took the fork from her hand and waited until we had finished our shot to start in on my cake and try separating myself from the party.

"Hey it was great to meet you, but I've gotta get going."

"Where you going in such a hurry?"

"Up to San Jose."

"What's going on up there that's so important?"

"Picking up a friend at the airport."

"Why not have them take a bus? They have one that brings you here from the airport. I don't even think it makes any other stops."

"I'm sure there is, but I said I would so I am. Enjoy the rest of your birthday celebrations."

"Well thank you. Travel safe."

"You too Denali. Nice meeting ya."

I pulled myself away from the crowd and walked to the beach where I continued to the furthest end of the cove on what turned into nearly an hour long stroll through the sand. When I got back a little while later I found Wes relaxing.

"The guys still fishing?" - Patrick

"Yeah. If they're not back soon they're gonna miss the surf lesson." - Wes

"Wanna go with me to San Jose?"

"Nah man. I wanna stay here and surf. You. mind?"

"All good man. Just wanted to offer you an out."

"I appreciate it. I'm good though."

I was indifferent about their decision to come with me or not. If someone came I would get some one-on-one time and a shared set of eyes while trying to make my way around the city, but otherwise I was happy enough to cut loose for a bit and enjoy an evening drive on the mountains alone. After getting myself ready I left the hostel and with the glare of the setting sun as my guiding light I made my way up the mountain and towards the city. Half way up I began asking myself why I was driving three hours to pick up a grown adult when I knew an efficient bus system existed. But as always I was to blame for my own inconvenience. When I originally agreed to this I had told her that she would have to find us and that she'd have to make her own way from San Jose to wherever we were, but once it all became so mixed up I agreed to meet her at the airport since I couldn't give her much notice on where we would be or how to get there. Figured there was no point in starting someone else's trip as confused as my own if I could do anything about it.

Although we had driven this same route on the bus before I still found most of my views approaching the city to appear brand new to my eyes and memory. A bus is great because you get to look far and wide, but there's a different intake of the landscape when you're the one driving it. After topping over the mountain a steady drop gave me a great view to my right of a low valley surrounded by green coffee fields, a common sighting by now, but one I was still savoring. For some reason I couldn't stop thinking about what type of view you could have from the middle of that valley on a clear night. I would never know, at least not on this trip. But it had to be beautiful. There's no better view than one that involves a valley beneath the stars.

I ended up arriving around an hour before her flight was set to land so I drove to a side street about a mile from the airport where I waited her out with a short nap. Anyone with common sense would have been more alarmed to snooze on a dark road by the airport, but sleeping in unsafe spots around the world at this point in my life had sadly become quite the normal thing. From what I can tell the nap lasted around 45 minutes until I was awoken by a text informing me that she was exiting the terminal. I knew I had a little time until she got through customs so I sat there for a minute waking up and then got myself to the airport. It took a few minutes more than I expected but somewhere around my 5th rotation through the parking lot I spotted a short curly haired girl waving me down. As I pulled over she threw her things in the backseat and climbed up front giving me a big hug the moment she got in.

"Hello there friend. Pleasant flight?" - Patrick

"Yeah it was great! I got on their wifi and did a bunch of research. Have you seen a volcano yet?"

"Let's not talk about volcanos."

"Uh okay. So you don't want to see one?"

"We can. But they really want to find a waterfall to jump off. You game?"

"If you need any suggestions just ask me."

"Of course."

"So what's our hostel like?"

"It's pretty cool. They have surf boards for rent if you're interested. You okay sharing a room tonight?"

"That's fine."

"Good. And I thought of a fee for picking you up."

"Okay, what do I owe you?"

"Nothing big. But tomorrow you're getting me my own room. I need an evening of peace."

"I can deal with that."

"Good."

"Are you guys having fun?"

"Yeah I'm enjoying myself so far."

"Good. What are we doing tonight? Do I need to be dressed up?"

"No, there's plenty going on at the hostel if you wanna do anything."

"Do I have my own bed?"

"Not tonight. But you can bunk with us."

"What if one of them brings someone back?"

"Not something I would worry about after last night."

"What happened last night?"

"I'll tell ya later. Oh, and while you're down here, try not to mention anything about work. They don't exactly know about the bartending. Leave that out if anything happens to come up."

"They don't know you used to bartend? That's such a random thing to keep a secret."

"Look, I don't wanna get into it, it'll just make my life easier if you don't. Cool?

"Yeah, that's fine."

"Thanks. So how's everything at home?"

"It's good. Just busy with work and the wedding."

"Have a date for everything yet?"

"No. And of course it's the only thing people want to ask me. I wish I hadn't announced the engagement yet. I shoulda just left it at us moving in together."

"You mean with Marcus or with the announcement?"

"Stop it. I mean with telling the outside world. It's so much easier when you keep your shit to yourself."

"Agreed. So which are you more excited about? The wedding or finally getting a bigger place?"

"To be honest they're both a little annoying. We still have so much stuff to figure out."

"What kinda stuff?"

"Just a lot. I've never lived with anyone else before."

"You live with kids and you still haven't figured out boundaries?"

"It's different."

"Why even bother getting married? You've already got kids and all the good stuff that's supposed to come along with it. Maybe just live with the guy and enjoy each other?"

"It's not about that. I want to share my life with someone."

"You don't need to be married to do that."

"Leave me alone and let me live my fantasy for a minute."

"Alright fine. So how goes the home shopping for this fantasy?"

"Annoying. He keeps trying to push us towards a place with more rooms, but I wanna keep our first place on the smaller side."

"Why does he want more rooms? More kids on the way?"

"I don't know who he thinks is gonna have them."

"You don't want to have any more?"

"I did when I only had my two. But he already has a daughter and with her moving in I just don't know. Not sure I can handle four. Three already sounds like a lot."

"Sounds like it's going to be an interesting summer."

"It should be. I'm gonna be moving the whole time."

"That sucks."

"Yeah. I'm gonna miss the area we're at now. It's so convenient. I can walk to my gym and wash my car without leaving my parking lot."

"Sounds nice."

"It is. What about you? You've got some big things coming too!"

"What do you mean?"

"I'm not sure exactly. Marcus was telling me you're up for some type of promotion here soon. You're going to get a raise and all of that after your next 90 day evaluation and then they're gonna talk with you about it."

"See that. Go on vacation and they wanna promote me. Seems I'm doing great."

"I'm really glad for you. I told you everything would work out."

"Yeah."

"Okay. You could at least pretend to be excited."

"Oh I am. What's the job exactly?"

"I don't know, it's good news though. They like to promote from within."

"I get that."

As we drove I found myself remembering a day in my senior year of college during which I was a part of an internship program run by the university. As a sort of career day we were able to meet with a few people whom had participated in our same program years before, some recently, some decades past. I sat there in class disheartened to find that with each new speaker I found myself progressively concerned about the future I was walking myself towards and forever instilling me with the thought that such things should be done to you on your first day of college not near your last. At the time I didn't have the awareness to know that I was also the victim unenthusiastic workers and poor public speakers, problems which if solved could have sold me on each path with far more passion. Yet I still knew then and there that the paths before me were unlikely to be the ones I would take. It wasn't any fear which kept me back from grad school or any of the jobs which could have been taken after graduation. I only had one fear. And it wasn't failing. Truth was I was never afraid of failing, I was just afraid of succeeding at the wrong thing. Something I knew I would do if I continued on my scheduled path. Ironic as that then led to levels of indecision and overwhelm for which I had not been prepared.

When we finally pulled up to Jaco I found the same parking spot from earlier and got situated as Renata got her things together. We got to the front desk and the clerk checked us in once Renata paid the twenty dollar fee to join our room. After that we went upstairs to find the guys sitting on the roof with a circle of chairs holding a few new friends obtained in my absence. I introduced Renata to the guys and she got herself acquainted as we all settled in. The others were polite, but she took a natural liking to Austin when he noticed the background of her phone was her daughters playing with some friends and he countered by offering to show her pictures of his own kids. She embraced the offer and he brought out his cell phone and started to scroll through the highlights of his own family until he paused on a shot of his wife surrounded by their three kids.

"And there's the lady taking care of them while I'm down here. That's the wife." - Austin

"Patrick. I found some gringos of my own so consider yourself free if you wanna use your night to find those hookers again." - Myles

"Hookers?" - Renata

"Ignore him. You guys catch anything?" - Patrick

"Fuck no bro. Those river crocs were no joke." - Myles

I stood there and gauged the circle which had been formed before my arrival. To my left was an open spot to the side of a blonde girl in her twenties who I was almost certain I had seen working at the front desk earlier. But what I noticed most about her was that she was wearing a thick hoodie, like thicker than you would need even if it were cold, which it wasn't.

"Anyone sitting here?" - Patrick

"Nope. Are you the Patrick who left these guys with me all day?"

"That would be me. And you are?"

"I'm Ansley."

"Nice to meet ya. So what do I owe ya for today?"

"For what?"

"The three of them alone all day...there must be some damages. The boards. The hostel. Something?"

From inside her hoodie a few laughs came before her next statement.

"No. They didn't damage anything."

"That's a first. Glad to hear it."

"And where did you run off to while we were surfing?"

"I had to go pick someone up in San Jose."

"Well are you gonna get a chance to ride the waves tomorrow?"

"Probably not. I won't have time before we leave."

"That sucks, where you going?"

"Who knows. And it's not really a big deal. I love the water and all, but I'm not in any hurry to go surfing."

"What's wrong? Can't swim? Bad balance?"

"I swim just fine. I just prefer being close to the shore. Being in the deeper water kinda freaks me out."

"Oh come on. What is it? Are you afraid of sharks?"

"Afraid. No. But I don't need to be in close quarters with them."

"Oh my god are you serious? There's nothing closely quartered about the ocean."

"When everything can swim faster than you the whole place might as well be close quarters."

"Sharks though? That's what you're worried about? You'll get yourself knocked out by your own surf board way before you ever see a shark."

"Oh that sounds so much better. Sign me up."

"Come on are you really gonna let something stupid like that stop you from even giving it a try?"

"It's amazing how anyone I know who grows up surfing can't understand why the rest of us are hesitant to share an environment with natures oldest killer."

"I understand. I just think you're over reacting."

"Perhaps, but this is one downside I'll keep protecting. No need to leave my feet dangling in the open ocean any longer than I need to."

"I'm telling you from my own experience that you don't have anything to worry about. Especially not here."

"Where are you from that you've got such confidence about this?"

"I grew up in Australia. Just outside of Perth."

"So you're practically from the most dangerous waters in the world? Land too for that matter. No wonder you escaped."

"We do have sharks, but it's not as bad as they say."

"Not as bad as they say? Even the fuckin' kangaroos can drown you there. What brought you here? You know there's still crocodiles right? You haven't escaped anything."

"Wasn't looking to. Just needed a place with some good waves. That and this job as the surf instructor for the hostel."

"Not enough waves back home?"

"There are. But I wanted to try somewhere different. It's nice to change up your environment every now and then ya know."

"You're preaching to the choir on that one."

"Glad to hear it. Any of your travels ever taken you near Australia?"

"Sadly not. It's on my short list of places to go next. Waiting on the money and patience for that flight."

"Yeahhh it's kind of intense. I fell asleep, woke up, and still had time to need a nap again before we landed."

"If I were you the flight back would be enough to keep me from going home anytime soon."

"There's plenty to do that without a flight getting in my way. But if you're really against it that much then make sure you get in all you can when you do visit. That side of the world has a lot of spots worth trying to catch."

"What all would you suggest? What is a must see?"

"That's a hard one. Crazy as it sounds I would actually tell you to go down to New Zealand. The Northern Island is gorgeous. I took a road trip around it last summer and I still wake up thinking about it."

"I do love a nice calm road trip. Chaotic ones too. Whichever."

"Me too. One day I'm gonna take a road trip through the states."

"Where do you wanna go?"

"All of it. But I'm gonna start in California. I wanna cruise up the Pacific Coastal Highway like they did in *Big Sur*."

"You know about Jack and them?"

"Of course I do. They have a few of his books here. I'm fucking obsessed."

As the night continued we discovered a few more shared interests beyond the Beatnik writers, but overall it was hard to relate to the combined cultural and generational gap created by our semi-British understanding of the world. Still she was easy to talk to and had read more than the average person. To such a level that was even able to talk to me about Ernest Hemingway's favorite writer Owen Wister and his book *The Virginian*. Which was a sadly underrated piece of work by those outside of its generation. Or maybe that's just the opinion of one Virginian. Either way I enjoyed our talk. One which was eventually thrown off by the tired voice of Renata to my right, "Pat? I need to get some sleep. Could I get to the key to our room."

"Yeah of course. Here ya go. It's room 303."

As Renata left Ansley informed me she was about to do the same, but not before offering up a free surf lesson for tomorrow should we decide to stick around. As she walked away I sat there for a bit and enjoyed a view of the stars who were uninhibited by clouds and slowly winning the battle against a moon which though bright, was still far from drowning out the millions. And no thought of my millions could drown out the one floating in my head now.

Why had I never thought to come back in the capacity that I had been called for on this trip? I probably could have done so much sooner had I tried. Translating could have been an option all along. One which had only fallen into my lap with the help of Myles. Which I suppose is how any good idea comes around. Through the voice of a friend in this helpful world of ours. Though not realizing another option for my life abroad is part of why I never left. I thrived off the surroundings. And though I knew what I was doing. I was always worried once I left that the option to come back would be forever gone. Not because the location would be gone, but I knew if I left at such an early age I woulda forced myself to settle down and never returned. Only to live my life forever talking about that one sliver of adventure I had for a brief period of my life. When I left and made it up to the room I found Renata curled up on the far side of the bed with all of the covers pulled away from my side. Luckily the temperature was pretty mild so I managed to fall asleep within a few minutes after maneuvering a bit of the sheets in my favor.

Day 9: Inside The Lightning
Quepos, Costa Rica

Today the room woke in unison to the annoyance of an alarm like days before, but this time it wasn't coming from my phone. When the beeping first started I instinctively patted my pockets and was met with no relief as I got up to see Myles rising from his bed with his alarm still buzzing next to him.

"Come on guys. We gotta get going if we're gonna see this damn Volcano. Austin get your ass up."

"Volcano?" - Patrick

"Yeah dude. Tired of sitting around all day. Get your asses moving. Austin come on!"

As Myles continued to berate the room Austin rolled over and argued against any orders sent his way.

"Dude. Fuck yourself. I'm not moving right now."

"Come on man you can sleep in the car." - Myles

"Fuck that. I'm taking a shower before I do anything." - Austin

"Yeah dude just let us chill a bit." - Wes

"You guys are lame. I wanna actually do something with our day for once. Come on Austin I'll get you some food on the way out." - Myles

"You're worse than my damn kids. I done took you fishing yesterday." - Austin

At this point I decided to chime in and put some decisions to our fate.

"Are we coming back or should we take our stuff?"

"Grab it all. We can try to get down to the Caribbean side before the day ends." - Myles

Renata had been ignoring the talking with closed eyes and open ears, but now she turned toward me and put her hand on my shoulder.

"Is he always like this? I was hoping to sleep in."

"No this is new. He's usually knocked out until noon. Come on though. You can rest in the car."

I got up packed up and made my way to the rental where I began loading up my things. As I moved a few things around to make room I was approached with a tap on the shoulder and some light aggression from a voice behind me.

"Where do you think you're going? I thought we had you talked into a lesson today?" - Ansley

"Apparently we're heading to a volcano."

"Do you know which one you're going to?"

"The Arenal Volcano I think."

"You should go to this other one outside of San Jose instead. It's called Poas. You won't be able to get near the Arenal this soon after the eruption."

"That's kinda why we wanna see it. Isn't it still smoking?"

"Probably not. And all you'll get is a view from the bottom anyhow. That's not worth the ride. Poas has a small lake in the crater and the drive up is gorgeous. Trust me I know what I'm talking about. I don't just surf here."

"A lake in the crater? That does sound neat."

"Still not as cool as surfing, but here, let me know if you all come back through in the next few days and I'll take you out on the water."

"We'll see what happens. Anyways, nice to meet ya. Good luck down here."

Although I was not hyped about the idea of surfing. I didn't necessarily give a damn about the volcano either. I would have rather stayed by the beach for the day and see if I could talk myself into getting up in the water. Had I not I still could have spent my day on the beach. Another one of those times when I missed the days of operating without the obligation of an anchor. Or in this case a sail that wanted to make his own wind. From there we left Jaco and drove up the coast until we came to a large bridge which crossed over a steadily flowing stream of soot and brown water. As we approached the bridge we were met with a sign which said, *Crocodiles. Use Caution.* Which I found uncomfortably casual. I mean if there's not a crocodile, then there's no reason to raise any alarm, but if there is a crocodile…well then one should exercise more than casual concern. They all wanted to stop and take a look so we parked at the end of the bridge and walked our way towards the middle along with a few other people who had shared the idea on their morning drive.

When we got to the middle of the bridge I looked down and saw a line of crocodiles sprawled along both banks of the river. Though a more than safe enough distance away I still felt an instinctive reluctance at even leaning over the concrete barrier separating myself from the prehistoric killers within my sight. No matter how many hours I spent watching Planet Earth or much I enjoyed wildlife I had no interest in interacting with something willing to kill me and save me for later. Mind you most of these things were nearly twelve feet in length and none of them were less than eight. While my mind surveyed the sight memories of crossing through a shoulder high stream at night started to haunt me with the reality I had once made for myself. In fairness it was a case of complete ignorance, it's not like I actually knew the magnitude of the potential danger. Still it spooked me to think I had once unknowingly shared these waters at night with the same creatures I saw below me. Once we finished gazing down we continued up the mountain and were soon urged the dashboard to pull off and align ourselves with a gas pump advertising itself as the last one between there and San Jose. As we parked an attendant showed up at our side with his hand out to receive a credit card.

"Cuánto quieres?"

"Fill it up please."

As he started to fill up our tank the doors opened and the crew headed inside to buy some drinks. I didn't wanna stress about this all day, but I still had no idea what we were going to do once we finished up. With all of our stuff in the car we had a lot of options, but I wasn't quite sure where would be the best spot to go. I know the guys wanna make their way down to the Caribbean, but I really don't think that's the most logical of decisions given how far away it is tonight. We wouldn't get there til nearly midnight. Once the gas had been pumped I sat there about five minutes until I saw the group making their way back. As they all got inside the car I noticed a few cases of *Pacifico* being loaded into the backseat. I started the car up and waited for everyone to get settled, but I noticed that we were still without one of our travelers. Austin, Myles and Renata were all in their seats, but where the fuck was Wes? After waiting another two to three minutes he came calmly walking across the parking lot without his shirt and got into the car as if nothing was out of order.

"You good dude?" - Austin

"Nipples are a bit cold, but I'm good." - Wes

"Where the fuck is your shirt?" - Patrick

"You mean *MY* shirt. *MY* fucking *Subaru* shirt that I let you wear. That one?" - Austin

"Trash." - Wes

"Why the fuck is my shirt in the trash?" - Austin

"Dude. I don't wanna hear it. I yelled for you guys for five fucking minutes and no one came to help me." - Wes

"Help with what?" - Patrick

At this point Wes started laughing and gave us no help in deciphering the broken words he was using to try and explain himself. Though we eventually pulled together that he had found himself in a stall without any toilet paper and had tried yelling for us for almost ten minutes. And apparently he was even brushed off by a man in the stall next to him before he was forced to use his shirt to make do where the lack of toilet paper could not.

"You nasty mother fucker! I hope you know you're getting me a new shirt." - Austin

"Fuck you dude. I don't know why you're worried about running out of clothes. You fucking leave tomorrow bro." - Wes

"That wasn't some tackle box shirt bro." - Austin

"I'll give you one of mine I got with me if you need another shirt. Stop stressin man." - Wes

"It's not about that bro. It's a fucking *Subaru* shirt. You just don't do that." - Austin

They all started drinking as we pulled out of the gas station and had the first round of beers down within a mile, all at the encouragement of the front seat where Austin sat with a case of beer between his legs. We directed ourselves to the Poas Volcano and discovered that it was just north of San Jose about two hours away. We drove along and avoided the majority of the city traffic by curving around the top from the West as we approached the highway which led downtown.

As we cut away from the city my mind went to wishing I were in a video game because a sky view of my surroundings would have been ridiculous to see. Each time I topped over a hill I saw bright fields of green sitting on the bends of rolling hills steadily making their way down the mountainside. The hills looked like they could be perfect for sledding if this climate ever allowed for it. The road continued to wind up the mountain range seamlessly dipping in and out of bridge covered creeks as we passed a few scattered homes and bodegas marked by narrow driveways and unique mailboxes. Beautiful flowers decorated the fronts of homes and gardens were scattered amongst an array of stray chickens and roosters regardless of the size of the dwelling. But all of this started to become hazy as the drive up thickened with mist and clouds making their way across the range. As we increased in altitude the cars temperature gauge dipped as low as the 40's and I was feeling ever less certain about my decision to wear shorts. The higher we got the denser the clouds became and it didn't look like the situation was going to change anytime soon. Still we pushed forward and eased our way up the road and towards a gated entrance. Though I knew the higher we got that we had missed out on our chance to see the Volcano today.

The guys had been plowing through cans of *Pacifico* the entire time and I had lost track of who had drank single digits and who had drank double. Even Renata's tiny self had managed to down at least six by this point. She was relatively quiet on the way up, but when she finally loosened up and started talking she quickly became like one of the guys and the energy in the car swayed out of my favor as the cases of Pacifico continued to empty in the forming of new memories filtered by both backseat drivers and 5% beers. I was glad to see her having fun and embracing the guys. Not that I should have been surprised. She was no stick in the mud and she knew her fair share of hidden bars throughout any city she had ever shown me.

When we got to the gate our party was interrupted by the discovery that they wanted $20 a person to enter and the current forecast indicated that we were unlikely to get much of a view of the crater. And for once I voiced my opinion rather than going with the flow and wasting our $100.

"Guys I don't think this is going to be worth it."

"Can we fish from the crater?" - Austin

"No. And I'll let you all waste your money, but I think we're going to be wasting more of our time than we already have if we go through this gate."

I didn't necessarily feel like this, once you've driven that far why not go the extra fifteen minutes, but at this point I was trying to figure out how we could salvage the day and another hour of delay would do nothing to help that. Because once we paid to go through, we would go through the ordeal of more driving, parking, and hiking to try and get the best possible view of a bad situation.

"Fuck that. Not wasting anymore money on this trip. There's a river close by, lets go check it out. I'll have the GPS take us." - Myles

"Alright man is everyone good with that?" - Patrick

By now they were all sufficiently drunk from a long day of tearing through *Pacifico* and soon enough they would be black out drunk which I welcomed at this point. As I made it to a major exchange the road split off to the left and then continued down a flattened gravel road. I started to slow down as a hand from behind reached forward and landed on the seat belt covering my left shoulder with a voice attached yelling.

"Dude! Turn around! We gotta ask those guys where the good fishing is." - Austin

"Move your fucking hand! That seatbelt is choking me." - Patrick

We pulled off the road and found ourselves parked in front of two teenagers walking with book bags on their way up the hill.

"You all from around here?" - Patrick

"Ask him where the good fishing is." - Austin

I spoke with the guy for a moment and started to feel out the situation. While the entire time having to ignore the combination of questions coming from the back seat and a seatbelt that continued to fasten along my collar bone as a member of the backseat pulled on my side of things.

"See if they know anywhere we can go to sneak up and see that Volcano." - Myles

"Ask him where the good fishing is." - Austin

"Yo shut up I'm trying to talk." - Patrick

"Well what's he saying." - Austin

At that point I finally turned around and yelled for what was probably the first time in years.

"I don't know how you expect me to ask them anything when you won't shut the fuck up! Now be quiet and let me fucking talk."

Sometimes I wished I had it in my to yell with more regularity because from time to time it managed to get things done and this was one of those times. Unfortunately it's too out of character to even be angry enough to need to yell to bother honing in on the skill long enough to reach the proper volume. After turning forward I exercised a rare gift of situational control and used the electric window to mute Austin from our two new friends as I sat there and took in what the kids had to say. Upon their instruction we continued down the road and found a small lake where a deli of sorts sat with a sign indicating they sold fish bait and licenses to capture a certain amount of trout from a nearby river which ran through the property. Austin saw the sign and almost jumped out of his fucking seat when we pulled into the parking lot.

Upon inquiry we were told we could fish in the pond or the river for the day and that there was a fee per fish if from the pond. It was Austin's last day so he didn't really care what he had to pay to get it done and happily handed over a wad of cash from his wallet. We all got out and the guys drank another beer before taking Austin's gear inside. Inside I helped them fill out their fishing licenses and then stayed behind as Austin made his way up the river with an empty bucket and his fishing gear. Luckily Myles decided to follow him up and alleviate my concern about his whereabouts as they both started fishing while I joined Wes by the pond.

"Where's Renata?" - Patrick

"She went to find some food I think. We gotta sober up. Those roads are gonna kill me on the way down."

"If you throw up in the car I'm gonna have Myles knock you out."

"I'll be fine man. I just need some food."

By the time the guys came back Renata had returned with a bag of chips and a few sandwiches to share as Myles and Austin made their way back up to the car. When they got close I saw Austins bucket was filled to the brim with fish and Myles was had the lighter load carrying the rods and a small bag at his side.

"You sure we can take the bucket with us?" - Patrick

"Yeah dude. I already took care of it." - Austin

He wedged the bucket into the trunk and covered it up with a towel on top. As I closed the trunk I could hear the fish still flailing about in the bucket.

"Dude. Why didn't you get them filleted here?"

"Man. I know how to do all that."

"That bucket better not spill."

"It'll be fine dude. I promise."

We drove off about a hundred yards down the road before I noticed a white Camry coming up behind us with its lights flashing. As it got closer it rode my bumper so I slowed down to try and let them pass. Unfortunately they maintained a car length behind me and continued trailing me down the mountain for the next mile or so. We continued along until the road came to a crossroads with a convenience store and a few buildings at each corner. I pulled off into a parking lot and waited for the car to pass, but instead it turned and parked directly behind our right tire blocking us in. I looked around and saw a small store, a few homes, and a local police station across the street. Well that's convenient, at least we're able to get some help if we need it. As soon as the car came to a halt a lean dark skinned woman stormed out and started screaming at us. She pointed to the bracelet on Austin's wrist and she started to scream at him and started reaching in to smack the back of his head while she screamed something about calling the cops. I asked her why she would call the cops and she said something about cutting a fish. I stood there for a moment looking around, somewhat lost in the translation myself. While they were most likely guilty of whatever she was mad about they seemed genuinely unaware of what was going on.

"Guys. She's saying something about a knife?"

At that the guys kinda looked around as Austin's face lit up with the memory of a drunken set of motions before he left the pond.

"Oh fuck dude. I bet her filet knife is still in my bag."- Austin

"What?"

"The knives and shit. Sorry bro. They're in a towel wrapped up in my bag."

I knew I couldn't afford for the moment to become more of a scene than it already was so I popped the trunk found her filet knives sitting next to the bucket of fish. According to what she said Austin had paid for six, but had also taken almost twice the daily limit on catches. I knew

Austin hadn't understood the rules of the place and figured that the money he shelled out had covered whatever he wanted to do while he was there so I decided to solve this by reaching into the drivers side door panel and pulling out a wad of twenties. As she continued to berate them in Spanish I took the money and walked over to her where I grabbed her palm and placed $140 inside of it. I was annoyed to place myself as a member of whatever the fuck had happened and the way she may henceforth think about us, but there are occasions where it's just easier to live the role the moment has assigned to you. Especially when all of the circumstances make it so easy to fall into and the cops are across the street. If I played the *I don't know role* she woulda caused a scene. It's always a little tough being the translator and delivering bad news. But I gotta say, in this particular case it's even worse being the voice and having nothing good to say. Especially delivering bad news to the group compared to delivering it to the individual.

"Señora. Please just take this. Lo siento." - Patrick

She looked down at her hand and then behind me to see the sad state of my drunken friends and silently walked back to her car with her filet knife and gear under her arm and the extra cash in her hand. From there she backed out without taking notice of any oncoming concerns and shifted back into drive before speeding back up the hill. As her car backed up and made haste up the hill I looked back at my friends. As I walked to the car I hated knowing I was forever anchored in her mind as that person. It went too much against how I had tried to travel in my years abroad as I didn't see any duty greater to a traveler than to prove as a good ambassador for the lands from which they came. Even if only for the sheer advantage of being welcomed back one day.

"Let's get out of here." - Patrick

"Sorry bro. I got you when we get home." - Austin

"It's cool man. Just go back to sleep."

They all got in the car and remained quiet more or less for the rest of our time down the mountain. Partly due to the moment and partly due to the luxury of passing out. It started to my right when Wes passed out on the second turn and soon enough the only sound I heard was that of a lightly cracked window letting in the air from Austin's window. Driving down I wondered if I should be angrier at myself or them? It's not as if I didn't see what was going on all day and I couldn't claim to have been thrown into this without any warning. Our entire childhood had been a series of warnings leading up to this. So why did I think our time would go any differently? But why was it my job to accept this as their preferred mode once their inhibitions had been turned down? I guess it was my fault because I hadn't fought against it. But I hadn't fought against it because I thought they would get *pass out* drunk, not *annoy the fuck out of me* drunk. Now they may not be in deep sleep, but they had all closed their eyes and were placed slightly outside of the parameters of awareness. Which is perhaps the most vulnerable you could ever find these guys. Because when they were awake none of them could be held back by me or anyone else around us. A fact which has served as a gift and a curse. It's a gift to walk with, but it's a curse to deal with. Although it's one I had accepted about them from the beginning. And truth be told I had used it to my advantage when we were younger and there were plenty of times when it served me well. Only now did it annoy me. As do any inconveniences the moment they become ours to experience.

As we approached the city the highway came to a three-way split with the middle lane continuing into San Jose, the left leading towards the Caribbean and the pull off to the right went back to the Pacific. I knew we had to get Austin to the airport tomorrow so I figured it didn't make sense to make the four hour or more drive to the Caribbean. San Jose was cool, but we needed to wake up at a beach tomorrow. With that I veered off to the right and started our descent towards the coast. I kind of wanted to go to the Caribbean, but at this point I was more focused on finding the closest place to sleep. The next hour was quiet and I remained on auto-pilot as I directed us towards an unknown destination. I even began to enjoy myself as I put in my headphones and started to listen to a podcast which allowed me to get lost in another world for an hour so. When the drive put me in the blinding light of a passing truck Myles lifted his head and gave a look around at the surroundings as we passed a sign giving away our coordinates.

Jaco 10K

Quepos 65K

"What the fuck are we doing around here?" - Myles

This then prompted Austin to also open his eyes and take notice of the sun setting on the water ahead of us when it should be setting on the lands behind us.

"What the fuck man? I thought we were going to the Caribbean side." - Austin

I had been a bit lost in my own audio world at that point and even I was a bit surprised to see how far we had gotten.

"Sorry dude. I wasn't about to drive four hours both ways so you could leave before the sun comes up. I'm just getting us to a beach for the night." - Patrick

"It's all good. They got that beach with the monkeys down this way right?" - Myles

"Yeah. It's pretty close to where we're headed. And I'm sure they have buses to take you there and back."

"Why do we gotta take a bus?"

"Because, I gotta get Austin to the airport in the morning so I'm gonna have the car most of the day. You're welcome to come with me if you want."

"Fuck that. I'm done being in the car."

"Then you guys can stay here and go to that park for the day."

"Sounds good to me. Wes we can try and play catch with the monkeys. I'm gonna find us some tennis balls. Austin you ready to cook all that fish?"

"Fuck yeah dude. Can we get some more beer for tonight? I'm feeling thirsty." - Austin

"Yeah man. Hey, Patrick! Pull over when you can. We need another case or two."

"Will do."

For the next hour I listened jealously as the group talked about tomorrow's excursion and all of the cool shit they were going to see down there. Apparently the monkeys just run wild on the beach down there. The map made it seem like we were only a few miles away from Quepos when I had been passing Jaco, but the road which wound up and down the coast was not one which allowed you to gain a great deal of speed so the drive was taking a longer than I planned. Eventually the road diverted off to the right and towards the small cove of Quepos. Much like the places before, I had discovered this hostel via a quick Google search which sparked the trusty words of the strangers occupying the rating circles of the internet. A place where we see a user name with a few stars and an opinion and all of a sudden instant credibility is assumed without accounting for individual preference. Nor the consideration of what can reasonably be expected from a place or a service. Our drive through town had not revealed much nightlife and as we pulled to up to the hostel I could see that if there was a bad side of town, we were in it. I even hesitated a bit as I parked us along the cracked concrete of a broken sidewalk in front of a few run down buildings. But unless we wanted to drive another hour in the other direction, we were out of options for the night.

Conejito Escondindo sat at the edge of a narrow city block caddy-corner to a soccer field and a few small apartments. The first thing I noticed about our hostel was that it had more security than what I was used to seeing. Lining the property was a fence with a thin line of barbed wire running along the top with cameras at each corner. And next to the front gate was a tiny room with a guard who kept an eye on everyone going in and out. The homes across from the hostel were in disrepair with several latches lining the perimeter of the doors to ensure a safely locked home. At the gate we explained to the guard that we were looking for a room for the night after which he buzzed us in and let us into the foyer where we were greeted with an open door leading to an office on our right. Beyond the door's threshold was a small room with a four shelf library and a large fridge filled with drinks for sale at any hour you pleased. Behind the desk was a tall girl with dark wavy hair which she had pulled back in a ponytail as she sat Indian style in a pair of yellow shorts and a light green hoodie with the Brazilian flag in the middle. Looking somewhat surprised by our presence she rushed through the last bite of yogurt she had taken from the cup in her hand just before we walked in.

"Hola. Do you all have any rooms?" - Patrick

She nodded her head and finished chewing the rest of her spoon full as I looked down at a sheet of rates laying across the counter.

"Yes, I'm sorry. How many will you be needing?"

I looked at Renata and handed my passport to her as I started to walk away.

"You've got this one. I'm gonna explore." - Patrick

"Okay. I"ll get you your own room."

"Gracias."

From there she placed her purse on the table and started shuffling around as I heard her mumble something to herself in Portuguese, a habit she had unknowingly picked up during her time away. As I left the office I passed between the guys as they stepped up to the desk.

"Wes take care of our rooms. We gotta go get some stuff to cook with." - Myles

"Aight. Text me when you're back. I'm gonna go pass out for a bit."

As I walked through the courtyard my eyes shot across into the dining area and began to connect the dots of a face in the distance. I knew that face. But I didn't know it. He was obviously Germanic in all of his features and in some way familiar, but where did I know him from? For some reason it came to me that his name was Yann, but beyond that I had no further recollection. Every part of me knew I was right about his name. Though even with that confidence I had no idea why.

"Patrick?"- Yann

"Yes, remind me how I know you?" - Patrick

"This is wonderful. Almeré will be so happy to see you!"

"Excuse me. What? Who did you say will be happy?"

"Almeré."

Ignoring why I knew him I focused on the newest and seemingly more important piece of information to make sure my ears weren't lying to me.

"Almeré? The tall Swedish girl? She's here? How? Who are you?"

"Well not right now. I don't think she's back. She went to go get some food, but she'll be really happy to see you. She talked to me about meeting you on the bus ride up here today. She won't believe you're here. She kept saying she wish she had a way to reach you. Who am I? You met me in Boquete. I believe you turned me down for Spades. Big mistake my friend. I mopped the floor with them."

I could be a bit delusional at times, but that wasn't the case. I might have been tripping when we met, and I might have even harbored my doubts about whether or not our interaction even happened, but here he was actually saying those words to me. And as I realized this I thought how lucky I was to know that not only was she here, but she had also found reason to bring me up with some stranger she rode next to on a bus. He had done the ultimate bro favoring by alerting me and if I had to guess I'm fairly certain he had no idea of it. Though of all ideas I now had one which had to root itself in my reality. I didn't just have something to look forward to, I also had something to worry about. The two realities which were about to meet were not ones that I wanted to deal with, but there was no way I was going to deny myself the chance to spend my time with Almeré in order to avoid an awkward moment with my friends. This was one of those '*fuck it*' moments. I had always heard that lightning didn't strike the same place twice. And honestly, I have no reason to know if that's an actual fact, but I got the message. It's like the same person never being able to step in the same river twice. The person has changed and so has the river. Although this time the river had brought us both to the same place and the lightning she had placed inside of me was no less fierce.

As I departed from my run in with Yann I walked around looking for where I could sit and realized just how poorly the layout of this place was for my intentions. Even worse was the unfortunate news I got when I asked about the location of the beach which I thought had been a short walk away. Turns out it was less than a mile, but the whole place was used as docks for fishing boats and didn't provide for anywhere to hop in or for the boys to fish. Walking around I began to feel somewhat like a teenager in my angst at the possibility of seeing this girl again. It was an odd feeling. Something I hadn't really felt in quite a long while. After my first swing at the fences went south I had kinda accepted my role and never gave too much emotion to those I was dating and sure to leave along the way. Yet here I was having only met this person once and I felt an odd rush to the most excited parts of my brain at the drug which awaited me in her presence. But if I was going to ingest and without stress I was going to have to find a way to entertain my friends and seize control of my time to spend the most allowable amount of it with this blessing from the Nordic Gods. As I sat there thinking about what to do Renata came up and placed a temporary pause on my angst.

"Patrick. They only had one private room left and there's not enough open dorms so we gotta share a spot again tonight. I'll get you at the next stop." - Renata

"Took you that long to find all that out?"

"Well yeah. And I was trying to get some help from the front desk and see what there is to do around here."

"No worries."

"Are you hungry?"

"I can always eat. Sorry it got a little crazy today."

"It's okay. Your friends are a lot of fun. But I wish we had done more with our day than just drive around."

"At least you got to sleep."

"Well what else was I supposed to do?"

"Not complain?"

"I'm not complaining. I'm just saying I've spent more time in the car than I thought we would."

"You think I'm not annoyed by that too?"

"I'm sure you're annoyed. You seem annoyed now."

"Sorry. I'm kinda scrambling to figure out how to make tonight work."

"What's up? What do you mean?"

"Remember that girl I mentioned from the hostel up in the mountains?"

"The tall one?"

"Yes, her. Well, she's here. I haven't seen her yet, but I ran into one of her friends and they told me she's here. I'm excited. Like little kid on Christmas morning excited. You gotta help me distract the guys somehow. Take them out dancing or something."

"You think they'll follow me? They're trying to cook that fish."

"Fuck. Okay, where are the grills?"

"It looks like they're over by the pool."

"Alright. Then I'm gonna take my luck around the picnic tables. Do you know which room is ours?"

"It's that one over in the corner. You wanna follow me? I'm gonna go put my stuff inside."

"Yeah sure."

As we walked back we reached a room which held a bunkbed style set up but with a much larger mattress taking over the bottom.

"You can take the bottom. I"ll put my stuff up top."

"Sounds good to me. Do you need these drawers?"

"Nah. I'm gonna keep everything in my bag. We're probably only gonna be here one night anyway right?"

"I don't know. I guess so."

As we situated our things we locked up the room and headed back to the picnic tables where Renata tried to lighten the mood with a drink.

"Gonna get any food?" - Patrick

"No. I at least wanna try some of that fish since I had to ride with the smell of it all afternoon." - Renata

While we talked I sat there begging the universe to instill my friends with the same feeling of independence and will to explore that I walked with on a daily basis. Though not for any intrinsic benefit of their own, I just needed them to find something worth doing outside of this hostel. As I sat there trying to relax the time went by in a flash as one moment I was dazing off into the distance over the pool and the next I was drawn to the opening of the front gate where a tall figure in a blue sundress walked through with a set of bags in her hand. As she got closer our eyes locked and her face was filled with a happy confusion over the recognition of a friend made not so long ago. As she got closer she handed her bags to the figure of another woman which had remained blocked in my tunnel vision. As the girl took her bags Almeré hurried in my direction and engulfed me in a hug.

"Patrick! What are you doing here?" - Almeré

"We just needed a place to rest for the night. And here I am. What about yourself? I can't believe I'm seeing you right now." - Patrick

"I know. Wow. I'm glad to see you. And oh. We were on our way up to Nicaragua and our bus driver needed to stop off and let the engine cool down. Where are you guys off to?"

"We're staying here tonight then heading to the Caribbean."

"What's over there? You should come with us up the coast. Our bus has room for a few more people. I could help you finish the drawing we started!"

"I would love to, but I think we've worn out our welcome on this coast by this point. Plus they've heard so much about the Caribbean. I know they wanna see it."

"I don't think it's gonna be worth it. The waters were rough in Bocas. You guys might find a better time staying along the Pacific."

If it's not obvious, this is one of those times where I would change my plans if I were alone. It's not like I was married to one set of plans over the other. But adaptability requires a weird relationship with instability and the people I was with were not about it. And why would they be, it wasn't to their same benefit. And it's always easier to adapt on your own. But nothing happens on your own. It's always a character or a place that draws us into a new adaptation, or the need to adapt. I was in that sense a follower. A follower of the best which would have me. And this time, she was easily the best. She was like a recharge. I couldn't see any reason to not want to go with her. It went against everything inside of me to tell her no. Even in my annoyed state I was yet again calm in her presence. Who wouldn't want to drag that feeling out as long as they could? And the universe was giving me a second chance to do so.

As we continued to talk Almeré straddled the bench and leaned in with a bright smile forgetting about her food or her friends. As Renata returned I introduced the two and soon we all started talking beyond introductions. After a few minutes I had gotten so caught up that I had forgotten to keep up with the time passing and the inevitability of my friends return. I was soon alerted of their presence by the same girl who attended the front desk as she came around to inform me that the boys had been singing a bit too loud on the sidewalk and needed to be dealt with.

"Excuse me. Your friends need to be quiet. We have people trying to sleep." - Desk Clerk

"Sorry. I'll get them to calm down."

"Obrigado."

I wish I had not been such a nice person by cutting off the music in the car earlier, but then we probably wouldn't be here had I let them stay awake. With that unfortunate realization I walked towards the front gate and left Renata talking with Almeré as I went against everything I actually wanted to do and started trying to convince the boys to come back inside.

"Yo. You guys gotta come in." - Patrick

"What? Why?" - Austin

"So you can start cooking and let these nice people sleep."

"Got it. MYLES! Let's get this shit cooked."

With the boys back my neutral zone was now in jeopardy. I tried to deflect their presence by showing them where the grills were located. There was no real separation between courtyard, picnic, and lounge area. It all sort of meshed into one area creating too open of an atmosphere if you're trying to interact uninterrupted by others. You're not always in earshot but you are always in sight. I showed them where the grills were and tried to get them interested in some of the activities we could do around there tomorrow. If I was lucky a stomach full of fish would be all it would take to piggyback on their beer and let them all pass out finally. Once they fired up the grill I slipped away and got back to Almeré who was now sitting alone.

"Where did Renata go?" - Patrick

"She went to get us some playing cards. I think she's trying to smooth things over with the lady at the front desk."

Although I was able to delay my fate temporarily I could not fight the eventuality that Myles and the guys would find their way to the congregation of people hiding my current situation. Until then I sat and I enjoyed my conversation with Almeré who told me about her last few days and how she had ended up there tonight. I was almost ready to go for a walk with her when I saw the guys approaching. They had gone and brought Wes from his slumber and carried over a big plate of freshly cooked fish.

"Another one of your special friends?" - Myles

As Myles started his interrogation an increasingly drunk Wes sat down at the table across from us glaring at the girls face with an uncertain familiarity.

"Hey I know you. Weren't you at that hostel up in the cloud forest?" - Wes

My body was now on edge as Myles' face began to look as if he were putting together some grand puzzle inside of his ever processing brain.

"Ahh now I get it. So this is why Patrick wanted to come all the way down here tonight..." - Myles

With a confused look Almeré looked towards Myles and attempted to introduce herself.

"Hi. Nice to meet you. So you're friends with Patrick?"

"I guess you could say that. Patrick has had a lot of friends on this trip. Did you tell her about the friends you and Wes made the other night?"

At that point I tried to brush him off and continue talking over him since I had nothing to gain in this situation from his views on the evening in question. While we continued talking the guys drank a few more beers and peered around the room looking at what trouble they could find, but the whole time the looming presence of Myles sipping his beer across the table with an open ear had me wishing I had picked up Swedish at some point in my existence. It was such a shame to me to see which side of him was taking over. The drunken side which highlighted the persistence of his most annoying aspects. The sides which never interacted with the genuinely good within him. Jekyll and Hyde seemed to have a relationship with one another while his halves seem to hide from one another. And as both sides continued to battle I received more than enough signals to wrap up my night. Although if I am to be honest, she seemed to be handling them pretty well. As far as the heckles of friends went, she was passing that test with flying colors. Of course that was easy for her. For there was not much one could pick at.

"Geez Patrick. Looks like one of your graduates came and found ya. Almeré was it?"

"Yeah, that's me."

"How old are ya girl?"

"Twenty."

With her response he looked at me with a sense of wisdom and recollection on words I had previously laid at his ears. I had always felt hesitant about dating girls who were younger because at a certain point in life you just have too much more experience to play fairly with those who don't. It wasn't so much the stigma from the outside world, I could give a fuck about that, there was just something more satisfying about flirting with someone older than me that made me feel like I was fighting in my own weight class. And here he was able to use the hypocrisy of my own pursuits against me.

"Twenty? Would you look at that. *Don't give yourself that headache.* Isn't that what you said when I wanted to date that girl from the city? Remember the younger one I used to like?" - Myles

"Why don't you quit while you're ahead?" - Patrick

"Ahead? Bro, I ain't ahead of nothing. Hell, when I look around at what's going on I feel like I'm behind. I'm just trying to figure this whole thing out. Hmm lets see if you're twenty that woulda made you around eleven or so when he was teaching ya? Damn Patrick you really do a great job at keeping up with people." - Myles

"I think you're mistaking me for someone else." - Almeré

"No. I'm pretty sure it's you. Gonna go with my gut on this one. Not like Patrick is gonna tell me the truth or nothing. Only got my gut to rely on." - Myles

He was right in placing his focus on her age. It was the only thing about her he could even start to dissect with such little time spent getting to know her. Had he been in my shoes he would have seen what was keeping me in that seat. Still I held onto my hesitation at carrying any of my conversation into the realms of flirting. While I had been taught to believe no one was out of your league it wasn't a matter of confidence with this one. It was a matter of respect and a bit of uncertainty. And the penalty of losing her in the future for being wrong in my assumptions would be almost overwhelmingly worse than the benefits to them if I were right. By far a more difficult decision than can be explained. Plus, when it came down to it, she was still sitting there. She didn't have to sit there, but still she sat there.

As I sat there listening to him a flood of memories rushed back to me. Memories of leaving parties wondering if I would be allowed to return after some of the shenanigans he had pulled when we were younger. Usually fights inspired by the novelties of high school rivalries. Now for some reason he was doing the same type of thing. It was okay the times we were amongst unfortunate strangers, but amongst the people I loved I would have preferred to trust him to be diplomatic. Even though I knew deep down that this had nothing to do with the moment we were in and much more do with the conversations we have left unsaid between us. As I looked at them I kept thinking what a false indicator of maturity age actually was. There was no reason for the connection. One could lead to one, but one did not imply the other. Not when I looked ahead and saw a girl in front of me with plans for her life and moves making them happen. And that view made it hard not to elevate her above the alleged adults around her. Perhaps most of them only come off as adults because the world did not recognize the children hidden within the shells. The worst part about all of this was that it finally confirmed that our friendship had suffered more than I realized. I wanted us to pick up right where we had left off as friends, but not as the same hooligans we had been. As the situation got increasingly awkward I decided I needed to get my night fixed sooner than later. So taking that into account I looked down at my phone and connected to the hostels WiFi long enough to get on google and translate a few key phrases into Swedish. I had seen some type of balcony up top so I hoped I could find myself a hideaway. As I managed to find the proper wording I wrote one line on a post-it in my notebook and slid it across to her with a prompt for her to circle yes or no.

"Lets take this upstairs?"

Language is nothing more than association and reaction. Just like reputation. So once the understanding of words is unified, proper wording is everything. That being said, I hoped that the transfer of meanings wouldn't catch her off guard, but I also wouldn't argue against anyway interpretation she decided to act on. As she looked down and started reading I watched her start to scribble with one hand while holding down the pages with the other hand. When the notebook made it discretely back into my hand I looked down and saw her response.

"Meet you in 5?"

I closed the notebook and got up to go to the bathroom. As I began to move Myles got up and stepped in front of me.

"Where you going?" - Myles

I looked around for Wes hoping for intervention, but he was already half-way to the front gate.

"I'm calling it a night man."

"Come on man. I'm just fuckin with ya. Why don't you stick around? We have plenty of food for your girlfriend to join us."

I turned my attention back to Almeré and created the facade of a departure with a hug and a goodbye.

"Good seeing you again. Maybe at another time or in another country?" - Patrick

"I hope so. Maybe somewhere with a better view."

I walked away and towards the bathrooms where I took a moment to rinse my face in hopes of alerting my senses a bit. As I left the bathroom I stayed close to the wall and tried to avoid being exposed by the corridor lights as I got closer to the stairwell. As I the railing I gripped it with my left hand and swung my body into position to head up the stairs and took two steps at a time all the way up. As I got upstairs my stride was interrupted by a kid playing with a tricycle while his mother and older sister sat on the couch consumed by the evenings latest craze. Towards the edge of the rooftop were two couches and a table with a backdrop of rooftops and telephone cables carrying the shared signal of this weeks soccer game throughout the neighborhood. To the front of the building I could see beyond the street ahead and to a soccer field which sat off to our left. As I went and sat down on a couch towards the back I was almost certain I could hear someones T.V. playing through a tin roof in the next building. This was a great spot. If my friends decided to follow us up here we always had the option of roof hopping until they got tired of pursuing. Though that fantasy makes for a time where my knees preferred life were like a video game as well.

I was frustrated with how my day had gone, but enough Machiavelli had been pressed in my head to know that this was one of the times where the ends justified the means. And for these ends to have been acquired I had to go through quite a bit. Had anything gone differently about our day I would not have been sitting there awaiting such a surprise to close out my night. And had I not run into her again she might have just been some girl I met once and moved on from. Some fantasy forever chased. Instead the universe had found a way to present me with another chance to absorb the presence of someone who had already provided me with more peace than most. As I laid on the couch pondering the ins and outs of everything that had happened I let out a deep sigh and closed my eyes while I enjoyed the only moment of peace I had experienced all day. As one more sigh left my body I was met with a newly familiar voice.

"No need to stress. I don't think anyone noticed me." - Almeré

"Well that's one win for the day. Glad you could make it."

"Of course. I can't stay long though. We've gotta head out early tomorrow."

"Understood. Look. I'm sorry about my friends."

"It's okay. Can't believe those are the guys you chose to come with you on your first trip as a translator. You must be one of those that likes to make your life complicated."

"I'd say my current situation seems to speak to that pretty well. Thanks for understanding though. I know they're a lot to handle."

"No worries. I have two brothers. I get what boys can be like when they decide to gang up on you. Give them a break. They'll lighten up by morning."

"I'm not actually as annoyed as it may seem. I'm just frustrated that I keep trying to show them a good time and somehow it turns into this. Or some other shit I gotta deal with. I guess I made the mistake of wanting to relax."

"Maybe they're just bored here. I mean there's not a lot to do. Or maybe this is their good time. Who knows."

"That's possible."

"Maybe you should take some time to yourself."

"Maybe. Guess I shoulda stayed in my role and gone along with how they really wanted this trip to be."

"What do you mean?"

"This shit is nothing new. It's just like it was when we were kids. That's why I say it woulda gone a lot smoother if I had been the host they wanted down here. I didn't do my job right on that one."

"Well if you think they need distracting then why not bring them up the coast with us? I'm sure no one would mind. Plus they'll have new people to hang out with. Most of our group speaks English like it's their own."

"Your patience with them is impressive, but we can't. One of them has to leave out of San Jose tomorrow. So after that we're probably just gonna make our way over to the Caribbean side."

"Why do they wanna go all the way over there?"

"They want to try their luck fishing on another coast."

"The water was really rough back in Bocas. It's probably the same way up the entire coast."

"Yeah, but that's what they've got their sights on. It's where we were supposed to be this entire time."

"Oh. So, I guess I won't be seeing you for a while then?"

"I've not hated agreeing with someone this much in quite a while, but I would be willing to bet you're right."

"Well maybe you'll make that trip back to Europe happen sooner than later?"

"I hope so. I've been thinking about arranging a trip to Ireland or Spain sometime soon."

"Well we could meet up if you make it anywhere close enough to visit by train."

"Well now that we've got each others info we won't have to hope lightning strikes the same place twice for us to see each other again."

"Lightning? It's not storming."

"I know. Never mind. It's just a saying we have."

At this point her phone lit up with a message from her travel partners alerting her that it was now less than six hours before they had to leave.

"Ugh. They're right. I've gotta go. My bus leaves in a few hours."

"It's all good. I gotta be up early too. Fucking shit."

"Before I go, do you mind if I write something in your notebook?"

"Of course not. Gonna try and draw me real quick?"

"No. We'll have to save that for next time."

"That's a raincheck I look forward to."

Without further hesitation I took my notebook out of my back pocket and placed it into her hand. As it landed in her palm she started flipping through the pages until she paused on a blank one and placed the pen to the paper. Using her left hand to shield her words she began scribbling in a combination of big swoops and fine lines which carried on for the majority of the page. When she finished she closed it up and slipped the notebook back into my hand. As we said goodbye she leaned in and wrapped a set of long arms around me as she planted a kiss on my cheek before drawing herself back. I've had to give a lot of goodbyes in my life, but this was one that I hoped wasn't final. I knew any goodbye could be the last, but their finality is now our own fault in a world where the interconnectivity is so limitless. I don't know if you've realized this, but we now have the ability to travel faster and farther than anyone from the days when we used to measure the passing of time by the seasons of what we ate. When seasons were seasons and when seasonal was only a now and then type of thing. Though it's all a comparison to what we already know. I guess that's why we marvel at the passing of a comet and only smile at the sight of a shooting star. There are plenty of them out there, but the ones which really capture us only come around once in a while. Walking away she paused,

"Can I ask you one more thing before I leave?"

"About what?"

"That girl in Mexico."

"Yeah, sure."

"Were you ever mad at her?"

Having never been asked the question I paused and looked down for a moment with my mouth still breached from a momentary loss of words.

"It's okay. I'm sorry. I shouldn't have asked that."

"No, it's fine. I just never gave it any thought. I guess the short answer is no, I mean, I can't be. Her passing was too much of a life changer for me."

"Yeah, it just seems kinda unfair how she kept you in the dark."

"Can't be mad at that. That's just human nature, it was probably the easiest thing for her to do in the middle of a complicated situation. Maybe it's like they say, a monkey doesn't let go of a branch until it has a firm grip on another. Can't be mad at which branch you are for somebody. I don't focus on that. I Just focus on what I took away from it. Before then I thought I was invincible, I never even thought of my own death. To be honest, the strangest thing was knowing that someone with whom I had shared secrets was no longer around. Knowing I have certain stories where the only other witness for them isn't around to reach to help you remember the details. That's the type of stuff that sucks."

"I get that…Okay I lied, one more question…How is it a good thing to think about your death? I try not to do that…"

"Okay, maybe not good, but eye opening, ya know? Here, lemme try to make some sense of my thoughts. Okay, the week before she died she was really stressed. Like super stressed. I don't even remember what she had going on anymore, it doesn't matter, but it was your typical modern life shit. And I know it should't matter, but anytime I think about it, it kills me to know her last few days on earth were spent stressed. Stressed over shit that didn't end up mattering in the end. So now whenever I feel myself getting stressed or annoyed I try to remind myself that it's not worth it. Actually had to use that lesson a few times lately. Does that answer your question?"

"Yeah, it does," pacing in her mind for something to say she continued with a brief pause and then leaned back in my direction, "Hey Pat? Don't be a stranger. I'm really glad we met again." - Almeré

"Me too."

When she walked away I sat on the couch and closed my eyes. And were it not for the sound of another set of feet pounding their way up the stairs I might have ended my night then and there. Instead I looked up to see Austin placing himself at the top of the stairs where I had last seen Almeré's height fading with each step that took her slowly out of my life.

"What up man?" - Patrick

"I need some cigarettes." - Austin

"There's none left?"

"Dude I've asked everyone and there's not a jack left in this whole fuckin hostel. I just need you to walk me to a store."

"Why didn't you guys pack a carton for the trip."

"Next time we will, but that's a problem from yesterday. I gotta solve this one tonight. You got the keys bro? My wallets in the back."

"I think they're in the room. Let's go. I'll spot you."

"Fuckin right. Gracias Señor."

From there I walked down the stairs and saw everyone had moved to the picnic tables at the end of the kitchen and were sitting in a circle around Myles. They didn't seem annoyed so I continued forward without issuing apologies and made it outside where I found Austin waiting to explore the town which had long fallen asleep. As we walked, a few blocks turned into seven, and each storefront we passed was as abandoned as the alleyways on either side. The streets were safe, but the row of cabbies still looked at us like we were out of our element. Like we instead belonged safely within their vehicles.

"Sucks you're leaving tomorrow." - Patrick

"Lies. I bet you wish we were all leaving."- Austin

"Perhaps, but of all people I don't want you to be the one to go."

To my right Austin continued to strut with his bulky chest now showing through his unbuttoned shirt and over-exaggerated stance.

"Dude I'm amazed you're still able to make it to the gym with kids and all the work you do."

"Shit, you're just seeing after a week of sweating off all this water. I'm lucky I still look alright. I don't make it like I used to. The only real exercise I get is chasing the kids around. That's the goal this year, getting myself back in the gym. I was so good about it for a while. My dad told me my body was the only thing that wouldn't leave me. Everything else. Jobs, friends, even the best of them, kids, all of them eventually go off and do their own things. I see you managed to keep yourself in line too."

"Yeah. And I thank you for that."

"What's that?"

"Getting me into the gym."

"Me?"

"You don't remember that? You took me to that guys gym outside of town back in high school. If you hadn't done that I never woulda had anywhere to workout or anyone to teach me what I should be doing in there."

"I guess so man. I took so many people over to *Big Phuqs*. I shoulda started asking for commission. Could probably put my kids through college."

"Never too late to ask for that back pay."

"Nah. Be better off opening my own gym now."

"Lemme know. I'll sign up."

"Oh bull-fucking shit. You'll visit twice. Three times tops."

"Well maybe you can build in a rate for the less frequent visitors. Plus I'll give you that sit-up bench. It's just been rusting away in a storage shed."

As we moved down the street I opened up my phone and decided to send Renata a text to see if she wanted anything from our expedition.

"I'm on my way to the store. Need anything?"

By the time we reached the store I still hadn't received a response. When we got to the door store Austin looked in and started dictating instructions in my direction.

"Dude ask him if he have any weed-o." - Austin

As we entered the store the cashier started laughing as Austin hit his head on a halfway shut metal gate which had been rolled down as a sign that closing time was near. Then the two men went through a brief transaction followed by a five dollar loan on my part and from there we got on our way. As we walked outside I looked across the street to see a parking lot filled with a few groups of guys and their tricked out cars holding center stage as their trunks stood open with speakers blasting a mixture of heavy metal tunes, one of which we both recognized. With his right arm raised up Austin extended a hand mangled into the shape of horns as one would at a rock concert and started to scream in praise of his favorite band.

"Fuck yes! Dude they're playing Pantera! I'm fuckin goin over there." - Austin

Before he completed his sentence he started walking across the street imitating the movements of a man working his way to the middle of a mosh pit. At times bumping into the guys standing around the car in hopes of getting them involved in the craziness. Since they all seemed playful in their acceptance of him I went up to the one with the natural alpha position in the group,

"Sorry it's his last night here. Lemme know if he's being a problem and I'll take care of him." - Patrick

"No man he's good." - Tico

"Thanks. He's a huge Pantera fan." - Patrick

"Badass. Let's get that shit turned up some more then. *Oye! Subelo!*" - Tico

"What's your name?" - Patrick

"I'm Julio, y tu?" - Julio

"My friends call me Patrick. And that's Austin. Gotta admit I'm shocked to hear Pantera down here." - Patrick

"What's wrong? Think we can't afford MTV?" - Julio

"No no. That's not it at all. I'm just surprised you're fans. The music is heavy even for rock fans sometimes." - Patrick

"Not this fan. The heavier the better. I saw them play in Mexico City back in '97. Best show of my life. My dad took me when they were opening up for Kiss. Been a fan ever since." - Julio

As our conversation got deeper into music we started to go back and forth, at times addressing each other in Spanish, and at others going on in sentences of English. A skill which he seemed to possess with great fluidity. As we continued to talk he looked at me with the same suspicious eye I had seen many times before.

"Yo where are you from?" - Julio

"America." - Patrick

"Where did you learn your Spanish though? Your accent is *almost* perfect."

As always I found it hard which answer to give to this question. It hadn't been picked up in any one specific place. The foundation had been set in college by Puerto Ricans in the dorms and later enhanced with the beautiful vocabulary of Colombian writers whose works had been gifted to me by women who wanted me to know how to say more than *mucho gusto*. And who could forget the number of dinners I spent sitting across from Bolivians discussing the ins and outs of regional politics over a table covered with *lengua de vaca* and *sopa de mani*. Cows tongue and peanut soup for those not in the know.

"A little bit of everywhere man. But short answer is I lived around latinos for most of my twenties. What about yourself? How did you learn English so well?" - Patrick

"Mainly the *Looney Tunes.*"

"Like from the subtitles?"

"No. It was all in English. When I was a kid my cousin used to smuggle me cartoons from our family in the states."

"Why would you need to smuggle cartoons?"

"My mom was crazy strict and locked up all of the movies in the house. So my cousin started bringing me anything he had recorded back home."

"Your parents seem very unalike."

"Oh they were. So glad they divorced. If they hadn't I never woulda been able to go to concerts or any cool shit like that."

"Interesting. I'm still processing the *Looney Tunes* thing. I didn't know Bugs Bunny was so well traveled. Thought the NBA was his biggest jump out of cartoons."

"Yeah that stupid rabbit taught me more than I'd care to admit."

"Makes sense. I Mean. I learned via music to start with. Pretty sure the only Spanish word I learned from the *Looney Toons* was 'Andale! Andale! Arriba!'"

"Taking lessons from Speedy?"

"Only about what pace to keep."

As we stood there discussing the intricacies of the *Looney Tunes* Austin approached us without a shirt.

"Haven't you lost enough clothes for this trip?"

"Not lost bro. It's hanging off that guys mirror."

"Better than the fate of your last shirt."

"Don't fucking remind me man. That fucking idiot."

Standing there I looked around and thought how these guys reminded me of friends I had made many times throughout my twenties. Friends made in groups where I started as the foreigner invited to a party and became a regular just in time for me to move to another country. Which of course was my fault and my choice for keeping on the go, but if I wasn't doing that then it became hard to justify what I was doing down there. Without exploring one country after another it would have just been the same day on repeat after a while. As we stood there talking I observed a few moments of truly lost translation as Austin looked to me for help without understanding that those around him were speaking in perfect unadulterated English. Once he broke that barrier in his mind he went on for the next few minutes embellishing the details of his fishing adventure including everything from the size of the fish to the secluded nature of the river. The locals embraced his story and as we continued to stand around they dragged us further into conversation with the offer of a few locally made brews. I gave in and stood there drinking a beer while Austin downed two in the same time and continued to impress the locals. Unfortunately we had to be early and while that didn't really concern Austin on his last night I still found myself edging us towards an exit as I knew I would be awake and operational earlier than anyone else around me. Once we said our goodbyes and separated ourselves from the crowd Austin realized he was already down half a pack of cigarettes due to his drunken and generous nature.

"We can grab you a pack on the way to the airport." - Patrick

"Nah man I'll make these last two last. Trying to quit when I go home."

When we got to the gate Austin started to light up a cigarette and dropped his first attempt from his lips as we stood there.

"So you remember how this gate works right? It locks right away, so don't let this rock move until you want to come inside. I gotta get some sleep."

"Thanks for today man. I had so much fun."

"Glad to hear it. So you'll be up early morning?"

"Yessiree. Good to go."

"Open your phone and show me your alarm."

"Patrick, I got it."

As I left him I allowed the door to ease shut and continued through until I came upon the now empty courtyard. Where there was once noise and annoyance I now only saw a few dimly lit picnic tables with randomly placed trash spread along the ground and table tops. To the side of the furthest table was a drunken Myles, sprawled out on the floor with a snore coming from his hoodie that was audible even a few feet away. I wondered, much like a distant relative, were it not for our history, if I met these people now, would I choose them as pieces to put in my life? We are born into circumstance, but we decide our lives by dictating which characters and scenarios we put our energy towards. I understood that it had been my choice to inherit the responsibility for our cleanliness, as it had been my choice to inherit all of these burdens. But until I knew where we were staying tomorrow it was best to keep our options open by not pissing this place off anymore than we had. With that I walked around a few minutes cleaning up our mess and any residual mess from the night as a whole. It's so weird. You never understand how youth slips away until you're expected to be the adult. And when they expect you to be the adult long enough that becomes the norm. And that went for society as well as your friends. I was a man who usually believed that you were in control of your circumstances. But I had not understood the role I had been chosen for today, or the role I was putting myself into for the entire trip for that matter. Today and all other days regardless of geography or moments in time.

After cleaning up all I could I turned off the lights and walked to the hallway where I heard a blend of reggaeton and techno coming from a speaker on the other side of a tightly closed door separating me from my final resting place. With the knob turning slowly my biggest hope was to slip in unnoticed and hidden by the noise, but as the door opened I adjusted my eyes to see that the noise had harbored a great deal more than I had expected to see. And perhaps even more than I could ever hope to be a part of. At least that's what I figured when my eyes were first met by the sight of two naked girls curled up against each other in the bed I thought was mine. A situation which led to a momentary pause as I looked around the corners to find my belongings and confirm my right to be there. Though it was not the sight of my book bag which confirmed my situation as much as the undeniable view of Renata's mane of hair covering the face of a bodily blessed girl next to her. Someone I could never truly pick out of a line-up, though I would never forget the figure or uninterrupted tan which ran down her entire body. After a few moments I was released from an innate hypnosis driven by testosterone and curiosity and started backing up to exit. As I closed the door with even more ease than I had opened it I watched as a ray of light slowly faded from their bodies and the final smells of perfume and sweat left the air around me.

Now as a testament to how tired I was I quickly got over the scene and moved back into the mode of searching for a spot to rest for the evening. Admittedly an eighteen year old version of me might have stood with my jaw hanging just a bit longer, and it's not like I didn't have some questions, but by then I was tired enough to start hallucinating so I needed to find myself somewhere to lay down. Unfortunately I didn't see which dorms my friends had gone to earlier so I couldn't even steal the bed that should have belonged to Myles. I looked around for a flat surface to sleep on until I remembered the couches upstairs and decided to go see if they were vacant. Thankfully they were so I plopped myself down and leaned back until the inevitability of exhaustion led me into a light squeamish sleep.

Day 10: Solomente Yo
Quepos, Costa Rica

When my alarm went off I opened my eyes and immediately felt the warmth of a leather couch gracing my cheek as I laid there curled up in a ball patting my pockets to silence my phone. As I got up and stretched I reached around to make sure I had all of the things I needed for my morning to begin. My notebook, phone, pen, keys...fuck. I had gotten so caught up going for cigarettes that I hadn't thought to find the keys before going to bed. As I stumbled around for a moment I made my way over to a sink and began rinsing my face to alert as many of my senses as possible before heading down the stairs. When I turned off the sink I started walking down the stairs until I saw Almeré sitting at a table rushing to get her food separated into portioned containers. Seeing her plan out her meals was a testament to her experience on the go. That type of discipline takes more out of you when you're not at home. I stopped halfway down uncertain if I wanted to re-open our goodbye as I heard her friends remind her of the urgency surrounding her morning.

"Almeré! We gotta get going. The bus leaves in 15 minutes."

"I'm coming, Just give me a second!" - Almeré

I looked at her with a brief feeling of dismay as it sunk in that no chance encounter would bring us together again on this last neck of the trip. And I would not be getting my coffee on repeat anytime soon. Sure I would see her again if I tried to, but for now our chapter would have to close. Long ago I had learned that even though circumstance may be what bring two people together we now live in a world small enough to create your own repeat visits once you've decided seeing someone again to be a necessary encounter. Once she finished packing her food she threw the containers in her bag and joined her friends at the front door before they all ran to the bus which was set to leave any minute. As she jogged onto the bus I watched the tip of her ponytail bounce and the soles of her white chucks trail behind as the bus doors closed and she left my field of vision for the last time since. A moment which led me to promise myself that this would be the last second chance I pass up. Now and forever.

I got downstairs and tried to imagine where the keys could have ended up. The only logical spot was back in my room so at the risk of breaking up another party I decided to go and chance my way through through the room. Not just for the keys, but I also needed to get my belongings together. I had no idea if I would be returning before the group decided to check out so I figured it would be a good idea to have my stuff in order in case they were kicked out before I returned. When I opened the door to my room I was greeted by the still bodies of Renata and what I assumed was the same girl from a few hours ago with a bulk of white covers separating them. Again I took advantage of the radio still playing to go through the dresser in search of my keys. As I started rummaging through the night stand I heard some movement from behind me so I grabbed my bags and eased my way out of the room.

As I went outside I approached the drivers side door and found it unlocked as I looked in to find Wes stretched out across the backseat. That lucky mother fucker. I quickly checked and saw the keys were not in the ignition as I opened the door. Had he fallen asleep to music and killed the battery I might have had to strangle him. The door opening had not alarmed him so I smacked his legs to wake him up as I popped the trunk.

"Wes. Get up. Get out." - Patrick

"What?"

"It's time to go man. I gotta get Austin to the airport."

"Lemme just go with you to San Jose."

"If you go you'll miss seeing the monkeys on the beach today."

"Can't we just drive there after?"

"No man. We won't make it back in time. Now get up and get out."

"Dude don't leave me in charge of them."

"It'll be easy man. A bus heads that way every hour until 2 P.M. You just gotta wait for it at that corner opposite of that soccer field. Now come on dude I gotta go."

"Alright fuck. I'll get up."

"And I don't know which dorm they're in so I need you to help me find Austin and get him out here. We need to get going."

"Our rooms are in the back behind the pool. 501."

"If you know where your room is then why are you out here?"

"How the fuck was I gonna get any sleep? The kids above me wouldn't stop fucking talking and then Myles was making so much noise in the kitchen that I couldn't sleep in the hammocks. And I figured the car was the safest bet so I wouldn't get left behind if we got kicked out."

"Well we're not kicked out, but I do have to leave. Make sure you tell Myles to stay out there as long as you all want today. I won't be back for a few hours."

After rolling around for a minute he folded his blanket around his two pillows and got out of the backseat and made his way through the hostel courtyard where he disappeared out of sight. While I waited around I got the car straightened up and adjusted everything to my liking until Austin appeared at the front gate with his bags. He stood in the doorway swaying in the daze of a weeklong hangover. By now I've gotten everything ready to go so all that's left is for him to load his belongings into the trunk, which he did right before landing in the front seat and falling asleep. On the way out I finally noticed the odd combination of one way streets which took you on forced journey through the entire town before you could make your way to the exit. Either a planning flaw or a great accidental tourist trap.

Only a few miles outside of Quepos reality showed us that we should have allowed for more time as we came up on what appeared to be an accident stopping the flow of traffic. Austin remained unaware of the obstruction ahead so I sat for a few moments while I waited to see if we would be waived along. As we sat there I saw the line of cars behind us growing until a few started to make U-turns which led me to believe there was another way around for those in the know. In times like these one must trust the locals.

"Hey man! Does the GPS work here?" - Patrick

Austin rolled toward me and shielded his eyes from the sun as he muttered,

"You don't know where you're going?"

"I do. But I could use another route if we wanna make it to the airport on time."

His response was no help so I opened up my maps and started to zoom out until I noticed a few roads appearing to run in the formation of a grid system beyond the palm trees to my right. I scrolled and saw an entrance to the series of roads behind us so I decided to do my own U-turn and get around this mess. After I turned around I followed some other cars onto a service road and began driving down a trail of packed clay which looked like it was being used as a roadway to connect the many thousands of acres of palm fields around us. As I looked around at this overly harvested crop I found myself struggling with the idea overburdening the ecosystem for softer skin when some people are still working on getting food. By this time the truck in front of us was throwing up so much dust that we couldn't see the road ahead which really sucked because it was starting to get bumpier the deeper into the trail we went and If I popped a tire here I would be completely out of luck. Maybe that's why they demanded such large deposits for the rental. As the frame was rocked by a pothole Austin jerked up from his seat and opened his eyes to his new surroundings.

"Bro? We good?" - Austin

"Just a necessary detour. Don't worry."

He squinted as he looked around for a bit trying to process the situation before laughing to himself and turning back to his pillow. When I saw that we were coming up on an area to cut back over I turned left along with the truck in front of me and started to make my way in the proper direction of my final destination. We eventually made it down another series of roads until getting back to the main road where we continued along up the mountain unobstructed by traffic from thereon out. As we reached the top we passed by a large roadside farmers market where a few trucks were selling fruits and empanadas as others unloaded wooden crates filled with freshly picked food from around the area. I wanted to pull over but that didn't seem worth the stop until all of the vendors had arrived later in the day and I could browse the selection without any worries of time. That being the case I made myself a promise to stop there before the day was done, but for moment I continued along to the airport.

When we made it to the airport I found a parking spot after which Austin began to wake up finally noticing that we had stopped moving. As I got out and gave myself a full body stretch Austin started organizing a series of items which had fallen off his lap on the drive up. As we unloaded his things I offered to walk him through checking in before security, but surprisingly he urged me to go ahead.

"Nah I'm good man. It's *boleto* and *bolsa*. I got a note in my phone. Here ya check it out, lemme know if I spelled them right. It's some of the Spanish I heard down here..."

Grabbing his phone a moment I looked down and saw a list of s cattered words, only a few making sense, *Donde esta el bano? Weed? Tienes mota? How much? Cuantos por mas? Cerveza? No me gusta tequila. Pescado. Donde? Is it far? Muy lehos? LOW SIENTO!*"

"Yeah dude you're good. Kinda. Take away that *W*."

"Boom. Delete. *W* gone. Thanks for taking care of us down here. It was nice to not have to pay attention for once."

"No problem buddy, glad you had a good time."

"Yeah man. Just wish I had gotten some more pictures to show the kids though."

"I got a few you can show them. Here look at these."

I lifted my phone and showed him a picture taken from the rooftop of our hostel of Myles and him standing in the grass a few feet from a pair of iguanas with a proximity effect made by the capability of zoom. As he looked at the photo I took out my notebook and separated the tiny insert containing all of the fishing terms I had written down for the trip.

"Here man. Take this. I didn't use these much, but maybe you'll find something to do with them. If the kids gonna talk to you, let it be about something you wanna talk about. And if you ever decide you wanna learn it, take some time to re-write it in your own handwriting, it'll help out a lot."

"Thanks man."

As I walked him through the airport I began to look around at all the people coming and going. This was not an airport filled with people waiting for connections, it was a destination. Those coming were pleased, and those leaving were unsure why they're leaving. Although amongst all of those going here or there one of them walked confidently towards his gate. As I watched him leaving and couldn't help but think about the world his flight would soon return him to. A world much different than the one he had been living in for the last ten days. He served as a healthy reminder of just how far away I was from the type of reality he existed in on a daily basis. I had forgotten to consider what these guys were living back home all together. They had so much more responsibility in their lives than I did. Wes may have had a little bit less. Comparatively speaking to the others of course. But in the end they all had some pretty busy lives; kids, businesses, decisions. I only had me. And because of that perspective I was unable to see the type of journey they were hoping to have. I think in a lot of ways they were hoping for a story to tell. Something to be told in circles of wine and beer over the next twenty years sitting around the front porch.

Once he was through security I stepped outside and enjoyed a view of the mountains and felt the fresh air around me warming up from the afternoon sun which was now positioned directly above. I felt a rush of freedom as I was able to breathe a sigh of relief knowing that the most important task of the day had been completed. All that remained was dealing with the fact that I was missing out on the best chance any of us would get to see monkeys on this entire trip. An offense which was somewhat lightened when I realized that at least that meant the others were safely occupied for the rest of the day. Which meant I had a little bit of time to myself if I wanted. The idea of calling Matilda to spend a day wandering around the city seemed like an obvious way to go, but I knew regardless of what I wanted to do there I still had to to adhere to the reality that I would need to be back in Quepos at a reasonable hour.

Making my way to the car a part of me considered just driving around all day. I had a nostalgia for a time I was never a part of; a time in America where the road had been opened up by the freedom of four wheels and a few bucks. Growing up I had always wanted to have the type of road trip where I could just take off and go, seeing what happens around each turn. I had once tasted this chance when I spent a brief time living outside of Los Angeles along the beaches of Santa Monica, CA. Unfortunately I did so at one of the notoriously broker times of my life and was unable to take full advantage of the adventure I would have loved to have lived along Americas golden coast. Even if I were to spend my day driving it made the most sense to go back towards the coast and make the best of a few things along the way. It's not like I hadn't passed a lot of spots I wanted stop at over the last few days. As I started driving away from the airport my mind recalled the hostel in Jaco and the surfing lesson I missed so I took a moment to find the girls number. I wasn't entirely sure I was up to the idea, but if I was going to learn to surf what better situation could I ask for.

"Hey Ansley this is Patrick. What are you up to?"

"Hey! I'm on my way to a cookout. Where are you?"

"Leaving San Jose and trying to decide what to do today. Was considering a lesson if you had the time."

"I don't have any boards with me, but come meet us! We're heading to a cove about two miles from Jaco. I can give you a lesson after."

"Okay. You all need anything?"

"Some watermelon if you can. I'll send you my location and see you soon!"

I drove until I reached the top of the mountain and stopped in front of one the farmers markets to search for fruits and I found two perfect watermelons. Which honestly seemed excessive, but it was hard to talk myself out of such a great deal at $3 a piece. After placating my hunger with an empanada I loaded up my new purchase and got back on the road in the direction of Jaco while I waited on a location from Ansley. When she sent me her location I entered it into my GPS and saw that I was only an hour and a half way. When I arrived I came to a small pull off that had no other cars parked and only the smell of a smoldering grill to alert me that others were around. I got out and started to walk towards the beach where I saw a four wheeler parked a few feet ahead of a fire burning underneath of a makeshift grill. Tending to the fire was a man I recognized from nights before. Omar, the man who had unknowingly given me the assist with Gabi and her non-hooker friend. I saw Ansley as she started to walk towards me in a blue bathing suit with another pleasant figure following close behind. She smiled as she approached and reached out for a hug which dampened the front of my outfit.

"Patrick! So glad you made it." - Ansley

"Me too. How goes it?" - Patrick

"It's good. We decided to come here earlier. Gonna be a one on one lesson today?" - Ansley

"Yeah. Looks like it."

"Well if you wanna surf we're gonna have to wait til we get back to the hostel. This area isn't meant for a beginner."

"No worries. How long before the barbecue gets going?"

"Soon. Omar is getting all of that together right now. And here this is my friend Denali. She might join us out on the waves."

"Well look who it is. The guy who takes your shots and ruins your dessert." - Denali

"Well I hope I can bring peace to the issue with a few things I brought?"

"Watermelons. That all you got?"

"Didn't know I needed more. Excited to get surfing?"

"No. I'm more of a swimmer. Speaking of which, I'm going to go get in the water. Here, finish this before the ice melts."

With that she handed me her drink and pulled a pound of silky hair into a pony-tail before walking waist deep into the water and taking her head underneath. Still in my khakis and no position to swim I diverted my attention to the left and saw Ansley helping Omar prep some meat for the grill. Debating my options I decided to opt out of running to go the car to grab my bathing suit and instead stayed behind to cook with Omar as Ansley went to join Denali down in the water.

"Your amigos have any luck catching fish that morning?" - Omar

"Yeah we found some trout up by Poas. You been there before?"

"I've fished everywhere this country has to offer. They woulda had better luck on the boat with me and my buddies. We brought back a whole load of fish the next morning. But river trout is very good too. Did you get to try it?"

"No. I didn't have the stomach to eat that night."

"Oh my friend. Big mistake. You must change that."

"That and a few other things. So is this how you spend your days off?"

"Every day is vacation when you live by the beach my friend."

And with the mention of vacation Ansley chimed in and interrupted our conversation with some bad news.

"Omar. We might have to fix something at the pool when we get back." - Ansley

"I thought you said life was a vacation here?" - Patrick

"Well...once in a while they make me to show off my famous handy work." - Omar

When the proper stretch of time had yielded us with some medium-rare steaks and seared vegetables I stood around and ate the food in a rather barbaric manner and without any regard to the unburnt status of my tongue. After we ate I was directed to sit down in a patch of sand shaded by the palm-trees as Ansley pulled out a bottle of spiced rum from her bag.

"So what supplies do I need if I'm gonna start surfing on the regular? Seems less cumbersome in the supplies department than snowboarding." - Patrick

"Not a lot. Just a solid board and some waves. The bigger the better. Once you know what you're doing."

"Well speaking of the beach factor I've been wondering. How do you deal with the downgrade in surfing here?"

"What do you mean?"

"Well. Where you're from has like the best waves in the world. If you're going to travel halfway around the world to surf then shouldn't you have at least gone to the best spot in Costa Rica? How did you find yourself here?"

"I found out about the hostel from this foreign exchange student in my neighborhood last year. She was around when my parents went through their divorce and we were around the same age and became really good friends."

"So she's from Jaco?"

"No, but her cousin runs the hostel so she hooked me up with a chance to teach surf lessons in exchange for a place to stay."

"So are you on a break from school?" - Denali

"No. If anything it's a break from my family. Actually let me correct myself. We don't have a family. We have three adults who can no longer be in the same house."

With an awkward pause in her response Denali leaned back.

"I'm sorry to hear that." - Denali

"It's okay. I knew it would happen eventually."

"Did they argue a lot growing up?" - Patrick

"No, but my grandma told me they had problems from the start. Apparently they were going to split up, but once I came along they decided to figure things out."

"That's awkward." - Denali

"No it's cool. I'm just gonna let them figure out what type of family they want to be before I change my tune."

"I know what I said earlier about not wanting to fly back, but eventually you're gonna have to. Not that there's anything wrong with surfing and chilling for a few years. Just don't mess up your future to prove a point to your parents." - Patrick

"I won't." - Ansley

"What are you going to do when your visa expires? Don't you have to go home then?" - Denali

"That's an easy fix." - Patrick

"Easy? Do you know how much paperwork that is?" - Denali

"He's right. I just gotta leave the country once every ninety days. When I do that I'm gonna take a few weeks and travel around and then probably come back here." - Ansley

"You don't wanna go back home?" - Denali

"Why would I? If my parents aren't going to act like adults I don't need to deal with them. It's not like I owe them anything. They made me. I didn't ask for the favor."

As they continued the conversation I checked my phone to review a few messages and found a theme showing up on my screen.

"Yo where you at?" - Wes

"Hey did you make it to the airport?" - Renata

"Dude. WHERE THE FUCK ARE YOU??" - Myles

I looked down, uncertain what to say back. I could be back in an hour if I wanted, but I had no reason to rush, and they probably weren't back from the beach yet so why not allow myself another hour. I told myself I would ride the moment as long as it kept taking me today. I had no real desire to get back on the road at the moment. And for as long as I was welcomed I figured why not hang around people who weren't causing me a headache. Especially on a night like tonight when I found myself around a group of people whom had taken the chance to live the life they wanted once life had given them the right excuse to do so.

"Hey. I don't mean to interrupt. But what's the plan for the rest of the day? Just trying to figure out my plans."

"We'll be heading back pretty soon. Omar has gotta get back to fix something at the pool so if you want to go back with us we can get the boards waxed and take a few runs." - Ansley

"No. It's getting a little late to start that." - Patrick

"So does that mean you're leaving us?"- Ansley

"Not yet, but soon." - Patrick

"Don't you think it's time for you to stop being in a hurry on vacation? Walk with me and I'll drive you back on the four-wheeler afterwards." - Denali

"Ansley you coming?" - Patrick

"No. I gotta help Omar tonight."- Ansley

Ansley turned and cupped her hands around her mouth as she yelled in the direction of the fire as Denali looked over at me with the beginning of her plead.

"Come on. Don't make me go alone." - Denali

"Do you wanna just drive back in my car?" - Patrick

"No. It's too nice out. Let's walk."

"Alright, but someone is gonna have to get me back here later."

"One of us can drive you back on the four wheeler. Now let's go find a place for you to make up for my birthday cake."

"The watermelons weren't enough?"

"I never asked for watermelons."

We left our campground and walked along the shore until we made our way to an empty bar with a blender and a pile of fresh fruits sitting on the counter. I ordered a mix of papaya and banana as Denali looked over at me.

"Are you gonna get a shot with that?"

"Nah I'm good."

"No you're not. You're on vacation and you're doing a terrible job at it. Here let me help you. Excuse me bartender, can we get two shots por favor?"

She reached over and handed the bartender her credit card as she leaned against me and finished signing her bill. As the bartender handed her the shots she slid back and placed one in my hand which I pulled towards my face for a preview of the aroma about to be ingested.

"Tequila?"

"Too strong for you?"

"Not at all. Just not what I wanted after all of that papaya."

"Well drink liquor and nothing else. You'll be fine."

Once we left we started walking along the beach in the direction of Jaco while enjoying the final fading of daylight in the distance and a steady drop in the warmth of the sand beneath us. From there we started talking about everything from her job to her time spent living in London where she had a house, plants she never had time to take care of, and the cat that felt more neglected than her unfinished home office. Though I tried to comfort her by telling her the cat appreciated more neglect than any of us would care to admit. When we got closer to town I followed her lead and found myself seated on the patio of a restaurant placed on a corner at the first block on the outskirt of town. By now I felt a bit of a buzz from the days sun and shots joining forces. When the waiter arrived she stopped flipping through the menu and ordered a round of drinks.

"Look, I'll have this one since you ordered it, but after this I'm finished." - Patrick

"Would you just enjoy yourself. I'll get you some food to soak it up if you're worried about driving."

"I'll be fine. I'm just not much of a drinker."

"It's vacation. We all do different things. No one back home believed me when I told them I was turning my phone off for my month away."

"Then why even have it on you?"

"I'm using it as a camera. It's just on airplane mode all day."

"That's a great idea."

"I thought so. I had to get away from my phone going off every five seconds ya know what I mean?"

"More than you know. But unfortunately there are still a few constraints I must live by and that means I gotta get going. It's gotta be after six by now?"

"Oh I think it's closer to eight."

"Fuck. The guys are gonna kill me if I don't get back soon."

"What are you supposed to make it back for?"

"Nothing special I guess. It's just that I'm traveling with them, they paid for me to be here. I feel like I should go back."

"Well they might have paid for you to be here, but I am the one paying for your drinks."

"Touche."

After we ate I urged us out of the restaurant so that I could start getting home. I knew the longer I stayed the more I was pressing my luck with my friends. But at this point what was the difference? Would they be slightly less mad at me now than if I return in an hour as opposed to now? Truth was I was already fucked. But at least I was having a good time. More so than I could claim to have had in a while in such a scenario. The dating game had become very convoluted back home, and explanations of my state in life were not well received by those looking to anchor their lives with the next stable guy they met. Often resulting in nothing more than an interesting conversation and a goodbye filled with lies of *next time*. So why walk away now when I had found a different situation? Even if it only ended in conversation.

"Seriously, why are you in such a hurry? You're like the least fun person ever." - Denali

"Now that's just plain lying."

"What have you done that's so fun? I haven't seen anything yet."

"Well I don't *do* fun things. They just kinda happen."

"Well what's the last thing that *happened* to you?"

"Well I got to meet the President."

"Of where?"

"Panama."

"What was he doing in Costa Rica?"

"He wasn't. He was just on a walk through Panama City."

"Did you guys do anything other than talk?"

"No. But he did get us tickets to go see the canal."

"That sounds like the story a government intern would tell me. What's something you did that was actually risky?"

"I'm not sure if this counts, but I once drove naked through three states."

"Excuse me?"

"You asked for something crazy. There it is."

"Wait, what? You did what?"

"You heard me. I drove naked through three states. South Carolina, North Carolina, and most of Virginia."

"Why would you start driving naked in the first place?"

"It wasn't like I planned to do the whole drive like that."

"Why would you do *any* of the time like that?"

"Well I was dressed and ready to go. And before I left I went to the pool to say bye to my buddy. He had been letting me stay there while I had this weird two-week gap in my leases. And one of his roommates was drunk as hell and pushed me in the pool. So I got a towel afterwards and went to the car to change off. But all my shit was still in the trunk and I had hurried inside so I sat on the towel for a bit and dried off. Figured if I drove a bit my clothes could dry off with the windows down. It was already midnight so it's not like anyone was gonna notice."

"So how did that turn into three states?"

"Well like I said, I made the mistake of putting my clothes in the trunk earlier on so I had to go through the backseat if I wanted to change once I was in the car and undressed. And there was no reason to rush since I had like six hours of darkness to keep me hidden. Plus it was dark and humid, so it's not like the clothes were drying fast."

"That's not adventurous, that's stupid. At least you did it at night. But how did no one notice you that whole way?"

"Just luck. Had a close call though around Lumberton, North Carolina. There was this stretch through town where the speed limit dropped to 20 MPH and about half way through town this cop starts riding my bumper. I don't think I've ever been on edge in my life."

"You and Ansley make me feel boring."

"I thought you said you're out all the time?"

"Well yeah, but those are business dinners. Or final dates that I don't know are final dates. That becomes old after a while."

"I guess so. I never really had that type of social life. I mean I had fun, but I can't relate to how you're living over there."

As we walked along I looked up and appreciated the moonlight for a moment. Not that it was shining, but that the clouds were letting us see it. All around me the sky was open and the cove was lit up by a duality of strength created by not just the moon, but its reflection off the tightly enclosed waters. The beach was fairly empty aside from a few bodies remaining still in the distance.

"I think it was called Thukpa." - Denali

"What?"

"Thukpa. You asked me the other day if there was a dish I could make. I can't really cook it, but my grandma made it for me a few times and I really loved it. It was this spicy soup from the mountains. And *sel roti*, it's like a long donut they eat as dessert. When I get home I'm gonna try to find a market with the ingredients I need."

"I'm a fan of spicy. I expect the recipe or a sample mailed my way once you've got it down."

"And what are you gonna send me? I thought you were the cook."

Continuing to talk we slowed down and found a place to sit in the sand just a few feet away from a set of palm trees. Over the next few minutes we went on in pointless conversation talking around anything other than parting ways. It was then I decided to see if my night was finally going to end or if I was going to be explaining my absence to my friends even later than I had previously expected. I only knew a few older women in my life, but not many of them would waste their time, though not all of them would reveal their intentions. As I formed the next line in my mind I stood trying to see the situation for what it really was and relied on my best observing instinct.

"I wish I had a room here tonight." - Patrick

"Why? You getting tired?"

"Well that's irrelevant. But no, I would just use it to test out our boring ways by inviting you to come back."

"To your room?"

"Yeah. If I had one."

At that she paused a moment and placed a palm fill with sand onto the top of my hand.

"Well tell me. What can do we in a room that we can't do on a beach?" - Denali

Pleasantly surprised at the lack of truth in her previously unassuming presence I looked back at her unsure what to do next. But certain enough at what to say.

"What an amazing answer..." - Patrick

As she leaned in on me I braced myself in the sand and enjoyed the pleasantries of a first kiss for long enough that my shoulders started to burn at the duality of weight being supported at such an uncomfortable degree. Soon enough my awareness took me away from the pain and to the recognition of voices passing which accompanied the shadows of bodies passing between us and the moonlit shore.

"Stop! Stop." - Patrick

"What, what's wrong?"

"We gotta move. There's too many people here."

"No one is watching us. Stop worrying."

"What about that inlet over there? There's fucking crocodiles around here. I know I said I would take you to my room, but how about we just go to yours?"

"You're overreacting. And we can't. I'm in a dorm."

"I am not overreacting. I'm just refusing to be the tourist who died that way. Now I thought you said the best part of traveling now was not being broke while you do it."

"I said I wasn't broke. I didn't say I was rich."

"Maybe we can find an empty bungalow."

"We're not breaking into a bungalow."

"I thought you wanted to be more adventurous?"

"Don't start that. We're under a full moon. This is adventurous enough without breaking and entering."

"I don't suppose you rented a car for this trip?"

"No. I've only needed to drive once since arriving."

"What did you drive?"

"Some SUV Ansley loaned me."

"What kind was it?"

"An older Land Rover I think. Why?"

"I think that's the one I saw parked there when we first came up on the hostel. Those things are perfect."

"What do you mean perfect? It's not ours. What if someone comes to use it?"

"Now you're the one worrying about the unreasonable. No one is picking up guests this late. No one will even be in the parking lot. I'll make ya a bet."

At my urging we both got moving towards the hostel and

approached the entrance to a dead end street which led to the parking lot for the hostel. When we got to the parking lot I spotted a white Land Rover Discovery parked a few spots down from a street lamp meant to add security to the area. I walked up and tried my luck by reaching around to the gas tank where I found the key sitting next to the gas cap. This was clearly a community car being used by all of the workers. And this spot was the go to for most old trucks. Hell, we probably weren't even the first people to do this. I opened the door looking around as I got in to make sure no one saw us as we rushed into the backseat. From there we went through your normal routine and started kissing one another while we took off each others shirts and wedged them into the cracked windows to make some curtains for added privacy. Facing me with her legs straddling my waist she grabbed my hands and directed them to her torso where they rested under a set of perfectly full breasts, still covered by a veil of red lace, causing a boyish anticipation that I knew she could see on my face.

"Well Mister, done this before? You seem like you have." - Denali

"What's that supposed to mean? You're the one who was trying to fondle me on the beach."

"I still think our last spot was better."

"Well this is a first for me too. Let's hope we can enjoy it."

"Is that supposed to make me feel special? I was hoping the first partner of my new year to be a bit more confident."

"Feel as you wish. I'm not one for expectations in…"

Before I could finish my sentence she put her hand behind my neck and began consuming my bottom lip, unbuttoning my pants as she did so. Filled with excitement I moved my hands up and grabbed a handful of what I should soon see, trying to scoot off my pants at the same time.

"Here let me help." - Denali

Swinging her right leg off of me she sat next to me and slipped out of her matching red underwear, revealing a thin line of interruption in her otherwise naturally tanned skin. Both now ready, she established control and made herself comfortable, briefly digging her nails in my back as she did. Despite the concern for being caught we soon lost track or care over whether or not we were causing the SUV to rock from the outside. At times I was almost certain she was gonna rip off the handles meant to keep riders in place when they took a sharp turn. And though she seemed to be enjoying herself, I hate to admit I found my posture and the position itself a hindrance on the full potential of enjoyment the situation would have normally allowed. A problem which she did her best to fix each time my frustration became noticeable or my focus had somehow directed away from caressing her skin. When the curtains had served their purpose I rested my face on top of her breasts and let out a sigh, the moisture from my mouth now mixing with a dew of sweat on her chest. As I rested there catching my breath, I felt the beating of her heart, slowly rejuvenating with deep gasps of air as our pulses steadily evened.

"Well, you still have the energy of a twenty-something, or was it twenty plus twenty?"

"Don't push your luck."

"We're not friendly enough yet to joke around?"

"We're getting there. Aren't you glad you decided to stick around?"

"Didn't feel like I had a choice. Miss bartender here with the shots."

"I knew you would leave if you didn't drink. You're antsy."

"Yeah. I would have."

"So here we are."

"Yeah. I like tequila. It's been good to me. I don't know why it gets so much bad press."

Laughing she gave me one more kiss before putting her shirt back on.

"Any chance you wanna hop in the front and take me back to my car?" - Patrick

"So you're finally ready to leave?"

"Don't even. I've been trying to leave all day."

"Well unlike you I rather quit while I'm ahead. So let's get out of here and I'll go grab that four-wheeler they have outback. But first I wanna know something."

"Go for it?"

"Is it better being naked in a car with some company?"

"Absolutely. Plus I feel confident even if the cops did come it wouldn't be as bad as if they had pulled me over that night."

"Why do you say that?"

"Well they would at least understand what got me here."

"So you're admitting the urge to drive naked is not as universal as you'd like it to seem?"

"It's not too late to hop in the front and find out for yourself."

"Guess some things I'll have to leave up to you."

We refurbished the curtains and got out of our handmade hideaway without anyone noticing and returned the key to its original hiding spot. On the way out I noticed a ton of sand on the backseat, but no matter how much I tried to brush it off I couldn't seem to get it out. While I continued cleaning she went to get the four-wheeler from behind the property. Once I was done cleaning I stood there waiting at the end of the driveway readjusting my outfit until my motions were interrupted by the revving of an ATV rolling up on my right. As she slowed down she didn't surrender the drivers seat so I hopped on and grabbed the handles at my side. A set of blinding halogen lights lit up our way as she hit the throttle and sent us speeding into the sand. As we drove along I felt a quenching in my abdomen which got worse with each bump we hit. Hoping to counter the feeling I clenched my hands on the side as she drove closer to the water and splashed up a mixture of sea water and sand which collected itself into a light clump on both of my calves for the remainder of the ride. When we got back to my car I got off slowly and made it through a quick goodbye as I held onto a straight face and did my best to hide the deep breathes holding back an ever queasier stomach.

After she left I got in the front seat and looked down at a list of missed notifications and a clock telling me I was indefensibly late. Aside from already feeling sick, I did't look forward to the greeting I was bound to encounter once I got back. I had only set out to give myself a day without the stress of others. And I should have been enjoying every bit of that now, but even then my body wouldn't let me. That uneasy feeling from earlier came on stronger with each mile I drove and it wasn't long before I was compelled to pull over and throw up in the middle of the road. I was happy to have been on a long stretch of road where I was able to see in either direction for quite a ways. Ahead of me a set of lights approached from about a mile away, but behind me was all clear. After a few deep breathes and washing my mouth out with some water we had I got back in and continued my drive. I wish I had been in charge of the speed regulation happening on my ATV trip earlier. Perhaps then I could have avoided this. Although I had to admit it made sense. I wasn't used to drinking and I certainly wasn't used to mixing that with motion. The closer I got the more my senses returned to me and I started to dwell on how I was going to explain my day away. I can't tell them what I did, but I also can't tell them that I wanted a fucking day to myself. I can't stand there and say how I had fooled myself into think that this would be a vacation for me as well. I guess I had forgotten what it was like to travel for the first time and how much I would be needed.

When I arrived back in Quepos a great deal of relief hit me as I parked along the sidewalk and was able to let my nerves finally ease up. Which they did the moment I stepped out of the car and started to dry heave in front of the hostel. Which of course worked out great because when I looked up there were Austin and Myles smoking a cigarette with the guard. I debated using the moment to my advantage by just claiming some sort of sudden sickness, but I had waited too long to pull the trigger on that decision so I wiped my face and walked towards the gate. Once I was in earshot a voice chimed in from behind the fence.

"Where the fuck have you been?" - Wes

"You followed that girl somewhere again didn't you? I hope you at least fucked her this time. - Myles

"Dude. I'm not doing this right now. I feel like shit. Renata, let's not crowd my side of the bed tonight okay?

With that comment a look landed on her face that confirmed for me she had not heard me when I tried to sneak out either time. But that she now understood what I knew and what I didn't know. As I continued on I was reminded there is no greater annoyance than be to sick and in need of sleep. The body competes with too many urges at once. Which mine did as I spent the rest of the night tossing and turning in between pacing around the hallway trying to keep my food down. Of all the nights of sleep, this was the worst. My mind had felt tired many times, but this was the first time my body felt the wear just as harshly as it went through the seesaws of karma to end my day.

Day 11: Shore to Shore
Quepos, Costa Rica

When I left the room this morning I found Myles sitting at a picnic table with a half-eaten peanut butter sandwich in his right hand and a glass of orange juice in his left. To either side of him sat groups of two and three getting their day started with their own styles of breakfast, all of which looked enticing. When he noticed me he looked up to speak and went about chewing.

"So what's the plan today?" - Myles

"I think we should chill on the beach and hit the road after the sun goes down." - Patrick

"That works. I could use some downtime."

"Then let's find a spot up on the way and we'll make our way to the other side sometime later."

"Sounds good to me. Do you know where we're gonna stay?"

"More or less There are a few towns around Limón we should check out. Other than that I'm open to suggestions."

"And what about somewhere for today?"

"I heard about a beach with black sand from all of the volcanoes around here. That could be cool to see."

"That sounds neat. Wanna get everyone together?"

"There's no rush. It's only an hour or so up the road."

"You talk like that's normal."

He was right. Our views of normalcy had become very skewed. With regards to, but not limited to, talks of distance and plans to span it. Over the next few hours we made no hurry in departing and closed out our accounts before easing up the coast to Playa Negra where we arrived and the local palm trees put me through a brief but embarrassing moment of parallel parking before getting out to gain our first view of volcanic sand since middle-school science class. At first look it was not one perfect shade of black as I had recalled. All throughout its rich texture with a rumpled appearance like the fur of a jaguar. As we got to the sand it was instantly apparent that one needed to wear sandals on this beach. And even then each step splashed up a scattershot of scorching hot sand which would reach midway up your calf and keep itself baked on until you thoroughly scrubbed. As the guys ran towards the water Renata hung around and kept herself close to me. I could tell that she wanted to talk, but I'd yet to settle my feelings on the topic that I'm sure was on her mind.

"This is awkward." - Renata

225

"No it's not. If you have one of those open relationships that's between you all. Now I know what Marcus means when he says you're the most fun girlfriend he's ever had. I guess that's why you wanted your own room so bad? You don't have to be embarrassed. Just tell me the truth."

"I'm not embarrassed! I just. Ugh!"

At that her face had more red than her statement had lies.

"Alright fine, I'm a little embarrassed. I thought the door was locked! Please tell me you didn't see anything."

"Nothing more than she saw. Ya know. I've got a lot of things I'm working my way through, but I'd settle for understanding how you got some random girl into our room so fast. It took me all fucking day to do what you managed to do in a few minutes. You can keep your embarrassment to yourself, but teach me how you managed that."

"She wasn't random. It was the girl working at the front desk."

"The Brazilian girl?"

"Yeah her."

"How the fuck did that happen? She wasn't with us."

"No, but I was trying to help calm the boys down so I went in the office and asked her for some playing cards. Then we started talking and got caught up and the next thing I knew we were back in the room."

"That seems like a lot of fucking steps skipped. And what did you think was gonna happen when I came back?"

"I thought you went away with that girl somewhere ! I didn't expect you to be back…"

"You give me far more credit than I deserve. Marcus is the one who deserves the credit, finding a girl who is as open as you, with all of your shit together. That's awesome."

"Well no. Not exactly. He doesn't really know about this. And not like this time, like this side of me. At all."

"And you've not let him in on this because…?"

"I tried to bring it up once as like a hypothetical, but he started acting all weird about things when he saw I might be serious. He was drunk though so I don't think he remembers."

"So do you have like a girlfriend back home then too? I didn't even know you liked women. Let alone that we had such similar taste."

"No. Don't be stupid. I don't have a girlfriend or anything. There's not enough hours in my day. This sort of thing never happens."

At that she paused and looked up searching for a number.

"Okay, like three times. But we weren't dating the first two."

"Interesting. So when did you break out of that shell? I hate how interested I am, but I really can't believe I didn't know. We practically lived together for a fucking year. And this is only with girls right? You're not hanging with any other dudes are ya?"

"No. There's no other guy. Look, do we have to talk about this?"

"Yes. Yes we do. I can't walk in that room and just not ask you anything after what I saw. Especially when it was supposed to be my room in the first place. You're my friend. I want the story."

"Ugh. I hate you sometimes. Okay fine. It's not like it's a big deal. It only happened once the whole time I was around you in Mexico. And you wouldn't know anyone I was dating when I got back home. But that all ended when I got home then I got pregnant, the rest is history. So yeah."

"Was that so hard?"

"No, but this isn't how I wanted you to find out."

"I haven't found out anything? How did it happen? That's not the whole story."

"She just reminded me so much of the first girl I was with back in Rio for some reason. I think it was her accent."

"No, not her!"

"You mean the first time?"

"Yeah. In Mexico, who was it around us?"

"Oh it wasn't there. That's another story. I'm not telling you that one. My first time was in Rio before I met you."

"Who was she?"

"My dance instructor."

"Can't blame anyone for getting seduced on the dance floor."

"We were actually on the train when she made her first move."

"How did you find privacy for that on a train?"

"I mean, that's just where we started. We went to her house after that. And she was very smooth. I let her take the lead."

"So it was like a date that went well?"

"No. We both lived near each other and one night we ended up in the same car on the ride home. She came to say hi. Next thing I knew we were chatting it up and somewhere before home she made her move."

"You didn't see it coming? That also seems really quick. You must have been giving her signs in class. Or she was bold as fuck."

"Not really. Her feet were swinging me into her lap before I even noticed how close she had gotten. And I wasn't flirting. I don't think."

"Guess she knew what she was doing."

"I feel like you're judging me."

"Oh I'm not judging anything. I'm actually a huge fan of the whole thing. I thought I made that clear. I just don't get what dude is gonna be mad about that? I say just tell Marcus what's up. You got away from him and this happened in just a few nights. So it's clearly not a drunk thing."

"I told you I already tried that. I told him we should go out one night and pick out a girl and he got really weird about it. He backed out at the last minute."

"Really?"

"Yeah. Some guys are more old school than you would think."

"Well, how did you sell it to him?"

"What do you mean?"

"Well did you say why you wanted to do it? Like did you tell him you were bored? Or did you make it sound like you wanted to be adventurous? Who knows, maybe he was worried about what the boundaries were for that kinda situation. You ever think that?"

"You think any of that makes a difference?"

"I'm not really the best person to ask on the subject. I would imagine most guys who find out their girlfriend is into girls won't end up being mad about that information. I thought it was one of those things that sold itself. Can't say I'd be against it. Though I had a buddy tell me he realized how bad he was at going down on girl after he saw a girl do it. But that led to growth. We all need growth."

"I just don't think he's about it no matter why I wanna do it. This sucks, he's supposed to be the one talking me into these things."

"My point exactly. Maybe he's not old school. Maybe he's like super freaky and you don't even know it. Maybe he's the one afraid to ask you."

"I highly doubt that."

"He's so simple."

"Like missionary all the time simple?"

"No. But he's not a complicated guy. I messed it up. I was way too into the girl. She was so hot."

"What if he wants to bang a dude? Would that be ok? I mean you gotta be ready for whatever he throws at you when you open that door."

"Eh…do I really?"

"Probably not to that extreme. But still. Worth considering. Do you like women more than men? Or is it kind of a tie?"

"Neither. It' just so different with a girl. There's no judgement with your body. It's just so much easier."

"Do you feel he judges you…? He's not exactly in shape…"

"No, I guess I'm just freer with women than I am with men. But I love men. Well one man. Marcus. I just really like girls."

"I don't blame you. I totally get it. I love a woman's body. Truth be told I'm still surprised guys can get women to fuck us. We're pretty gross by comparison. Women are so smooth."

"Yeah. And sometimes you guys are so cold. It's annoying."

Listening to her justifications I had nowhere to go and no new words to offer as I had never had a conversation with Marcus about women so I had no idea how he felt about any of this stuff. I had done my best not to involve myself in that part of the friendship as a way to keep neutrality where needed, especially since I had been friends with her before him. Nonetheless I was curious as to why he felt as she said he did.

"Well how much does he need to be cool with? Do you want some type of open relationship?"

"No. I don't know what to call it. I've always been attracted to women, but it's not like I'm gonna leave him for one. I don't think he'll understand. Guys and girls are so different. They both make me feel something that the other doesn't," interrupted by a few moments of hand shuffling and silence with a set of eyes darting around for clarity, "I know I want to be with him. It's not like I'm gonna leave him or any-thing. I love the guy, I love the family we're building. I just wish he was a little more open minded. In all sorts of places really."

"Geez. I thought your latte order was complicated."

"I'm not complicated! I'm just annoyed."

"Look it's cool. I'm just fucking with you. Do what you want. I would just be worried about marrying someone that you can't talk to openly. Especially about sex. Fuck. Maybe ask yourself if you're really sold on the future you're making."

"I know I want to be with him. Just leave it alone."

"Aight cool. I wasn't attacking ya, just chill."

"So are you mad at me then?"

"Stop saying mad. No one is mad. I was never mad at you. I was just pissed I didn't have anywhere to sleep. I was fucking exhausted."

"Well I didn't mean to make your day any worse."

"Well drop your concerns about all of that. I'm more mad that I missed out on meeting the monkey's than anything else. But now that we're done with all of that, how did you enjoy yourself in my absence?"

"It was kinda overwhelming. I'm pretty sure one of them stole a granola bar from my bag."

"The boys or the monkeys?"

"The monkeys."

"Okay. Just checking. Did you get to high-five one?"

"What?"

"You know. That thing two people do with their hands."

"I know what a high-five is weirdo. And no. I didn't high-five any monkeys."

"Then you didn't have nearly as much fun as I would have. Oh well, maybe I'll catch them another time. Thanks for taking care of the guys for me while I was gone."

"I still can't believe you left us all day."

"Well, I'm glad I did. I needed a few hours of me-time."

"Where'd you go?"

"Don't worry about that."

"Whatever Mr. Shady The guys were pissed you weren't answering your phone."

"Oh I bet."

While Renata and I had been talking Myles had taken the liberty of hooking up our hammocks in a set of trees off to the right of where we had parked. Once he was finished he abandoned them and made his way over to us as we tried to take the conversation back to beaches.

"Come on man. Gotcha a spot to rest before the drive. Plenty of shade." - Myles

"Thanks man. I'm comin." - Patrick

"What time you wanna get going?"

"Sometime after five? Get the most of the daylight."

"That works. I'm gonna go walk around a bit."

As I started to relax I set my alarm and slipped into a coma which lasted for several hours. By the time I woke up three hours had passed and I felt the most recharged I had felt in quite a few days. As I tried to get moving I turned my head to look beyond the folds of my hammock and saw Wes and Renata both spread out on towels absorbing the afternoon rays. When I got up and suggested we get moving everyone gathered their stuff without argument and made their way to the car. If I had to guess they couldn't handle any more of the heat being put off by this unique brand of sand. And to be honest I can't really understand how they had managed to handle it this long.

The drive started with a late-90's playlist led by Renata who dozed off in the back along with the others soon after she starting the two-hour shuffle. I drove them as they slept and we made it into the city around the same time rush hour had finished dying down. As we were driving through San Jose Myles woke up and suggested pulling off to buy some groceries. Shortly after I saw a sign for a Wal-Mart so we got off the next exit and made our way to a full parking lot where a series of evening shoppers attempted to navigate their way through the traffic of those leaving. Once we parked Myles announced he was staying inside to sleep while Wes asked for a favor from the back.

"Yeah me too. Can you grab me some pasta?"

"Yeah I got ya. Does it matter what type?"

"Rigatoni if they got it."

We went inside and grabbed a few days worth of food and managed to make it out of the city as the last traces of daylight sat reflecting on the upper panes of the only tall glass building the city had. Making our way up the mountains I was reminded about the situation on the roads around this area of the country. Which is to say, they were completely fucked. I mean the roads were paved and all of that, but how they were used was sometimes hard to manage. I could never tell if I had the right away or when I was driving in the wrong lane, or what the hell was going on. I just stuck close to the right side when possible and hugged an annoyingly dark trail while remaining delayed by the presence of mist and rain. Which was made worse by the fact that this route had an unusually high volume of tractor trailers on it which meant I had to keep myself peeled to the road for a good forty-five minutes of solid maneuvering before I was able to give my cortex any type of break once we got started. By the time I reached the bottom the others had fallen asleep and my eyes had grown tired from the overly focused hour I just went through.

As we got within the city limits of Limón our GPS took us on a route through a mixture of neighborhoods on the outskirts of the city. As we drove along the streets became crowded with teenagers on dirt bikes and a few scattered cars left over from a 1980's American extradition of outdated and beaten up automobiles. Once we made it away from the outskirts we were taken down a series of gravel roads which directed us to a two-lane road heading down the shore and ultimately isolating itself as the only means of transport along the coast. While veering to the right I peered off to the left and saw a line of lights slowly bobbing across the dark horizon ahead. As any port, this one was there was for a reason. One of the two, though which one first I shall never know. Someone was leaving, or someone was coming. But at one point, enough of both was happening to create the need for a harbor, and then a hotel, and pretty soon an entire shipping lane. And depending on the moment in history these lanes carried spices, food, and often slaves. Something which would make itself apparent on the faces of the local population.

For the next hour we drove between Limón and Puerto Viejo where crashing waves followed us on one side while sparsely populated farms hurried along on the other with a light glow from the moonlight exposing the silhouettes of the occasional two-story barn and the never ending fields of palm and bananas crawling in each direction. We traveled that route uninterrupted until we were met by the distant glow of a town nestled in a cove about an hour south of Limón.

When I had come here years before the entire town shared one street light after sunset and only offered a payable option for lighting if you were playing basketball at the court along the sand. And now I saw how much that had changed as we eased our way into the town limits to see the streets glittering with newly installed lamps guiding a line of overcrowded cars in and out of the narrow streets which seemed momentarily populated beyond their intended capacities. As I approached we were forced to slow down and wait on two drivers lacking confidence and skill as they attempted to pass each other without hitting the other cars squeezed along the sidewalk. Sitting there I looked down to my left where a line of palm trees parted the road from a fifty foot stretch of Caribbean sand and a warm turquoise sea. If my memory served me right the town went to my right a few blocks all the way to this steep hill which had a soccer field and the towns only graveyard. Both elevated to remain out of reach from rising waters. It intrigued me then and even more so now how they were protecting the dead before considering the living. Although I knew it was there for now all I could see was the moonlit outline of palm trees at the top of a hill overlooking the city. As I caught glimpses of the storefronts I kept thinking I would recognize a spot here or there, but the facades had changed as had the names. Or perhaps I was giving too much credit to the memories of a younger me. The town only had room for a few small hotels and I couldn't help but think how lucky I had been to have gotten to know this place as a hideaway before it became a destination.

"Is this where we're staying?" - Wes

"Nah. There's no openings in town. We got a spot a bit farther down the road." - Patrick

"Is there a waterfall around here?" - Wes

"I'm sure there's a few if we ask." - Patrick

"I wanna go snorkeling." - Renata

"That won't be a problem. I saw somewhere to rent snorkeling gear when I was searching for spots for us to stay at earlier." - Patrick

We drove about two more miles until we found our next home, *Hostel De Fronteras,* sitting on the right next to a bike shop and a driveway which led to a small home barely visible through some lush foliage. The hostels property was lined by a tall wooden gate with palm trees at each corner and jungle growth hanging down over along each wall. I parked the car and walked towards the front door where I found a doorbell with instructions for those arriving late. After reading I buzzed the desk until a body started moving its way through the courtyard in our direction. When the gate opened a rather bronzed man with dreadlocks to his waist waived us in and explained we could keep our car there for the night. The driveway cut down the center of the entrance and two both sides a row of cotton hammocks lined the edges with exotic plants growing throughout an otherwise open acre in front of the actual hostel. Which of course was made up from the two house-sized structures facing the road. Each with open air living quarters and room for four next to a kitchen which connected the two houses on the bottom floor. Beyond the entrance to the kitchen was a stone path to the outdoor bathroom and shower. It was somewhat of an outhouse by definition, but to call it an outhouse seemed somewhat insulting given the quality. The floors were covered in smooth pebbles and a tall stone wall extended to the ceiling where a three paned border of opaque glass let in natural light while still providing privacy to a very spacious set of twin shower heads. After taking our names he directed us to our room and informed us the upstairs had been rented out by a family of Spaniards who were prone to early mornings of loud music. Which he said didn't make a difference because it was likely that we would be woken up by the local howler monkeys before anything else.

Once we got our room together I left and went to get myself a shower as the others walked towards the fence and exited the gate. Just like the showers before, this one was cold. Mild by most standards, but colder as a result of a light breeze making its way through cracks along the edge of the stone. When I finished up I found everyone had left and assumedly gone to explore the beach. Underneath the calming rotation of a loose fan I sat and thought about taking myself down to the water in-order to say I had stepped in both the Atlantic and Pacific in the same day, but instead decided to take advantage of a rare peace and quiet to try and fall asleep unnoticed in a hammock out front before everyone got back. As I did that I remembered being struck by the deafening silence my first time visiting a place like this. And as I closed my eyes I fell under the spell of a light breeze cutting through the palm trees swaying above me as that same remembered silence drowned out any thoughts passing through my mind or the world around me. Though this relaxation would only last for so long before a late night nuzzle from the local dog jerked me awake and led me back into a room filled with sleeping friends and wet bathing suits.

233

Day 12: The Falls of BriBri
Puerto Viejo, Costa Rica

He wasn't lying. Somewhere just before sunrise the branches and everything above us started shaking and loud howls started coming down as the local howler monkeys began their day in a rather noisy manner. Those noises continued on long enough to take away any choice we had on whether to stay in bed or not. And that decision became easier once the family of Spaniards caught up to their natural time-zone and started moving around without concern of the idle bodies below. As the bed next to me began to move Renata kicked off her covers and turned over in my direction.

"Wanna go for a morning swim?" - Renata

"I'll walk with ya to the beach. We'll see about the swimming when I see the water." - Patrick

Wes had now sat up and was wiping his face while glaring at his phone.

"Wes, you coming with us?" - Patrick

"Nah man. I'm gonna take the morning to myself. I gotta send a few emails for work. We'll go on a walk later." - Wes

"Sounds good." - Patrick

From there I went to the kitchen and poured myself a glass of water. I hadn't been told anything specific about the sanitation here so I held up the glass a moment and examined the clarity as Renata joined me with her swimsuit and beach bag.

"You ready?" - Renata

"Yeah. Just checking something."

As we left and closed the gate we noticed a small dog making its way through a hole at the far end of the fence. When he had squeezed himself under he shook off a blanket of dust and came strutting towards Renata.

"You think he belongs at the hostel?" - Renata

"He probably belongs to a few." - Patrick

"Do you mind if he comes with us?"

"He doesn't look concerned with how I feel about it either way."

Across the street was an opening in the trees which had a trail leading down to the ocean. Both sides were lined with short palms blending into a forest of mangroves a few yards beyond the tree line. About halfway down the trail was a house set back into the brush with a patio and a screened in porch; one of the few I had seen in my time down here. On the porch a dog was stretched across a white throw rug which blended nicely with his thick fur. The dog stuck out to me as one of the few dogs in the area that had a groomed appearance. If not groomed at least not allowed to roll in the sand. Which was good because his fur looked like hell to deal with. He remained unresponsive to our presence as we passed by and made it to the end of the trail.

Entering the beach I stepped over a few twigs and a line of debris left behind by the early morning tide still retreating to the warm Caribbean seas. When I took my first step onto the beach I crouched down and took my time to peer at a tiny crab until my moment was interrupted by our stray dog who was now at my right side. I put my hand behind his neck and started to scratch just below his right ear as he leaned into me and left a patch of wet sand attached to my shorts and the upper half of my shins. Stupid dog had it so good down there. I wonder if Maslow's hierarchy of needs even applied to something which has reached levels so high as to be nourished by strangers while cushioned by the softest of sands in the Northern hemisphere. As he left my side I walked around for a while throwing some deadwood for my new friend to fetch as Renata trailed behind with a lazy stroll through some crashing waters. Our tagalong was surprisingly obedient with returning anything I threw considering he had no trainable past. This continued until I found myself facing a palm tree which extended outward at a favorable enough slope for me to consider climbing. I had never been discouraged from climbing trees as a kid and this trait had managed to follow me into my adult life. Only these days I tended to take a second look to make sure not too many people are watching before I start climbing. With my first few steps I edged out until I was over the water washing up on the sand below. I wanted to go out a bit further, but it looked like this part of the tree had been receiving water for so long that there wasn't a chance I could find some footing any further. When I got down Renata waived me over to look at some seashells she had found.

"I'm gonna take a few of these home to my girls."

"You think you'll ever bring them down here to show them life?"

"Yeah. But they needs a few more years before I bother with that."

"Have they been on a plane before?"

"No. But we did a few days on a train through Canada and they were fine, so I know they can handle sitting still."

"Good for them. I'm still working on that skill myself."

"I say you're doing pretty well these days."

"Eh. Only time will tell. I'd be lying if I said I wasn't getting antsy. This whole thing makes me miss being down here."

"You just need to start using your time off and getting away once in a while. You were in the tropics for so long. It probably feels weird being home. I felt weird and I only did two years."

"Yeah maybe."

When we got back to the hostel Myles and Wes approached me with their decision to ride into Puerto Viejo to check out a few markets before going onto some waterfalls they had read about.

"You guys know how to get there?" - Patrick

"Yeah man. He gave us some road names." - Myles

"How far is it?"

"It ain't far. Said we can be there in bout an hour."

If I was driving I wanted to get more details than the name of the last turn, but after talking with him it seemed that our friends sense of direction was a bit foggy, much like his brain. So we stopped along the way at a surf shop, but no one seemed to be able to give us perfect directions. This was actually something of a good sign because it was likely that it would be somewhere generally free of tourists if I was having this much trouble figuring out how to get there, but I still needed to know where to turn.

We arrived in town and found a parking spot next to a row of palm trees. When I got out they had all gone in their own directions and I stood there starring at the water looking at the same white and blue fishing boat bobbing in the clouded waters as I had used as a landmark years before. Behind me the streets had been overrun by drunken frat boys changing the vibe of the streets and local dive bars. I had spoken so many times to people about the greatness of this once hidden gem. I hate to think I had been even a small ripple in alerting the outside world of this location to the point of its detriment. Because now those ripples of conversation had reached into the minds of many, some of which had made their way down here tonight, and many others who had left their mark long before me.

Eventually I managed to get a few more road names and the name of the falls, Bribri. Which was also the name of one of the major indigenous tribes still inhabiting reservations in the nearby jungle. When everyone was ready to leave we used an outline of directions collected from three groups of people I spoke with in the town. All I understood was that I was going to be taking a sharp left at some point after getting out of town and from there I needed to pass a tiny blue house and take a right into the woods. Great. Logic not withstanding I followed the guidelines to our destination and made our way out of Puerto Viejo until a series of gravel roads led us to a small sign for Bribri falls. As we drove down the final road we came to a point where a small stream had flooded over and at their encouragement I hit the gas and went through. But a couple hundred yards later we came across a second crossing where the water was more than waist high and moving a bit faster.

I decided not to take the chance and we pulled to the side as I told the guys I would stay to keep an eye on the rental if they wanted to continue by foot. Not that I didn't want to go, but I was a little edgy about leaving the car alone in the middle of a jungle. Plus I knew I wasn't likely to get full use out of the falls. I mean, I'll jump from a cliff into the ocean, but a cloudy river filled with rocks, no thank you. The group agreed with my proposition and took a bag with them as they crossed the stream. As they continued forward I walked down to the river where I found myself treading through ankle-deep water to get to a rock overlooking a small set of rapids. While I was crouching down I heard the sounds of a small group coming down the trail behind our vehicle. One-by-one a line of kids made their way out from the trail and passed the car. I had grown to have much faith in children, but two of them looked around and pulled at the door handles as they passed by. Opportunists, but not quite thieves. Luckily they had opted out of the opportunity to just mug the shoeless guy standing on the rocks. Which they could have done with great ease as eleven was an admittedly high enough number of eleven year olds to combat me from this vantage point.

Soon enough I found myself bored with the inability to wonder beyond sight of the vehicle and decided to return to it in order to organize the trunk and attempt to cultivate some sense out of the potluck style packing which had taken place. After organizing the trunk I sat with my feet dangling off the back of the rental and closed my eyes for an unknown amount of time. My best guess is two minutes. I was only brought back from my daze when I started to hear a group of people from across the street. As I opened may eyes and turn around I was greeted by the sight of my friends walking towards me. All still dripping wet and with no hope of drying in the humid air. As I remained on the trunk the guys walked passed me and Renata opened the passenger door to get inside.

"Where you going?" - Patrick

"I wanna see something." - Myles

As I got in and turned the car around the guys continued down the road and drifted to the ditches on the right hand side once they had made it about a hundred feet. That detour took them down to a row of thick trees about 8 feet high with dark green leaves projecting upwards, each exposing a cluster of bananas on their underbelly.

"What are they doing?" - Renata

"I think I know." - Patrick

I put the car in park and got out as Wes started to yell in my direction.

"Patrick! Bring my shoes! I'm gonna try and hit these bananas down." - Wes

I opened the trunk and grabbed a shoe from the newly organized stack of clothes and tossed it to Wes. He caught the shoe and pulled his arm back like a football and launched it at the tree. To our mutual dismay the shoe merely bounced off the bananas, causing them to shake briefly, but making no bountiful impact. The next series of sticks and small rocks faced the same sort of failure.

"Patrick, come here. Maybe we can bend it enough to reach." - Myles

I walked over and planted my back against the tree and attempted to push my weight against it while using my feet to anchor me in, but the harder I pushed the further my feet sank and slid away from my position. As this showed to be the same result for all of us the guys gave up and started to spread out in search for any bigger sticks or rocks that could be thrown in a last attempt.

"Dude. Gimme that rock." - Myles

"No man I got it." - Wes

"Make sure to aim for the stem."

"I told you I got it."

"Alright man. I just wanna get these fucking bananas."

As Wes launched the rock he nailed a shot breaking a small bunch from their grasp on the underpart of the branch. We ran to the fallen bananas and grabbed a few before heading back to car. On our way back I noticed my hands had some sort of irritation on them from the prickly side of the branches which I had been bracing myself against while trying to push down mother nature.

"Times like this I'm glad I only have girls." - Renata

Once the guys dried off we got in the car and made our way out back to the main road along the shore. When we got into Puerto Viejo Wes nudged me from the passenger seat.

"Can we stop here real quick? I need some food." - Wes

"You don't wanna cook tonight?" - Patrick

"Nah man. I don't have the energy for all of that. That waterfall kicked my ass." - Wes

"Well that's what happens when you belly flop from twenty feet high." - Renata

I pulled off and parked in front of a bar at the center of town where the crowd had finally died down and the streets were for once less scattered with the presence of people. As we got out of the car Renata noticed a sign posted on the corner that caused her to look back at me with some excitement, "Patrick! Look at that sign!"

Salsa Lessons, 8 P.M.

Followed by Salsa Dancing 9 P.M.

Club Limón

"Would you guys wanna go?" - Renata

"Yeah I'm down. I can't speak for them, but they're probably down to come along too." - Patrick

"Okay great. Can you give me a few minutes then. I need to see if I can find a dress for tonight."

"Alright. I'll go grab some food until you're done."

When she ran off I walked across the street and grabbed a kabob from somewhere I thought I remembered as having been a grocery store years before, but the inside was nothing like before. I had been in so many small towns sometimes made me wonder how much my mind played tricks on me and how much I was just plain wrong. The thing I had no doubt about with regards to my memory was how diverse the people here looked. They were such a neat blend of each type of skin that had come through the Caribbean over the last few hundred years or so.

The center of town had more artists and vendors selling their crafts than I recalled from years ago, and while I hated the crowds this one thing was a welcomed consequence of an un-welcomed circumstance. I perused a bit and debated grabbing a few things I saw, but I already had enough unpacked trinkets to deal with in a storage bin back home. Once leaving the row of vendors I crossed back to our car and waited with my kabob which slowly disappeared as the minutes passed and my friends explored the ins and outs of tiny shops scattered along the streets. Once they were all satiated or supplied we loaded back up and headed to the hostel with a photo of the itinerary for our night of dancing.

"I'm so excited. Look at this dress." - Renata

"I better come with some pockets. I'm not carrying your purse tonight." - Patrick

"Okay loser. I'll leave it in the car. You guys wanna come?" - Renata

"Yeah I'll come." - Myles

"What about you Wes?" - Renata

"I'm always about some dancing. Pat I'm done with this empanada, you want the rest of it?" - Wes

"Nah I'm good man." - Patrick

We got back to the hostel and I spent some time in the hammocks swaying with the forces of a steady breeze while the others went and occupied themselves for a while. I couldn't have been happier to just stay there for the rest of the night, but I still had one more thing to do. You see, learning to dance had been almost as good of an investment as learning Spanish. And this time I had the rare opportunity to not be the slowest dancer in the group. Which was way better than all of the other times before when I was with some girl holding herself back from moving as fast as she could while trying to avoid the dangerous steps of the amateur stomping in front of her. I wasn't an expert by now by any means, but I would at least be the best among this bunch. While I sat their waiting to leave I noticed Wes walk by holding his stomach. Then when it came time for us to go I noticed he was looking pretty pale in the face so I suggested that he stay, but despite my thoughts he urged me to not worry and got with us into the car. As we pulled out Renata put on some salsa music and Myles started dancing in the backset knocking into Wes with every few beats.

"What's wrong Wes? Why ain't you dancing? Come on' Pat turn up the music!" - Myles

"Dude. Just let me chill while we're driving." - Wes

In town we found a parking spot along the line of palm trees separating the street from the beach just a few moments away from the club. When we parked Myles opened the trunk and used the flat trunk space to rest his bottles while he mixed a few drinks. While we pregamed around the car we heard the salsa band introducing themselves to a crowd growing around the bar.

"You guys gonna go for a lesson?" - Patrick

"I'm not gonna be dancing on no stage bro." - Myles

"Someone needs to do a lesson with me. I want to get some practice before we get on the stage. Come on, at least come with me to meet some people." - Renata

It was just then that Wes leaned over and started puking in the sand.

"Only took a few beers to get it out of him. Better now?" - Myles

Wes responded with a series of moans before staggering about a bit and returning to sit on the bed of the open trunk.

"Well fuck." - Patrick

"You wanna drive him back? I can stay and keep an eye on your friend." - Myles

"I can go with you if you want." - Renata

"Nah. Go get started. I won't be long." - Patrick

When Myles and I went up to Wes he was still crouched over the sand trying to catch his breath and fortunately he only resisted our urging once before allowing us to move him into the front seat.

"What did you eat?" - Patrick

"It was those fucking empanadas." - Wes

"Maybe it was all that river water you swallowed. You took in bout a gallon per bellyflop." - Myles

"Maybe." - Wes

"Myles. I'll be back soon." - Patrick

"Renata come on. We gonna find you someone to dance with. Where's the instructor at?" - Myles

"You better keep an eye on her." - Patrick

"Shut up!" - Renata

"Huh?" - Myles

"Nothing. You guys have fun. Be back shortly. Don't lose each other." - Patrick

I closed the door and continued along the road as it ran parallel to the beach and curled me back to the beginning of the town. Wes moved his hand across the dash and sort of hit my forearm uttering something to me before passing out.

"Sorry man." - Wes

The pain in his voice was one I could relate to and I felt especially bad because of all the nights to be sick, this was the worst. Wes was one of the few people I've known to like dancing as much as a normal human being likes sleeping. When I got us back I helped him to the room and left him with the fan on and a bottle of water by his side. Although I gotta admit I didn't actually check to make sure it wasn't sink water. Once he was settled I got myself back in the car and returned to town where I found my old parking spot still open and hugged it up once again against the sand. As I approached the bar I heard a familiar song fading in the background and remembered a day when this music intimidated me as much as being in the front row at a strip club. When I walked inside I spotted Renata and Myles standing off by the bar talking to a few people. They both had smiles on their faces and drinks in their hands. As I approached them Myles threw his hands up trying to give a hug.

"Get our boy home?" - Myles

"Yeah. He's good. Why aren't you all dancing?"

"I ain't gonna do that dancing stuff in front of everybody."

I looked over at Renata and saw the bubbly smile of a girl a few drinks in.

"Well, you ready?" - Patrick

"Wait. Lemme finish this first."

"Give it to Myles. Let him hold it. We gotta make it before this song is over."

"Why what song is it?"

"*Suavemente.*"

"That doesn't tell me anything."

"Now you're the impossible one. It's an Elvis Crespo song. Come on. We've already missed enough good music."

With the last sip of her drink finished I pulled at her hand and led us onto the dance floor where twenty or so couples moved about in a scattered unison only really appreciated from a sky view. All around us brightly colored skirts and glistening high heels moved smoothly with partners often dressed in half-opened button down shirts. Glowing colors matched glowing cheeks and the vibrance of the room soon spread into my soul, reminding me of all I had loved about salsa in the first place. After a song or two we found our own rhythm and eventually made our way to a spot away from the speakers more towards the front of the stage where our attempts became the center attraction for those sitting at the bar tables scattered in front of us. There we fumbled through the motions of a few songs as the DJ went back and forth between salsa and bachata, each time causing me to take a few false steps before regaining rhythm. And although we seemed to move well together we were still no match for the couples parading around us, many of which had clearly been dancing since the days before I was still barefoot by nature and not by choice.

"Can we move? I hate being in front of everyone." - Renata

"Well you're dancing with the wrong person to solve that problem. How was it while I was away? Find any cute instructors I should watch out for?"

With that comment she squeezed my hand and gave me a glare that I had become accustomed to over the years. Unlike her I had always felt pretty comfortable on a stage. And that ease had led many to encourage a career in front of a court or classroom fairly early in life.

"I'm not gonna tell you anything I do anymore."

"Calm down. I'll get tired of pickin' on you soon enough."

"I hope so."

"I will. Now loosen up. This isn't how you dance. Do you even pay attention in class?"

"I'm trying to! This dress is too tight. I can't take wide steps."

"You didn't try it on first did you?"

"No. I didn't think I needed to. It's a small. I'm a small."

We continued on for a few more songs and once we were done we went outside where we found Myles lounging on a bench finishing a tall glass of beer as he looked up at the moon. It was still as bright as nights before and one glance up was enough to trap you for a moment. A moment that dragged on long enough for me to see he was being a bit pensive about something.

"Enjoying it out here?" - Patrick

"Loving it. You all done already?" - Myles

"We're ready to go if you are."

When we got back they both went to sleep while I sidestepped and took a walk along the beach. As I paced along the sand I found the calmest setting I had been a part of in quite some time. With only the sound of the ocean crashing up on my feet I stood and took in the sensation of cool sand on my toes and a humidity filled breeze on my face. A deep sigh of relief came through me as I remembered the night I had landed on the shore a few miles up only years ago. Reflecting back on who and where I was then I must say that not much had changed in the duration. My uncertainty then was no higher than it was in this particular now. The only difference was that back then I didn't realize it. Soon enough I saw I was at the risk of falling asleep if I sat down so I got up and made my way back up to the hostel. As I walked through the gate I saw Myles asleep in a hammock along the fence. With a breeze too strong too worry about mosquitos I piggybacked his idea and climbed into a hammock a few spots down. I was used to the inconsistency, but it felt weird not having slept in the same place more than two nights since we arrived. That was perhaps a misconception my friends had about me when I was away. They may have seen photos of me on the go or out doing this and that, but they had no idea how simple most days were comparative to just these few hours. I certainly never camped out and ran around from one spot to another like this for two weeks at a time. I usually did some no more than a three day trip here or there when the chance came up. Beyond that the only part that was still the same was how I lived out of my bag no matter what time I was in. Anyone who saw me on a regular basis could have told you that. I always kept it with me and eventually the items inside the bag evolved beyond needing a place on the shelves of my home. And of course that habit had carried over with the purchasing of a car upon my return. Now that I had a trunk I was practically void of the need for an apartment beyond the formalities of a bed. The last few months I think I've spent more time in my front seat than on my couch. The only limiting factor had been the lack of a nearby backroad to cruise. A need that this trip had thus far gone above and beyond at solving.

Day 13: Off the Trail
Manzanillo, Costa Rica

There was an unexpected silence in the air this morning as I awoke to a swaying caused by a warm breeze cutting across the property. This silence continued until I got up and made my way into the bathroom where I heard another set of sounds. Standing there from the other side of the stone wall came the sprinkling of water and the low humming of a Red Hot Chili Peppers song, I think it was *By The Way*. Anyway that song told me I at least wasn't losing my privacy to a stranger.

"Wes?" - Patrick

"Yessir." - Wes

"How you feeling?"

"Much better. Thanks."

"No worries. Next time stay home."

"Well hopefully I'm done gettin sick down here."

"I hope so. Watch what you eat today."

"I'm not gonna eat. I need to give my body a break."

"Good thinking...Dude, I'm sorry I left you, but I couldn't leave Myles in that town without you there. And I really needed some space."

"I don't know why I had to stay behind. Myles was the one being an asshole. I was just trying to get away for the day too."

"Wes. You completely fucked me. He never woulda known who that girl was if it weren't for you. He probably woulda said a few things and moved on if he hadn't known who she was."

He was quiet and all I heard was the sound of the shower until he let out a brief sigh.

"I'm sorry dude. I don't know what to tell ya. I was drunk as hell. I barely remember anything after we got to the hostel."

There was silence for a moment while I brushed my teeth before Wes chimed in again to tell me he had made up for being sick last night by being productive this morning.

"I finally sent my resume to a few parks out West. Hoping to get something started by summer."

"Hell yeah man."

"Yeah dude. I also noticed I'm spending dumb money at home. I've spent like no money since I been here and it's gonna be the same when I go out west, especially if I'm working in the woods all day. What I'm saying is I guess I don't need to work anywhere else this summer if I can get on at the parks. I've already got all the equipment I need, it's really just making sure I got the money for my bills while I'm gone. I'm sure I could sublease my apartment or something."

"Hell yeah. Makes sense. So where all did you send your resume to?"

"I sent two out to these parks in Montana. If I don't get one of those I'm gonna try one over in West Virginia and just go back and forth between the two jobs for a while. I know a guy that works there. He can at least get my application looked at."

"Glad to hear it."

"Yeah man. The time is passing, might as well get some things running in the background."

"Good deal man. Glad to hear that. Gonna tell Myles soon?"

"Yeah. But I don't wanna make it an issue until things comes through."

"I feel that. You'll have to keep me updated when we get back home. Love to know what comes your way."

As my visit came to a natural end we wrapped up and I made my way out and to the bar where I saw Renata looking into her phone. As I approached she lifted her head and started with a request.

"I'm hungry. Are you making anything for lunch?"

"What do you have I can work with?"

"I don't know. I left our stuff in the fridge."

I searched the kitchen and found that the majority of our food had disappeared, which was pretty odd from my experience in hostels. All together we only had half a bottle of water, olive oil, lettuce, carrots, salt, and some chicken. I held up a head of lettuce and looked over at Renata who was still sitting with her face locked on the screen.

"We don't have anything else?" - Patrick

As I stood there waiting for a response I became frustrated with her focus on a seemingly blank screen.

"What are you doing?" - Patrick

"'I'm waiting."

"For what?"

"For them to take me off hold."

"So I'm being ignored by someone who's being ignored by someone else from over a thousand miles away? This is fucked. Phones are fucked."

"Well it's my daughter and she's not ignoring me. She went to find my mom."

"Shouldn't they know vacation means you get to be left alone?"

"For someone who's been around kids so much you sure don't get them."

"That's because I didn't have to deal with them outside of a classroom."

While we were standing around talking Myles had done his own exploring and approached me with a new plan for our day.

"Guys pack up. I checked us in at a spot up the road where we can sleep in hammocks by the beach."

"What's it called?"

"Rocking Jay's. You heard of it?"

"I think so. It's like mainly hammocks and outside sleeping right? A little hippy looking?"

"I'd say that's about right. Get your shit ready. I got them holding us a few spots."

We packed up our stuff and had an awkward goodbye with the hostel caretaker who could not quite understand why we were departing to head elsewhere in town. But nonetheless he offered to help us with anything else if we needed before our trip was up. That's something I had always loved about the people down here. It was just like back home where the people treated you like they've known you forever even if they just met you. A place where the people were helpful to strangers and where they took some pride in the places they cultivated.

When we arrived we pulled into an empty parking lot and left our car running while we walked towards the front gate. I had heard of Rocking Jay's when I was down here before. At the time it was known as a must stop for backpackers traveling through Limón, but until today I had not seen the place outside of a few travel blogs. And on those forums it had been known as a party spot which is why I had avoided it after departing Panama. As we entered the lobby I gathered we were in a place that allowed for all the noise we could make if we decided to. The whole area was open-air and fully exposed with the exception of a few dorms off to the left. The backyard had about four acres of beachfront land with an intricate mix of small rooms and large patches of cloth canopies hovering over rows of hammocks all spaced about shoulder length from one another. In the center of the hostel was a small building covered in yellow and red graffiti which contained the bathrooms and a spray painted inscription of all Beatles lyrics running along the stalls. Not an inch of the hostel walls went without some type of elaborate mural and the majority appeared to have been done years ago.

At the front desk I found out they had a few regular rooms available so I opted out of sleeping in the hammocks and got a room for the next two nights with Renata. I loved the idea of the hammock to rest in, but I still wanted the availability of a bed if I could have it this far into the trip. They had a full kitchen, but full service was only available during lunch and dinner hours so once we were all unloaded we decided to run into town for some food. In town we found an Italian coffee shop curled along an alleyway with a beautiful white facade and colorful flowers dangling from posts on both sides which led to the main entrance and a purple door.

"You wanna get some food?" - Renata

"I don't have a shirt with me."

"No one's gonna care. Just come with me."

As we entered I saw that while the store may have been advertised as Italian the food, much like the people, had an ambiguous Mediterranean look. The menu was not one of Italian design, but the menu seemed to cater towards the community of health food enthusiasts. After siting down we were greeted in a distinctly Italian by a lean man with sharp features and a shiny black ponytail holding back a head of wavy hair.

"Good afternoon my friends, what is it you guys are feeling like today? Or more importantly, how do you want to feel?"

"I don't feel like eating right now." - Wes

"Someone had a late night? That's why you must have our special tonic. It will heal you right up." - Waiter

"Well, I wanna feel full. I'll have the No. 3 and a smoothie." - Patrick

As I pointed at the menu indicating my choices he began to recite a list of cocktails which was soon lost in the ether as Renata leaned in to ask me about her selection.

"If I don't eat all of this will you help me?" - Renata

"Is that is that even a question?"

"Well you ordered a lot of food."

"I'll eat. This'll probably be my last meal til we get to San Jose."

I loved places like this. The warm air was coming through the open shutters and above all of the inserted noise was an ambiance of waves crashing along the coastline only a moments walk from the front door. As I sat there my awareness continued to gravitate towards the two strangers running the shop. They both had a similar look implying that perhaps they had come down here together, but they didn't seem like siblings, nor current lovers. But I couldn't help but notice the causal nature between them which usually comes from the familiarities of romance.

The sandwich I ordered came with some toasted plantains and each dish looked better than the next as they hit the table. After chewing my sandwich into non-existence I used my winning record from earlier as confidence to get up and ask the woman behind the counter what ingredients she used to make it. She was just as kind as the woman at the bakery, but this time I did not have to wait for a phone call to confirm methods. She politely offered so I handed her my notebook and she began to write a recipe which I later noticed was a blend of Italian and Spanish written in cursive, making it basically illegible. It may have to stay buried in my book until I find a translator of my own.

Eventually we finished up and left with plans to head towards another beach Myles had found while we finished our food. As we walked back to the car my companions were sidetracked by a few souvenir shops set up across the street. As they went in I waited around and within twenty-minutes they were done and we got in the car and drove until the road ended a few miles down the road in Playa Manzanillo, a national park which blends the two coastal borders of Costa Rica and Panama. As soon as we parked the car Myles got out and started to walk away, patting me on my arm with encouragement to join him.

"Come on man. Let's go for a walk." - Myles

"We just got here." - Patrick

"So? You got all afternoon. Besides we ain't gonna be far from the water. Just walk with me some."

"Guys you wanna come with us?" - Patrick

"Where are you going?" - Wes

"Up the beach I guess?" - Patrick

"No thanks man. I wanna take it easy today." - Wes

"Do you. Patrick you coming?" - Myles

Myles took my silence as confirmation and started walking towards a set of trails running along the beach and into the jungle. As I followed him we trekked across a mix of wet sand and thin roots as the jungle grew along a path of scattered plant life. The trail led down along the water for a few minutes until we were impeded by a fence which slanted towards the left as an attempt to direct hikers back towards the beach. If you took their guidance towards the beach it brought you to a view of a rock formation rising out of the water about thirty-five feet with a small ecosystem of trees and shrubs growing on an acre of rocky habitat. He paused when we reached the fence and looked around real quick before placing both feet over the top and continuing forward on a thing trail through the brush. As we moved down this trail took us to a large natural staircase composed of thick mossy roots and dead leaves. After ascending about thirty feet we came to an opening with a series of paths to choose from. The one went along down to the shore and the other two diverted us at an angle further into the jungle.

"Let's stay on the softer ground if we can." - Patrick

"What? Why?"

"Because I left my sandals in my room."

"Why the fuck did you do that?"

"Because I didn't know we were going on an expedition."

"You wanna go down by the water instead?"

"Nah. Too much coral down there. Let's stay behind the tree line."

"Aight man. Just follow me. We'll walk a few minutes until we find a beach hidden over here somewhere. There's too many inlets for there not to be a beach."

My first thought as we sunk deeper into the green was how much different this type of wilderness was from anything we had grown up with. The amount of variety boggled the mind. It felt like every ten yards there was an entirely different ecosystem with a bed of vibrant undergrowth all around. And with each step we came closer to the possibility that we could be walking on pieces of ground which may have not felt a human step in years, if at all. With my knowledge of Myles I knew that had to be within his mind as well. The potential to be the first person to see something truly new was beginning to distinguish itself as a novel concept with each continued year of our existence on this planet. I often wonder how long it will be before there are no more chances to do something or see something for the first time. We were from a land which was once limitless frontier. Albeit frontier to those who had forced their way beyond the shores of the previously settled and nearly forgotten. And all of our young lives we had waited for the moment we could step into the shoes of the explorers we revered even if only seen by the audiences hiding in our own minds. Continuing to move in a direction further and further from the coast I looked around and tried to gain some sort of point of reference for where we were and just how far from the beach we were moving. All around me thick brown tree trunks rose from the ground with clusters of giant roots sprawling across a mixture of mud and dead leaves which made for a soft floor to walk on. In my mind the environment around me was a real-life encapsulation of all the encyclopedias and books I had loved growing up. From a time when I would flip through pages filled with exotic creatures and concepts yearning for the day I could explore these things on my own. And here I was this time getting to enjoy these same things with a friend who I knew would appreciate them the same as I had.

"This is how the whole trip shoulda been." - Myles

Hearing that I looked down at my muddy feet and then back at him with some confusion.

"This is the type of trip you wanted?"

"Why do you think I brought the hammocks?"

"To chill at the beach?"

"No dude, we were gonna take them camping out here."

"You thought that would be all we would need?"

"Yeah man. I've thought about doing something like this since I was a kid. Doesn't take much to rough it."

"We've done plenty of roughing it."

"What's the matter patty? You still mad them army men searched you up and down?"

"Fuck you dude."

"I'm just playing. What you think all that was about?"

"Who knows man. Guess we fit the description."

"Whatever. Someone tipped them off. Bet it was that skinny fuck we took to get us weed. Can't trust no one."

"You think someone had to tip them off? We weren't obvious enough?"

"No bro. You're just paranoid. That's half the problem."

"So what, are you completely mad about how this trip went?"

"No. I'm still glad I came. This jungle is badass. Why you asking? You made you came?"

"Well, I didn't know I was signing up to be a full time punching bag, but I'm glad I came."

"Well you ain't the only one who had your trip messed up."

As we turned a corner we came upon a bush filled with bright purple flowers and a set of blue butterflies fleeing a bed of ferns along our path. The colors pulled at Myles' attention and he pulled for a favor.

"You got your notebook with you? I wanna take this flower back for my mom. Lemme put it in the crease."

I handed him my notebook and he placed a tiny pink orchid in between the cover and the first page. As he squeezed the book lightly he extended it back in my direction. I returned the notebook to my back pocket and moved along the fern covered floor until I noticed a patch of grey and orange-tinged fur moving deliberately through a set of vines to my left. As I looked closer I saw it was the famous three-toed sloth. His dirty grey fur made him easy to spot and unpleasant to stare at. Myles walked underneath it and stood there for a few moments observing his every motion. It was this side of him that I had missed. It took a certain type of person to be able to stop and pause without concern for any annoyance at their delay. Because you knew if they were stopping it had to be something interesting. It was just a great relief to be with someone else who ran with their curiosities. It's kind of all I ever really wanted from my friends. We might have had as big of a communication issue as me and any girlfriend ever did, but Myles shared the same adventurous way of exploring the world as I did. I could complain about him or how much I wish he would just behave, but I still missed the guy. I only wish he'd come along like this before.

"I am glad I came. I forgot how much fun you can be when you wanna be." - Patrick

"Yeah. I'm a pretty decent time."

"Except when you're annoying the fuck out of me."

"Annoy you? Is that why you can't go two seconds without looking for someone new to leave us for?"

"I'm sorry. You're right. I'll stop being friendly. And just be like everyone else and piss off everyone we meet along the way."

"What are you talking about? I made so many friends on this trip. That woman at the bakery loved me."

"Oh yeah. Morning Myles is always loved. I just wish you knew how to be subtle sometimes. Cuz when you are everyone loves you."

"Whatever. You never cared how I acted when we were younger. I was always the life of the party. That's why everyone kept us around."

"False."

"Fuck you. We used to do this type of shit every weekend."

I couldn't deny how right he was. I had enjoyed having him as a friend because he always managed to facilitate a good time. And he was the best guy to take with you to a new town. People loved him. But at the same time there had been too many times that could have been fun, but instead turned into a headache. A night where a switch had turned and the better side him had taken a back seat to an ego filled with whiskey.

"Yeah. Which is why I ended up having to usually go the next time by myself. Why can't you just turn it down a notch sometimes?"

"I'm not hurtin' nobody."

"Don't pull that shit. You know some stranger couldn't get away doing the type of stuff we're doing back in our town."

"Who cares? I ain't gonna see these people again."

"It's not about that. You're fucking over the next group that's gonna encounter these people by leaving a bad impression now."

"You're overthinking this."

Maybe in his eyes I was, but based off of my memory, I wasn't. Or maybe it just wasn't how I traveled. Most of my past was filled with traveling to some small town to be met by the friend or family member of a contact I met while teaching. Which led me to erring on the side of caution more often that not. At least long enough to find out if my new friends were cool with mischief.

"No. The next time she sees another idiot that looks like you they won't have a chance. And it'll be because of you. Do you get that? If you're traveling you need to adjust to the area you're in, it's like a date, bring your best version."

"Well dude, maybe I wouldn't have to make my own fun if you didn't have us running all over the place for some girl trying to make your own date."

"Are you still on that?"

"Yeah dude. You took my vacation and turned it into a treasure hunt for some girl. Don't act like you didn't plan on us meeting her. I'm not that fuckin' stupid."

"I already told you, I had no idea she was going to be there. Believe me or don't believe me, I don't care. But I'm telling you, It was as random as that stupid volcano that got us here in the first place."

"Whatever man. I'm not mad at you for it. I just wish you would spend your time doing something more useful than chasing women and talking to strangers that you're never gonna see again. I can't believe you been up in D.C. all this time and you ain't come down to say *HI*."

"Well if you really wanted to spend so much time with me then why did you invite two other people? I woulda kept this one on one if you would have. Fuck dude. I was looking forward to a relaxing vacation with my best friend. I don't know how that got fucked up."

As my question went without response we continued walking and made our way to another area where the trees were separated by a fair amount of distance. In fact, they appeared to be either newly planted or underfed by the rains. Throughout this series of skinny trees was a giant ant colony which spread along the ground around us in every direction with small mounds creeping up on all sides to dump out the masses every few feet. As Myles continued walking I stayed behind and crouched down to observe the mounds of dirt piled up around me. All of which were serving as grand entrances to the civilizations below. The world of ants had been featured in my imagination and play times since I was a kid. Back then I couldn't get enough of their underground worlds and I always wondered what part I was standing over. The ants stayed in such structured lines that I was not a bit concerned about any bites as long as I kept my foot in the same spot. I was actually far more concerned about the yellow jacket I saw scouting out one of the large mounds in the center of the colony. He was scoping things out and leaving his scent to be picked up later by the soldiers who would return to raid the colony and rob the ants of their seasonal harvest in a battle which the ants would surely lose. As I was crouched down I had not noticed Myles staring at me from a distance.

"I don't get something about you. Why didn't you ever find some way to do more than live your days on repeat in some hot classroom? You coulda used that camera and at least gotten yourself instagram famous down here. Instead you got a masters in vagabonding. If you were gonna do that I don't see why you didn't write about all of this in a travel blog or something. What good is all this experience if you don't do anything with it?"

"Is that what you want me to do? Is that what I should be doing? Would that be the thing to make you think I was finally doing something worth while? Just making a damn spectacle of myself?"

"It's not being a spectacle you dumb ass. You're seeing shit no one back home sees. Why wouldn't you share it with everybody?"

"Dude just stop. I know you want me to, but I don't regret my twenties. I'm not mad at what I did or didn't do. Get over that."

I knew he realized I did plenty more than live my days on repeat no matter where I was. But there was truth in every insult, and he was right, I hadn't really done my due diligence to see where it was I was going back then. Or why I was doing what. And for that much I had to claim responsibility. I said I had wanted to give myself free time, but it wasn't about controlling my free time. It was about owning it. And getting the most out of it I could. Even when I didn't know what I wanted to do with it.

"Hell the only reason I thought you'd be good at helping me make that movie was cuz of how much you liked that internship you got by accident." - Myles

"It wasn't by accident. I just didn't realize what I was applying to."

"Same thing man. Just lucky your professor didn't find out your internship on the hill was you editing tape for your Senators YouTube channel all semester. I don't know why you didn't try and capitalize on that man. You had everything at your fingertips back then if you had just used your fucking brain."

"You always were trying to live others peoples lives. Just now you've managed to keep your claws restricted only to Wes."

"I'm not doing anything to Wes."

"You're not doing him any favors by paying him so much. He told me about his commissions. Are you kidding me? That's gonna ruin him for anything after this."

"It's better than him throwing his life away to go play in the woods with some college fling. That's why we have friends. Sometimes we don't know what's best for us."

"Do you know how many times I've seen you go against *'what's best for you'* down here?"

"What are you talking about?"

"Nothing man. Never mind."

"No go ahead. Please tell me what you think I'm doing wrong."

"Okay. Fuck it. I will. But I'm only gonna say this because if I don't there's no one else around you that will."

"I'm waiting."

"Whatever you do that makes it possible for you to stay fucked up all the time like it's no big deal probably needs to calm down. I know you. You're a fucking wild man, and your tolerance looks ridiculous."

"What I'm doing down here ain't nothin hardcore. It's just a few bumps. We're on vacation man, loosen up."

"Maybe not to you. But in the mountains you just spent your night going back and forth doing blow with that Brit once I told you no. And it's basically been your morning coffee every day since we been here."

"I'm just letting off some steam man. You don't know what a serious life is like so don't start pointing fingers at me."

"Okay then what about at the airport?"

"What are you talking about?"

"In the bathroom. I fuckin know what I heard."

"I got my life under control bro. Worry about yourself."

"You got it under control? If an Indian chief gave you a new name it would be *He Who Stays Inside The Spirit World.*"

"Fuck you. You don't know what you're talking about."

"Look maybe I'm wrong, but if not, watch yourself. That type of shit always ends up being an issue for someone with as much money as you. Look man, you're my fucking friend. I'm worried about you getting a bad batch. I'm worried about you going off the deep end. Fuck. I'm worried about you ending up like Sebastian. I don't know why the fuck you can't see that. I'm worried now that you've had a taste of the real stuff, you won't be able to find anything good enough back home. And eventually that chase is gonna kill you. So make your life as you like, but stop trying to control everyone else until you've got your own shit in line."

"I'm not trying to control anyones life."

"What do you call what you're doing to Wes?"

"I'm just trying to help him like I tried to help you."

At that moment I got a little agitated at him. Which was odd because it was about something I had not been agitated at before. Although the same truth had always been there. I had never been mad that he didn't come along and I had never felt let down by any of the situation as it played out on his part. Nonetheless, as much as I couldn't stand my own regrets about the subject I did not need to hear the false hopes of someone who had watched the journey from the outside while I scrambled from one problem to a-fuckin-other.

"Help me?"

"Yeah. That whole thing never woulda happened if it weren't for me. And I would've given you whatever you needed to keep it going if you weren't such a little bitch."

"Go fuck yourself. I never would have done any of that if I would have known you were going to ditch me at the last minute."

"You keep talking like I didn't wanna be there. What was I supposed to do? I had to take my business seriously man."

"I'm not faulting you for looking out for yourself. I get it. Just shitty because I never woulda put myself in that spot if it weren't for you."

"And what spot is that Patrick? Tell me because I never really understood how someone takes you for *ALL* of your shit? Did you help them load it all up and walk it home for them? I thought you were more of a man than that. I gave you the key to some kind of future and you sent it back to me."

As I listened to the anger present in his voice I knew it was my fault. I hadn't been straight up with Myles, I had held a few things back, from him and the story I shared. But that's because when we were younger, we were always smart enough or fast enough to not get caught. But that was as a team. When I was alone I didn't have the same awareness or proper reaction time to get myself out of trouble.

"I'm sorry for painting the wrong picture for you."

"What picture? You never told me anything. What happened? Was it a bunch of little kids and you're embarrassed to tell me?"

"If it really matters to you, I didn't get away with any of your fucking money. I got stopped by the cops and they took all of my shit."

"You mean you bribed them with all of that equipment?"

"No. Bribing is what happens when you come out on top of an exchange. I tried to bribe them and they shook me down for everything I had."

"Why didn't you just tell them what you were doing?"

"Dude I fucking tried that. They didn't give a fuck. I was breaking and entering, filming a movie without permits, and at that point hauling around a bag of cocaine. There was no believing me that night."

"Why did you have it with you?"

"I forgot it was in the book bag."

"How"

"Dude, It doesn't smell. It's not like weed. You never forget you have weed. You can easily forget you have cocaine."

"NO bro. Nobody keeps cocaine long enough to forget they have it."

"Fair point."

"So why didn't you say anything?"

"I told you I knew what I was doing. And I don't know about you. But I don't know many people who like admitting when they don't. Though I still think it wasn't that. I think a gringo walking with a camera asking people where to find the drugs was kinda suspicious to someone. Anyways. When they grabbed me I had cocaine and way too much cash to ignore. And my Spanish was decent, but it wasn't good enough to explain my way out of those factors. The first set dumped my bag out and the others stood there and kept me up against the truck."

"Why were you walking around with all of that cash? What the fuck is wrong with you?"

"I couldn't leave it in the hostel."

"So they just took the shit and let you go?"

"No. I'm not sure if they would have let me go. I wasn't handcuffed so I took the first chance I had and started running til I found the hostel. Then I grabbed my other bag and went for the docks. Luckily it was nighttime so no one saw me."

"How did you get out of there with the police looking for you."

"I went back to the docks and found this guy I had interviewed on my first day and made a trade for his help."

"What kinda trade?"

"I traded that Go-Pro for him to get me off the island. From there he took me to Puerto Viejo and hooked me up with some people from Atlanta who let me crash in their spot up the shore."

"Why didn't you tell me about this before?"

"Is that a real question? You know I never woulda stopped hearing shit from you. And dude if the money is your issue, keep what you were gonna give me. We can settle up that way if you please."

"I'd rather have that video of you running from those cops when they grabbed ya. I don't know why you seem so surprised the police fucked with you. That's the risk you took going down there."

"Well if I woulda had a cameraman as charming as yourself maybe we coulda gotten an interview with them."

"Fuck that. I woulda fought em and got our shit back."

"I don't doubt it."

"Fuck. I wish we woulda gone to them islands. I need to see that shit. Bet you're glad that volcano fucked everything up and kept us from making it there."

"Dude. It's not like I didn't wanna go."

With a raised eyebrow he looked my way and forced a response on my end, "Okay, maybe I'm glad we didn't go down there. They have my fucking passport. I can't get caught on that island again."

"Dude. They're not gonna remember you."

"Maybe. Maybe not. I'm not trying to find out."

"Well if you didn't get the good stuff on tape then what did you get? Did you at least make a buy?"

"Did you pay that little attention to the tapes?"

"I never saw none of that dude."

"You didn't watch it?"

"It's not like I could open anything up with all those stupid fucking passwords."

"Dude all that was in the journal I sent you."

"I told you man. I was really busy back then. I didn't have time to look around no journals. I just saw that you didn't send the camera or nothing else back. So I didn't know what to figure. And then you never fuckin called me to talk about a damn thing."

"Yeah. I know."

"So what happened? Was it just that awful? I figured we got last place in that competition and move the fuck on right?"

"Nah man. I. I didn't even send that shit in."

"What?"

"You heard me. I never submitted the movie. It wasn't even finished and ready for that. I sent you all I had and that was that."

"Huh. Aight then. Too bad."

"That's it?"

"Well what do you want me to say? Sucks you didn't at least turn it in. Even the fuckin unfinished version is better than nothing."

As we moved on I kept trying to remember some of the younger paranoia which dictated the *could and couldn't's* of my youth. It wasn't really about the trouble per se. At the time I was still trapped by the stigma around artists and I wasn't particularly shining in any of the arts enough to be willing to admit I wanted to live an artistic life style. Nor did I really understand what all that would have entailed. Given our differences in certainty I still found myself surprised he had not at least been curious enough to figure out how to watch what I had sent him back then. Especially since he had clearly kept the issue on his mind. Regardless of how it had been brought up I was glad that we finally had some time alone beyond a short walk to the bakery. This hike was probably how the whole trip should have been, but once we added others the potential of the whole thing became less and less. Maybe if we had come alone something could have happened to help us live the experience we were supposed to have lived together years before. Instead we both brought others and avoided the opportunity. Still all I could think was what a shame it was that it took so long to see him again and so long to tell him how it had really gone. Because it wasn't going to be the end of anything once he knew. It was just a new set of understanding to work from. Though anything after would be the fault of my own biggest mistake. Or at least the one I would say most impacted my life in my twenties. That was my lack of communication. I didn't communicate the ways that I should with anyone around me. Which was odd because from some angles I was on a mission to try communicate with everyone I could. But in doing so I neglected some of the conversations where my words were needed most. As our current conversation took a backseat we approached a maze of muddy roots where Myles noticed a tiny red frog hidden amongst the fallen leaves. One with a vibrant red body meeting a set of blue legs that seemed to stop at the waist, a trait which led the locals to calling this the *'blue jean frog'*. He had no aversion to fear or any thoughts about wondering if the frog was poisonous he just picked it up from its back end and started to give it a look. Further down the trail we saw an opening created by the greedy root systems of four giant trees all soaring a hundred feet into the air. Each with a spread of leaves that combined forces with its neighbor to create a football field sized canopy in above us.

"Holy shit, check out that tree. I bet we can walk inside." - Myles

Putting the frog down he bolted towards the opening of a tree which was large enough to fit two grown men through had we wanted to try. As we got closer the entrance revealed a series of vines hanging from the center, all of which were thicker than most rope and tangled amongst each other in a manner which seemed incomprehensible considering there was no wind or outside element to cause their intertwining. Upon entering Myles ducked down and reached up to grab one of the vines enough to stabilize himself a few inches above the ground.

"Give ya fifty bucks to climb up it." - Myles

I glanced up and down the length of the vines unable to see where they connected at the top and exercised a mix of logic and self-interest to say no.

"That's all you buddy."

As he jerked on the vines my eyes followed them up the center of the tree where they all disappeared into a tangled darkness sure to hold all sorts of life I wanted nothing to do with. Exploring is more than just seeing new things, it's also knowing when to move on to the next thing. And with that thought we continued on as Myles guided us through a twisting sequence of trails made by man and animal through time and the pursuit of something more. In following him we came upon an opening which led to a few acres of grass where I we spotted three capybaras chewing on some leaves and doing their best to stay hidden in the moderately thick grass surrounding one of the few pieces of land void of tall growth. Their brown fur hid them well among the patches of mud and clumped together they could have been mistaken for an area of grass after receiving too much rain. They seemed so tiny to be out in the open like this, but who were we to speak? We were out of our element no matter how much we wanted to try and be a part of this environment. We had lost our ability to live within it when we turned our back on nature and crawled our way into cities and the comforts of civilization. Now we could only hope to touch that existence again with brief interactions through preserved lands and sanctioned parks. Provided that the sun wasn't down.

"Myles, shh, look over there."

We both crept down and got a better look at at them as they started running away. As I watched them running off I heard a tone of concern that I had not heard in a very long time. One which implied a need to stop in my tracks.

"Patrick Stop!"

"What?"

"Don't move."

I paused and looked ahead to where our path met with an opening in the trees which was being blocked by a large husky like dog with scraggly grey and black fur. At the sight my mind took me back to a run-in with a stray dog years before and the imprinted reminders on my left leg which always served to not let me forget what could come from another unpleasant encounter. I looked to my left and right to see how far away I was from anything that I could climb up if the moment called for it, but the closest trees were too far of a run to consider as an alternative to being attacked. Next my eyes began scanning the ground in hopes of finding some sort of rock or blunt object to keep at my side.

"Stay still man. I got my knife on me if shit goes down."

At that moment the dog stared back into shifting darkness as a man came into view and adjusted himself along his side. I was immediately relieved to see two legs standing before us, in my experience it was far better to encounter the dog of someone than the dog of no-one when you're in the middle of the nowhere. Though the man was no slouch to be discounted. He had an undeniable presence, half a foot taller than Myles or I with a broad build and a slight belly that looked as hard as the tree trunks around us. His shoulders supported a brown satchel, and thick hands rested at his sides, with the right one only a hands length away from a machete hanging at his waist. A machete which caught my attention more than most I had seen. It was as long as a sword, sharp, shiny and all of the things you hoped to see attached to a stranger in the wilderness. He appeared to be as unbothered by us as his dog so we started walking towards each other with a slight hesitation. As we approached a smell wafted from his satchel which told me it was filled with newly harvested marijuana. As I started the greeting process we both stood there flanking him as Myles placed his hand down at his hip where he held a knife at all times. I knew I was the closest in reach if something went wrong, but I knew I had nothing longterm to fear with Myles around. And while I did not wish to know this reality, I appreciated the fact that the advantage was on my side if the man were to pull his blade. As we had our standoff his dog reached in and started to lick my hand. As I held my hand still I tightened my body and he told me not to be afraid of the machete at his side. I decided that this time I would not start with an exchanging of names.

"What brings you two here?" - Jungle Man

"Just searching for a beach." - Patrick

"Plenty of beaches behind you."

"We were hoping to find somewhere more secluded."

From there he stood for a moment and looked off at the setting sun behind us.

"Sun be setting soon. Best you head back."

"We will after we find what we're looking for."

At the finality of my statement the man looked at me and started to pass by. Pausing as he got closer to Myles. From my point of view the standoff between the two men had a palpable tension. We were probably close to his harvesting area and I think he was curious of our intentions. Meanwhile all my buddy could see was the challenging presence of a stranger with a blade in an area where the reminders and enforcers of laws are not around to judge or halt an altercation. I could see in his eyes that he was not scared of either one of us individually, but he saw a difficult situation with the combination. But the true power in the situation was with Myles. The perception of your own power is as important as the reality of your own power because it determines the confidence you walk with. And in his mind there was no perception, only certainty. What kinda power must a man possess when he can trust in his ability of fight just as much as flight? I could only be glad that I was with him. Even though this was not a situation which needed handling. In what felt like an hour, but was surely only two or three seconds, the man nodded his head at Myles and walked on by.

As we distanced ourselves from our new friend we walked along the trail a few hundred yards until a series of shadows moving above us caused me to stop and observe a primate driven world taking place in the canopy above. Myles noticed my pause in my steps and stopped to look up at the canopy. Looking up he drew in a deep breath of air and let out a well trained sound which mimicked that of a boar charging. The monkeys above us peered their heads beyond the leaves and continued to pace above us unbothered by the strange acts of my friend. It would take more than a few noises to disturb them.

"Great. Now they'll think that's how we greet each others."

"Dude. We gotta get those guys to come down. Those boys are bigger than the ones we saw at the beach."

"No. What we need to do is find a spot to get down to the water and we need to do it soon."

"Come on man. You don't gotta be afraid of that guy back there."

"I know I don't. I'm not thinking about that. I'm just looking at how much fun this is gonna be when we don't have any light to help us. We've already been out here over an hour so I know we've got a good bit before we get back."

"You worry too much bro. We got plenty of time."

Not far off from the monkeys we came to a large break in the trees which led to a trail that broke down to the beach below. Coming down the path it appeared to have some purposely placed logs on the gradual descent, both of which seemed manmade.

"I wonder who put these here." - Myles

"No idea. Just keep your eye out. These steps are worn for a reason."

The path led to an opening where the ground was a mixture of sticks and sand dampened from the early morning tide. The inlet appeared to be clear and around thirty feet deep in some areas where there was no coral. As I walked near the water, I hesitated to get in, remembering I was wearing canvas shorts at the moment so I decided to use my boxers to get me through the next part of my journey. Over the next thirty minutes I swam around the cove and looked up occasionally to acknowledge the changing shades from the pending sunset on the horizons around us, but the water was so refreshing that I found it hard to contemplate leaving regardless of what shit we were gonna have to deal with once we did. Even though the water was fairly choppy up top, the view was clear and provided for some fun swimming where I was able to see some shells on the sea floor tumbling in the current. Eventually I swam out a bit to see what would happen if I went beyond the cove, but the further I got the less control I had over which way I was drifting. Knowing that this was not likely to get better I turned around and started swimming full force back to the shore.

As I swam back from the edge of the cove I noticed Myles walking along a tree which had been uprooted from behind the shoreline and now stretched out thirty feet or so and hovered about five feet above the water. On each side the branches stemmed out and continued to keep their green color. I watched from a distance as he used the branches to balance himself on the walk out towards the edge. If I've not emphasized it enough, it's important to realize with all that happens next that Myles is not and never has been as we used to say, *"a little bitch"*. Myles is a fucking man, by all primate definitions of the word. So when I heard him scream my head jarred up without any delay to see what was going on. When I wiped my eyes I saw him dancing between two branches while he looked to either side with a noticeable sense of urgency surging through this body. Swatting his head he jumped into the water from the right side and started to swim away with his body submerged the entire time. When he resurfaced I only heard one word.

"Hornets!" - Myles

As I read the panic in his movements I dove deeper and started swimming in the opposite direction until lack of air forced me back up. He swam closer to my direction and then cut towards the shore until he was a safe distance from the fallen tree. As he got out and started to hold his arm I continued to swim until I met the shore.

"Fuck dude." - Myles

"What happened?"

"I got attacked by hornets that's what happened."

"You okay?"

"I think so. Those mother fuckers were huge man."

This was one of the few times in life I had heard Myles with a hesitation in his voice coming from a slight concern for the self.

"Well you're not hyperventilating. You'll probably be fine."

"I wish I had some ice. This shit fucking stings."

"You wanna get going?"

"Not yet. I wanna try and swim passed the cove."

"I think we've pressed our luck enough today."

"Yeah maybe."

He lightly patted his head where he had been stung and started to shake his head a bit.

"That thing does look pretty fuckin swollen."

"Alright fuck it. Let's get going. I'll lead the way."

I knew I was likely to be more motivated to get us out of there quicker since I was the one doing this barefoot so I instead insisted on taking the lead. As we got going I wanted to be slower at first because I noticed he was constantly reaching back to touch where he had been stung. At one point he stopped to look at the welt on his arm and forced me to stop and wait on him. As I stood waiting in the center of the trail my feet started sinking into the mud. The canopy had become a secondary source of darkness in our already dim surroundings and the light was getting so faint that all details were being lost. As I looked to my sides I realized that with the increasing darkness I couldn't see any of the insects around me and soon enough I would not be able to notice a spiders web until I had already ran into it. I started to think back to younger days and I remembered a trick I had once seen and reached down for the mud around me and spread it lightly onto my legs. I covered myself from knee caps to toes with a combination of mud and grime from the forest floor. I then spread the leftovers to my elbows and the back of my arms. Standing there I heard the jungle coming alive all around us. Birds faded as the sounds of insects chirping and frogs calling out to their mate in the night took over my bubble. When Myles finally got moving again I started running at full speed down a path which seemed to get muddier with each step. I knew the moon would only peer through here and there so we needed to take full advantage each time it did. We continued on a bit further before I started to feel a dip in the terrain which seemed to be leading my feet into the beginnings of a marsh.

"Dude. What the fuck is this?" - Myles

"I don't know man."

"I think we walked too far. If you wouldn't have been running I woulda been able to pay attention to where we were going."

"This from the guy who lost his wallet in between grocery stores."

"Fuck you. Follow me. I'll get us out of here."

From there we continued to walk and eventually I paused as Myles stopped and looked off to his right where he saw a familiar opening in the brush.

"Here it is. This has gotta be it." - Myles

We walked into a break in the trees where the grass had been split by a path leading deep into the forest. As we entered I had no way of knowing for sure if we were going in the right direction or not. But the further we got the less confident I felt about the feeling of the ground beneath me. He thought we were in the same grassy area as when we first saw signs of life running across the jungle floor, but I knew by the feel of the ground beneath my feet that he was wrong. The composition of materials under my feet was simply not the same. As we walked along a bubble of silence moved around us and the local cricket population hushed as our presence drifted along the forest floor. Parts of my mind began to wonder if he had wanted this to happen all along. Perhaps tales of a night hike up a jungle river such as this one had inspired him to take experience into his own hands.

"Dude I can't wait to get home."

"You're joking right?"

"No man. I ready to get the fuck outta here. I miss my cat. Next time I'm gonna go down to a resort and relax by a pool instead. I wanted to maybe come down here and retire, but fuck all of that."

I had no cat to miss, but I understood missing something. For as unattached as I hoped to be, I had grown fond of having a car again. The convenience of my own cockpit was easy to get used to and by now I missed the option of riding solo. But I didn't think about going back home to it. For that matter I hadn't given much thought to returning to anything.

"Why didn't you do that this time?"

"I wanted to see what the big deal was about this place. But I don't get why you liked it down here so much. What was it?"

I didn't know how to answer him. I couldn't begin to encapsulate my feelings for this place in a short explanation. It had been so welcoming to me when I first came, but that was a time when the world viewed America with eyes of adornment. And I was the American. But most of all this place provided me with such a new set of experiences that I never found the need to return. As the darkness thickened my eyes started making an outline of the world around me. I could only hope for the use of sound to do the rest. I needed us to stop for a moment so I could try and listen for the ocean. As we did I was able to hear a distant humming of water rushing somewhere just over the canopy. All we needed to do was find the coast and from there we could always find our way back. As we cut through the brush we must have disturbed something because out of nowhere a cloud of darkness came flying in our direction. I stood still as I saw the mass moving closer and realized that I was about to be surrounded by a swarm of fucking bats. As I closed my eyes I felt a breeze of tiny wings zing by me with a precision that avoided my body so well that it felt like my entire silhouette was surrounded by an invisible forcefield. After darting around us the cloud shot up and disappeared into the canopy splitting off from its unitary shape. I opened my eyes and a few feet away I saw Myles with his shoulders clenched and wearing a bright smile on his face.

"Dude that was so fucking cool! I think one of them touched my beard!" - Myles

"Dude that was awesome. Aight come on. We gotta fucking go. I think we're close."

I started to walk further and tried moving a bit faster to try and make up some of the ground we had been missing out on, but of course that didn't last long.

"Yo! Slow the fuck down. I can't see you!"

I heard him yelling so I came to a halt and listened to hear how far away he was from me. Which turned out to be an instance of poor timing because I had managed to stop in the path of some ants making their way through the forest. And by now the mud had thinned out enough to allow the whole troop access to my ankles. A fact I was soon painfully aware of as they bit down on any piece of exposed skin they could find. This of course caused me to say fuck waiting for Myles as I stomped my feet and attempted to brush them off me while moving a few more feet down the trail where I soon felt sand creeping into the texture of the ground around me. From that point the sound of water continued to get louder and the abundance of roots faded as I made my way through a maze of mangroves and into ever dampening sand. He followed me along this route until we came to a row of palms trees which opened up to a broad view of the beach and gave us a distant peak of the entrance to the park. Upon the progress of a few more moments we finally saw the flickering of a street lamp which stood where we had parked our car. A sight seen just in time because about then my shoulders started to feel a sudden increase in the volume of raindrops which had begun pouring down around us. As we finally got within eyesight I saw our counterparts leaning against the car holding their towels above their heads hoping for our speed to out pace that of the worsening storm. A sight which should have caused haste, but instead we both slowed our pace and tried to catch our breaths with an ever lessening concern for the rain. After-all, we were plenty dirty and the brief shower provided more relief than it did annoyance. Knowing his personality and the propensity to do so, I tried to discourage Myles from bragging to our counterparts at what a great time we had for ourselves, but of course he disagreed.

"Fuck that dude. They bitched out because of a little mud and you did this whole thing barefoot. I'm telling them everything." - Myles

As expected we were not received with cheers and applause once we got back and neither of them pretended to be interested as Myles's started talking about all the cool shit we saw along the way. On the drive back I saw our gas light warning us that we had about fifteen miles left. Not a concern since we didn't have to be on the road again until morning, but still something I needed to remember. Once we got back I squeezed us into a parking spot and got out of the car to go down towards the shore where I saw a fire burning in the middle of a group of guests.

"Where are you going?" - Renata

"Down to the fire."

"You're not gonna wash off first?"

"I'll wash off in the water."

With a concerned look held between her cheeks and eyebrows she replied, "Please make sure you wash your feet before you get into bed with me."

"Gotcha."

I'm not sure she knew who she was dealing with. I had always been willing to get dirty if need be, but it was my well-kept nature which had kept my barefoot self from being labeled a hippy by the locals during my time abroad. That and an unwillingness to grow out my hair to any length which would draw attention. I made it beyond her concerns and to the fire where a crowd of people sat enjoying a pleasant breeze which carried the smell of roasted coconuts up the shoreline and onto the roadside. As I stood enjoying the clam Myles approached me with his arm on my shoulders.

"What's up bro? Fucking got that adrenaline running through me like lightning. How you doing?" - Myles

"Feelin the same man. Had a blast today."

"Me too man. I needed that. And look I was thinking, if you think it's worth your time I'll have my secretary send that hard-drive to ya."

"Dude don't fuck with me. I know you don't still have those. That was damn near ten years now."

"I'm a fucking pack rat. I'm sure they're around my office somewhere. Hell, maybe in storage. You still remember the passwords?"

"I'm sure everything is out of date. I would need to find out what the software is. I would need a week of repairing the leaning curve just to figure out what program I need…"

"That's not what I asked."

"Yeah. I could get it all opened. Just might take a few days."

"Alright. Then I'll get to lookin when I get home. Just send me whatever address it is you use these days."

"Okay man. Will do. Thanks"

"Not a problem. Ain't doing any good locked up in my office."

"True."

"Who knows. Maybe they're better than you remember. No deadline in trying I guess."

I stood there for a moment aware that I had let the project go not because I was done with it, but because I was so busy scrambling to find a solution to my immediate problem that I had no time to be concerned with what could have been next if things had gone differently. Which is somewhat forgivable considering the state of panic I was in, but for as much as I was thrown off my balance after everything went down I was also somewhat relieved by how everything had led me to do some more thinking about the future I was about to step into. The whole thing had not been the reason I decided to stay abroad longer, but it had led to reflection which resulted in the decision. And it wasn't whether this path was right or this path was wrong, it was more a recognition of where my mind had gone so soon before I was supposed to enter grad school. Once I had my degree in my hand. My thought wasn't what to do with it. It was where to go now that I had it on reserve. And that type of thought process had perhaps protected me from a future I was never truly meant to live. Instead of searching for apartments or buying books I had gone off onto what was supposed to be another short adventure assuming it would go smooth enough to fit seamlessly into my previously planned existence. Perhaps an eternal curse of my soul, but in this instance it had made me aware that I didn't have anything more than mild intrigue at the path I was set to take and a curiosity in whether or not I could do it, but no interest in genuinely pursuing its labors to an end. Something easily proven by the fact that I had instead gone through more hoops than ever and set everything up for a documentary I had no business making. Though I hate to call it a pipe-dream as there was once a time I looked at it as a viable option for my future. That's really what I had hoped for when we started, the possibility of the project opening doors where I never thought possible. Though as always I was jumping ahead of myself, both then and now. First I had to take the time to sit and watch everything we had on file. And even after that it would take more to complete anything.

Before I had been motivated by a combination of things. Some which were obvious, some which even evaded my own awareness. In many ways I had hoped for my first attempt to serve as a worthy debut, but this long after the best I could hope for was to have something completed. And this time I could only go forward if it were really something I wanted to do instead of something someone was pushing me to do. That's really what mattered. Was it something I would want to do, and if not, then what? I had bailed on two futures that day and I had done nothing to go back to either of them. And my lack of doing so showed me the priority either of them truly held in my life. Which is why teaching had sat so well with me for so long. Not the act of teaching, but the position of being abroad. Either way I fell under the spell of a new life as one must when they opt to change their reality. Though I can't help but wonder what type of reality I could have created for myself if I had taken on my new situation as the obstacle to be tackled as opposed to the defeat of my path. With that motivation on my horizon I would need to find a way to keep myself settled a few weeks or months, whatever it would take to get the work done if I decided to commit to taking it on.

As he walked way I moved along pacing up and down the shore with my feet ankle deep in the crashing waves until I noticed a crowd gathering by the bar at the end of a long pass. At first I paid no attention, but then I saw an individual at a microphone being set up in the middle of the tables. A sight which could prove as inviting under the right circumstances. However, upon walking up I discovered they were transforming the place into a karaoke bar for the evening. With a mixture of locals and hostel singers alike signing up for their turn. A discovery which I found rather unfortunate because when it comes to singing I prefer self-awareness over self-confidence every time. And just as I was about to return to the beach I heard Wes calling my name with a set of waving hands ushering me over to a shared table. As I got seated next to him a waiter approached us and delivered some food which he and the others had ordered while I was away. Burritos and sandwiches from what I remember. They ate their share, I got the leftovers of course. While glancing around I found my attention drawn to a young kid performing a song which sounded like early *Rage Against The Machine* translated into Dutch. With a rebellious nature to the lyrics that was unmistakable in comparability. I had always admired anyone who could control a microphone and use it as their tool. I had used my voice, and I understood the power of tongue. And as the music faded I looked around and saw Myles on his way from the darkness beyond the courtyard with a guitar hanging from a strap around his neck.

"Where did you find that?" - Patrick

"Next to the fire. You wanna get on the mic with me? I just gotta find an AUX chord to hook this thing up."

"No thanks."

When Myles walked over to the DJ booth he tried coercing the cord out of the DJ's hand and the next thing I knew we were listening to *Family Tradition*, a country song with more relatability to the members of this community than I think that twang would have indicated. It was no surprise to see him enjoying his time in the spotlight. We were both products of youths which had helped us to become to center of attention in any circle we found. And I dare to say we probably developed this as a result of having older brothers to hang out with in high school. Often putting us in scenarios where we would be the only thirteen year olds at parties with eighteen year olds, forcing us to somehow grab the attention of the taller, more experienced figures around us. And as I recalled that time in my life, a smaller figure came up to side.

"Your friends look like they're having a good time. Gonna sing with them?" - Renata

"I know we're both learning a lot about each other, but you already know I'm not a singer."

"Oh come on! You don't know anyone here."

"It's not about that. I'm a talker. Not a singer."

"Then go up and commentate on their act in Spanish. Or tell a story with some jokes. I'm sure enough people will laugh."

"No no. I tried to tell jokes in Spanish this one time at a crowded dinner table. It went terribly. What about you? Why don't you go sing?"

"I will if they ever give up the microphone."

"Well wake me if they do. I'm gonna get out of here."

"You're going to bed?"

"Yeah. Gonna try to catch the sunrise in the morning. I'll wake ya up if you want."

With a cold bottle of *Pacifico* leaving her lips she shook her head and twisted her face at the thought of getting up early.

"Eh. You can try. I'm not making any promises."

By the time I had decided to take myself to bed the guys had transitioned to a playlist of *Blink 182* and were making their way through it as the crowd looked on in confusion. Normally I was able to block out any noise once I laid down, but tonight I found it oddly difficult to fall asleep as the images of my evening replayed themselves through a series of snapshots against the memory of hikes where my feet had felt dead leaves and acorns instead of vines and mud as they had today. Somewhere not blocked by a canopy. Instead a place where the light passed through a shrinking fall foliage with ease as it transformed the leaves into a kaleidoscope of reds, oranges, and yellows. A place I knew well from taking hikes as a child. And as the night went on my mind was filled with the memories of woodland trails until I woke up a few hours later.

Day 14: A Left At Limón
Puerto Viejo, Costa Rica

I woke up today without an alarm, the aid of the light, or any other annoyance which had accompanied any of my mornings thus far. It was like something in my mind just knew the sun was about to rise and I had to be up to see it. When my eyes first opened I saw glows of daylight breaking through the cracks of our room as Renata laid next to me still as could be.

"Hey. Wake up. Let's go catch the sunrise." - Patrick

As I turned and shook her she buried her head in her pillow and with a muffled voice answered my request.

"Can't we just see it tomorrow?" - Renata

"No. It won't be the same."

"Ugh. Why not?"

"There won't be a beach tomorrow."

She laid there for a moment and then reluctantly turned over before sitting up and pouting her arms down onto the covers.

"Okay fine. Let's go."

"No no. I know what *fine* means. I've had a girlfriend. You can stay."

"Ugh. Shut up. I'm coming."

We went outside and took the path to the beach until we found a spot where we could get a view of the sunrise without any branches hanging down around us. As the water rushed up on my feet I noticed they were far more sensitive to the cold water than ever before. Probably a consequence of the exfoliation the jungle floor had given me. As we stood at the edge of the shore we looked ahed and noticed that the sun would come up more to the right and above the canopy obstructing our view. While standing there we were approached by a lanky man with a ripped redshirt and disheveled hair who began to speak in a slurred Argentinian accent from a mangled smile on a face that looked like it had been awake for at least the last 24-hours. And at the bottom of all of this his bare feet showed that he had likely gone without shoes weeks longer than myself.

"Hola amigos. Soy Ernesto. I am a guitar player. Come with me to see the most beautiful sunrise in the world." - Ernesto

We brushed off his request but he kept insisting we follow him down a trail which was supposed to cut over to a more clear beach. His child like persistence at the fact that our sunrise was good, but the one around the corner was better seemed to work quickly on Renata and her feet started moving in his direction before I realized we had agreed. I began to follow her lead, but with a cautionary pause as I was again without

271

shoes and the morning ants were already out on their breakfast runs. This combined with the slight broach of sharp coral through the sand made me weary of our decision. We followed him and that decision along the trail for what ended up being a longer time than I had planned, or perhaps it was the constant pokes to my sole which caused the sand to drip a little slower through my hourglass on this experience.

When we reached the end of the trail we saw this crazy guitarist had not steered us wrong. The sun was breaking the horizon and quickly filled our surroundings with light and exposed a series of artifacts washed up along the shore which glistened as the atmosphere slowly brightened. I always found it neat to see how little light was actually needed to expose an entire landscape so quickly. With each degree it rose the light around us exposed an array of colors bouncing off the calm waters and our new friend found his way to a guitar which he had left earlier and began to play. As he started to sing along to the strumming of his guitar string he closed his eyes and went out with his music. At one point the song turned into a hum and soon the light vibration from his lips had stopped. After a minute or so it became apparent that he was no longer with us in this moment in time and we decided to leave him to his own devices. When we got back I was feeling pretty awake so I turned to Renata to see if she wanted to go out with me for a bit.

"Well I'm awake. You hungry?" - Patrick

"Sure. I saw some breakfast spot next to a bakery up the road yesterday." - Renata

"This place is dangerous. There's too many bakeries."

"Well you don't have to eat anything. I was just telling you."

"I know. And I was just telling myself."

Renata and I left and proceeded up the road until we found a series of small shops, one of them being the breakfast spot she had seen on our drive in. There were two open parking spots out front so we parked and left the windows down as we went inside. As I walked inside I was met with an array of breads displayed in baskets hanging on the walls to my right and a counter filled from top to bottom with local treats of every sort. At that sight I looked over and Renata and asked for a bit of her help with my morning purchase.

"Can we get some bread?"

"Why are you asking me?"

"Because I don't have my wallet with me so I kinda need you to pay for it. Spot me five?"

"I'll buy you bread. Just share some with me."

"That's the thing. I can't. I need a loaf to make it to San Jose."

"Why not just buy some bread there?"

"Look, just humor me. I'm buying it for a friend back at the hostel. And this bread looks legit. She will love it. I want to buy it here."

"Why are you bringing some random girl bread?"

"She's not random. I've known her longer than I've known you. Now are you gonna give me the money or not?"

"Well, you've never brought me any bread."

"I don't get any points for bringing you to Costa Rica?"

"Okay fine. Here take a $10."

"Gracias."

After she handed me some money I stood there and examined a few rows of bread until I found the perfect type, which ended up being a loaf of that made by the French with a rustic crust and a soft warm center. From there Renata ordered her food and we found a seat along a community table in the middle of the restaurant. I don't know whether to say or not it was a restaurant, there seemed to be waitresses, but none of them ever came up to us. And I have to say this time I might have over done it with regards to food. Renata got a little out of hand attempting to try a bunch of food on her final day there and I was the perfect culprit to aid in such an endeavor. So that being said we ended up with two plates stacked with food and by the time I left there I had a mound of starch and sugar growing in the pit of my stomach that stayed with me for the rest of the day. Once we finished up we went back to the car and made our way back to the hostel. As we pulled in we saw found the guys organizing their luggage and making the arraignments to leave.

"You guys wanna stick around a while?" - Patrick

"Nah. It's supposed to start raining. Might as well get going." - Myles

"And go where?"

"Back to the city? Maybe we can try to see the Volcano again."

"Sure. Whatever you guys want."

I had no desire to go and search for that volcano again, but I didn't plan to argue on our last day. Instead I decided to go grab my bag which was more or less packed and then took my few remaining moments to go enjoy a last wash of the feet by the sea before departing. I can't think of a moment I long for more once I step away from it. Despite living around tropical locations for so long I only managed the luxury of beach life twice and since those times I've made the ocean the last spot I visited before I ever got on a bus to leave a beach trip. Renata joined me down by the water and started taking some last minute photos of our surroundings.

On the way out we stopped to get some gas before continuing to cruise up the same foggy highway we had come down a few nights before. As we drove along the coast we saw evidence of the regions trade importance via the presence of a line of shipping convoys stacked with rows of containers almost as high as the captains tower. Once they reached Limón they would be unloaded and placed on a truck headed for the Central Valley and then dispersed amongst the rest of the country. As we followed the same route those containers soon would we were once again greeted with heavy rain which made the drive even less enjoyable than nights ago when I had been denied the courtesy of brake lights. Now I had the same issue, but with half-assed windshield wipers and a foggy glare obstructing my view for the majority of the time. When we got to the top of the mountain Myles asked if he could drive for a bit and I decided to deny myself the luxury of relaxation about the safety of the rental and instead exchanged it for another hour of sleep as he took us down into San Jose.

Without much conversation we had decided to make things easy and stay at the same hostel as we had our first night in San Jose. This may have been one of the only areas where I did not consult anyone on a decision and just directed us to where I thought we needed to be. Finding it was much easier this time around and we even managed to find a parking spot out front. I had not alerted Matilda we were close and I wanted to use this chance to try and surprise her with the loaf of bread before she saw us. When we got inside I left Renata to take care of signing us in while I walked towards the bar with the baguette wrapped up in my right hand. When I appeared her smile widened and exposed the lower half of her canines as she reached out to receive the loaf from my extended hand.

"I thought you said we were gonna go to that place together?"

"It's not from *Maria's*. Try it though, it's great."

"Thank you! Here, cut a few slices while I get something."

At that she placed the bread on a cutting board and handed me a knife as she backed away from the bar with her eyes darting around for a missing ingredient. As she scrambled through a few shelves she pulled out a jar of what looked like sugar, only heavier. She then placed the slice on the table and squeezed a combination of lime juice and what turned out to be crystalized guava onto the softer inside. And while I was admittedly hesitant about her chosen mixture in the beginning it wasn't long before I had eaten half of the loaf on my own.

"Where did you say you got this? I'll be down that way to do some diving before I leave." - Matilda

"It's down in Puerto Viejo. How's diving been?"

"It has been great since I got certified in Honduras and finally bought my own equipment. Now I go by myself every chance I get."

"Won't be using that certification much back home."

"If I miss it that much I'll open another hostel by the shore somewhere. Problem solved."

"Yeah, see how you like diving in the Atlantic compared to the Caribbean and then talk to me."

As we sat there she pulled out a pack of slim French cigarettes and lit one up with another from the pack outstretched in my direction. Instead opting just to share a drag of hers I mentioned that I was going to take the time to see if I had anything interesting on whatever film remained from my time on the islands and told her to make sure and ask me about it the next time we talked. I knew that would do one of two things. Either make me never answer her again, or make me somehow sit through all of that film before I committed to leaving my job. First, I had no need to give myself the stress of a job search and that task at the same time. And secondly, I needed to find a way to go about this with Renata. Naturally Matilda urged me to replace my situation with the pending vacancy at her Costa Rican hostel once more. Even pointing out the advantage long term seclusion could have to getting some work done. And though very appealing, I had to refuse. Wandering for the purpose of exploration had been amazing, but doing so with an aimless nature only needed to be a part of my life for a finite amount of time. I knew if I did as she asked I would return down to eventually find myself in the same spot years from now. This place had that type of power. It was pleasing. It was home. As much a home as a nomad could ever call anywhere. But in less than twenty-four hours we were set to head back to our true home. Of course getting back on the plane was still a choice away from becoming a reality. But that went for everything. The only question now was whether to climb a ladder which had been placed in-front of me or to build my own with all I had to ponder upon. No matter what I needed to stay focused on the next thing I did. Not that I was unfocused before, because I was certainly paying attention. However, if I had to give myself one true criticism, it would be that I wasn't planned. None of this happened due to my plan. I practically learned Spanish by accident. Purely a consequence required by my environment. I needed to make sure that my next ten years didn't happen on accident. Looking back from thirty to twenty I had undeniably lived a decade I was more or less responsible for, despite how unintended the results may have been. That's all I really had as far as insight, the true perspective of a decade led by my decisions. I am who I am because of those years. For better or for worse, all that jazz. Despite what narratives may shift about the existence or non-existence of time, one is unable to deny its passing and the reality of moments fleeting in a direction beyond our grasp.

To avoid that I needed to sit and focus on what potential could be hidden within those tapes, and what could be pulled from them. Ever since Myles mentioned them my mind had started going back and forth on whether I would want to deal with them again if given the chance. Knowing that even if I did I would have to find a way to reconcile the fact that there was still no real ending to the whole thing. And I hate to ruin it for you but we won't be going back to magically make that happen somehow over the next two chapters. As Robert Rodriguez had once said regarding his first movie *El Mariache*, *you never go back to reshoot, you just find a way to work with what you've got.* I even remember an interview where I heard him admit to having made the trailer for *Sin City* before the actors had even been casted. Creating a trailer that got enough notice to eventually do the whole thing the way he wanted to from the beginning. At that recollection I figured I might be able to try and do the same. Though for my situation I would need to see what I had to work with in the first place. I had a memory for places and people, but until I saw what the camera caught I wouldn't be sure how much optimism was just selective memory from a few good frames running through my head. I was keeping myself there to keep up with the promise I had made to myself when I finally left teaching, but that didn't matter if I wasn't enjoying the future it was leading to. I don't know why it didn't appeal to me. It's not even that it didn't appeal to me. It was more that I was afraid of succeeding at the wrong thing.

In many ways this was exactly the sort of thing I needed. For once something which didn't supply me with some new place to go, but instead with something new to focus on, with a specific outcome in mind. And as a nice collegiate full circle, completing some sort of film could help to show me that internship had actually paid off in some odd way. Ironic since the gap on my resume which followed the one impressive line ultimately became the only thing any interviewer noticed, eventually avoiding questions of my degree completely, noticing a lack of direction more than anything. And while I was often frustrated by their inquiries, I knew I had made it difficult for myself to find a place within the real world, and even more difficult for the real world to try to justify doing so on its' own. Of course now that it had, I would need to sleep on it before deciding if I was going to show it that it was right for its' hesitation all along, as perhaps even I was with mine.

Day 15: On The Return
San Jose, Costa Rica

I started my morning feeling more restless than I had in quite a while. It was such a weird mixture of sadness and completion overwhelming me the moment I opened my eyes. We needed to leave by noon in order to make our flight so I didn't really have much time to run around, but I didn't wanna spend my last few hours sitting around the hostel. As I got up I walked outside and stumbled over to the pool where I put my toes in the water to test out the temperature. It wasn't too cold so I decided to take advantage of another perk of my surroundings and hopped in for a quick swim. After my swim I climbed up onto a concrete wall to dry off as I heard the first sounds of guests moving about the hostel. As I got moving and went back to the room to get some dry clothes and gather my things I heard Renata's voice projecting from the bunk behind me.

"Psst. Patrick. Wanna go get a coffee?" - Renata

"Sure. Try to be quiet." - Patrick

"Okay. I'm gonna go brush my teeth and I'll meet you out front."

Once we got going we went north and found ourselves passing over the same train tracks which had served as the areas alarm clock for the last hour. After the tracks we came to an intersection with a large school attached to a church filling with students in matching blue and white uniforms. As they passed just below eye level I saw a series of faces which resembled that of kids I once taught. We walked through breaks in the line and continued up the street until finding our way into a cafe hiding among a wall of graffiti. Entering we looked to our left and saw a large blackboard with a chalk mosaic guiding guests through the process of harvesting and cultivating the cocoa plant along with a paragraph describing the origin of this particular cafe. We both ordered and waited at the countertop where three tall stools stood available next to a bulletin board of local events. The next room over contained a few tables and a mic stand with a tiny stage in front of a few tables.

"Wish we woulda known about this spot last night." - Patrick

"Yeah, reminds me of this spot by my place. So look, Marcus and I have tickets to a show at the IMPROV next week. You should come."

"Maybe."

"Maybe what? You love going to stand-up. Didn't you do used to improv in college?"

"No, that was a friend. I was in a talent show as a kid. Once."

"Oh. Well, still, I thought you said something about it to me before.

Anyways, you should come along."

"I might."

"Might? Whats wrong? Are you gonna be able to act normal around Marcus anymore or is this how it's gonna be?"

"You don't want me at dinner with you all so soon afterwards. I know I'll say something stupid."

"You said this would stay between us!"

"Oh it will, I told you, I'll stay quiet unless you leave him for one of your affairs and try to ruin him in a divorce or something. Then I'll be storming out of the woodwork for my commission as his lawyer. I mean you can leave him, just don't fuck him."

"Well let's hope it never gets to that…weirdo."

"You ever think he just needs a guy in his ear?"

"No. You keep your mouth shut."

"Well if no one else gets in his ear do you think he's ever gonna think differently about it?"

"Worry about your own girl problems. I've got this."

"Oh yeah, totally looks like *'you've to this'*. Look, I wanna bring this up with him, I'm genuinely curious. I'm just gonna ask him a few questions. I'll say I had a threesome or something recently, see how he reacts."

With a clear tone of doubt in her voice she shot back, "You think something like that will get it out of him? Good luck."

"Could work. Could not work. Gonna be fun to find out either way. Doesn't really doesn't matter what I say to him and or he says to me. All that matters is if you're two people who want to make it work."

"What do you mean?"

"Well that's all you need when you wanna get married. It's not that complicated. If you're two people that wanna make it work and you're always committed to that goal, then you'll make it work. Some old couple told me that once. So just ask yourself, and maybe even him, if you're two people that wanna make it work. And in the meantime, I'll try and see if he's like my friend or if he's got his own issues going on."

"Thanks. I uh. I never thought to look at it like that."

"I mean that's what a marriage is, something two people gotta work on."

"Maybe. Well, if it comes up, lemme know what he says?"

"I got you dawg. And yeah. I'll go to the show. Just tell me what night to be there."

As she continued I found myself focusing not on her words, but on what I really needed to tell her. A thought which had been dwelling since our first meet up at a cafe many months back. Even after consideration I didn't want the promotion and since she had gotten me the job I felt it fair for her to know what I was planning first. Especially since she would probably have to hear the lions share of the complaining from Marcus when he heard his own version of the news.

"I'm glad we're getting back on a weekend. It'll give me some time to get my life together." - Renata

"Speaking of getting our lives together. I gotta be honest with you. I don't think I'm going to be sticking around much longer."

"Sticking around where? What do you mean?"

"Look, I gotta be real with you. I appreciate how much you helped me when I needed it, but this wasn't really the type of thing I was looking for."

"What are you talking about? Do you mean your job?"

"Yeah. The job. The city. All of it."

"So what are you telling me? Are you quitting?"

"Well, I thought about it and I don't have any interest in moving up any further than I already have. I only ever really cared about the travel perks, but that's not reason enough to stay somewhere. At least not for what I'm trying to do after this."

"Where is this coming from? I thought you wanted to change life."

"Yeah, but I can't just hop into another commitment on something I wasn't looking for in the first place. And that's what this promotion would be."

"You are so frustrating. Seriously, why do you do this? And how soon do you plan to leave?"

"Depends. I can't be sure how long everything is gonna take, but I wanted to give you a heads up before I did anything."

"I appreciate that, but I hope think about this a little more. There's a lot of opportunities if you stay. Marcus is doing better than ever and he's only been with them for three years now. You know you gotta put in your time somewhere eventually."

"I get that. But it's just not what I'm trying to do. And you can stop worrying. I promise I'll stick around long enough for him to get that referral check. Not like I can just dip out on my lease right now anyway."

"Why is that when you're not reminding me of my headaches you're causing me new ones?"

"Shut up. You know you can't be mad at me."

"No, I can. But I'm not gonna tell you what to do."

"Look I don't know what to tell ya. I've decided not to double down on the same stuff I was doing before. That's what's up and I wanted you to know. Maybe we should just leave it at that."

"That's fine. I'll let that be the companies problem. And Marcus. Marcus will be fine. He's a grown up."

"Do you mind letting me tell him?

"You keep my secrets, I'll keep yours."

"Good. You know, maybe you could stay with the company and bartend in one of the lounges at another location to transition out. You've got the experience and you would still have a job."

"Do you get commission off of that too?"

"Just trying to help. Anyways, I'm hungry. Do you wanna get some breakfast? I think you owe me."

"I do, but can you wait? Matilda said she was gonna cook for everyone today. It'll probably be something really good."

"Should we head back then?"

"Yeah soon. I need to find a few things first. Do you mind walking around with me while I look around this market?"

"Yeah sure. What are you looking for?"

"I'm not sure. Have to see what catches my eye."

"That's no plan of attack for someone trying to plan better."

Truth be told I was looking for two things in particular; street art and gummy bears. The first of which we found when I came across a man selling some paintings from a tapestry he had spread across the sidewalk. Most of his work consisted of personal sketches mimicking the local wildlife, but my eyes were especially drawn to a few landscapes he had of the mountains running through the coffee zones. As I scrolled through his portfolio I ended up buying a piece and moving along to remain empty handed in my search for gummy bears. On the walk back it set in that my conversation with Renata was one secret she would likely not keep from her man for very long. Soon enough he would know I was leaving and I would need to figure out my next move sooner than later. Because while I knew very little of the corporate world, I knew that those on their way out were not often seen with the highest of regards. Especially not after turning down what those in their office would covet as an opportunity over an obligation. And especially not for an opportunity which was on the crazier side of likely.

When we got back I found Matilda walking around the outdoor kitchen prepping our meal with another worker from the hostel. They had already put a large portion of potatoes on the stove and were throwing some spices into a bowl of olive oil filled and grated cheese by the time I arrived. Once they had finished cooking everyone came over we all started eating along a set of barstools running the length of the counter. Through this I stayed alongside Matilda and her friend talking with them about their lives and what it was like living in the hotel environment. They had it so differently. At a hostel the staff is a much bigger part of the experience. Not just in making the experience for you, but for sharing it later when it's their time off. That's the difference between hotels and hostels in many ways. At most locations the workers live there and you're just as likely to see them in the kitchen or walking to the bathroom as you would any other guest. As we were finishing our meals Renata got an alert that her flight had been delayed and shortly after I received my own my email alerting me that the majority of the flights out of the city had been delayed by two hours or more. We took this extra time to hang around the pool and I spent a few moments helping Matilda clean the kitchen while we said our goodbyes. Of all the people I don't see enough she was someone I would really miss. I hadn't expected to see her, but that was the constant case. We didn't get enough time together. Not now, not ever. I always found it a shame that the people I enjoyed being around the most were the ones that I was pulled away from most often. Which I guess made sense since I had taken it upon myself to become friends with those living interesting lives on the go. Even though now it seemed the streamline of this shared existence was coming to an end as both of us would now be officially retired from the nomadic lifestyle. The only pain came in wondering which of my fellow explorers I would never see again. All of whom would go on to live lives far beyond my view. And many who would pass without my knowing at some point in life. For there is no obituary for the wanderers of this world.

Before we left Myles used the remainder of his wet wipes to give the car a thorough cleaning and even polished the wedges of the door enough to take away any suspicion that we had misused the car. And in fairness we didn't. That creek was barely an issue. In fact it had helped us because it gave just enough of an undercarriage cleaning to flat out impress them. Once that was done we loaded up and drove to drop it off. To my surprise they didn't give us any grief and returned the entirety of the deposit without any worry. After which we waited around until a shuttle came to take us to the airport. Once we got to the airport I realized we had overestimated the check-in process at the rental office and wound up pretty far ahead of the schedule. With that I took a few minutes to hang outside as the others went in to get their bags checked. As I stared at the world in front of me I thought about how much it had done in shaping who I was today. Almost as much as my hometown had, although the lifestyle during that time had spoiled me. And while it seemed nice at the time I can see that I allowed teaching to serve as the vessel facilitating my lifestyle for far longer than I should have allowed. And if I wanted to I could come back to this at any time. I could establish the medium of existence at any moment. But I needed to see that I could go and do something more with myself. With a final breathe of air I soaked up a view of the countryside and eased my way through the sliding doors entering the airport. Walking in I saw the guys still checking their bags so I took myself through security and waited for them on the other side. As I waited I found myself yet again being pulled to a screen of options being offered at the airports departure list. Here I was with the gifts of freedom and no certainty on where to go or how to use it. I had brought myself here many times, but I hadn't asked myself anything other than where to next. And this time it wouldn't be enough to make a change just based on location. The change needed to be an entirely different direction. A shift really. I guess that's what I hadn't realized before. I needed to adjust the course all together, not just the port I was visiting. And that's all I had been. A visitor. The entire time I had just been a person hopping around. I never made myself a staple of the environment around me, merely a neat character for the locals to get to know just long enough. And now that I had moved I can't deny that I loved the energy of being in a city like Washington. Our nations capitol had done a fine job serving as a hub for meeting new people from here and there, but there's plenty of jobs and places that could do just the same if I sought them out.

Once we entered the terminal I walked with Renata down to her gate where I received a half-assed goodbye and a smack on my shoulder before she planted herself in a seat by the window.

"Have a good flight. And don't be mad at me."

"Whatever. I'll see you next weekend if you still wanna come."

"Sounds good. I'll give you a call this week."

From there I walked back to our gate and found Wes stretched across a row of chairs as Myles sat finishing a crossword puzzle with his phone charging at his side. In their minds they were already home. Though the time between now and when we were home would come no quicker for me than it would for them. Any feelings to the contrary would be just that, feelings, not reality. Perception and experience. Neither of which gave truth to the length of its' passing. That's how it works. Time gives no favors, nor extra seconds, it just moves forward and we move on, unable to fight its tow no matter how strong our stroke, all floating along at the same universal speed. It's the only equalizer out there in such a manner. And the only thing we ever share simultaneously with the world as a whole. We are all granted the same twenty-four hours each day no matter where we find ourselves across this globe. Not even the sun can claim such a monopoly on our experience as time can.

Sitting at our gate I looked around and watched as those waiting used their final moments in Costa Rica in a variety of ways. With a few shattered seconds to my right being burnt by a family hurrying through some last minute packing in hopes of saving more space than time. And to my left a man sat reading at the speed of a calmly gliding index finger which paused on each period as the brain attached ingested the last sentence without concern for time or delay. His patience. Their panic. Both passing the same no matter which moment I watched. Whether one stood still or one moved forward with ceaseless ambition all that seemed to matter was the presence one embodied during the passing of the time their allotted in this existence. And our choice to control that presence sets the pace of our lives. And like it or not, I had chosen my pace a long time ago. But all choices could be changed. All paths challenged. All of this floated in my head until the time finally came for us to take off and I drifted through the line to the 7th row where I sat down and covered my eyes before anyone had time to worry whether I was buckled up or not.

Stateside Wanderer

New York City, NY

By the time I opened my eyes the landing gear had already locked into place and our flight was on it's final approach towards the runway. As we started to touch down I looked out the window and saw what looked like the Big Apple illuminated in the distance. At the surprise to the sight I turned to Wes and tapped him on his shoulder as he stared down at a magazine spread across his lap.

"Yo dude, are we in New York?" - Patrick

"You didn't hear the announcement?" - Wes

"No. I fell asleep before we took off."

"Oh. Yeah. They had to re-route us to Laguardia. Something about snow back home. They'll have us out in the morning."

"Snow and sandals. Perfect."

Once we landed I sat there waiting for the rows ahead to empty and kept my phone on airplane mode as I made my way off the plane and into the customs line. As I stepped through I was asked for my ID and upon a brief pause the agent asked me to step aside. I stood there for a moment looking down at a well deserved sandal tan and took a deep breath before looking up.

"Sir, step this way please." - Customs Agent

I picked up my things and followed him to a table where another man wearing blue gloves stood with a clipboard in his hand and a German Shepard panting at his side. Tilting its head ever so slightly at the arrival of myself and the agent. Once stopped I placed my bag onto the table and the agent began to dig through with a flashlight as the other asked me about the purpose of my trip.

"Are you traveling alone?" - Customs Agent

"Unfortunately not. Is there a problem?"

As I stood there he went elbow deep in my bag and pulled out my *Enos* hammock which he then unravelled until a clunky piece of metal fell onto the table.

"What is this?" - Customs Agent

"It's big businesses way to bind me with nature."

"Excuse me?"

"They're the straps for my hammock."

"You can't have these on the plane."

He placed the locks aside and reached in the front pocket where I had my notebook and a few loose items. As he grabbed the notebook the flower Myles had hidden inside for his mom fell onto the desk with all four purple petals still perfectly flattened. He looked up at me and then to the TSA agent on his left. The agent gave him a light shrug of the shoulders and indicated that nothing else had been found. He then placed the flower back into the notebook and stacked that with the hammock on top of my bag. Through all of this his dog remained unresponsive to my presence and the contents of my luggage. Good dog.

"Take your things. Welcome home."- Customs Agent

His voice was filled with the disappointment of a man who knew his instincts were properly placed, but poorly timed. As I made my way to the counter I was met with an apology and three new tickets for a flight departing at 8 A.M. Which obviously meant we would have to make it to the airport before sunrise. So much for sleeping in.

"Hello sir, here is the voucher for your room and your tickets to Washington." - Clerk

"Excuse me. Only a voucher for one?" - Patrick

"Well the room comes equipped with two queen-sized beds. That should be plenty for two?"

"That's great, but could we possibly get separate rooms? And there's three of us."

"Let me check."

Standing there I watched as she scrolled through the options on her screen and peered her eyes in any attempts to move this along.

"Okay. I can grant you one more voucher, but that's the best I can do."

"That works. Thank you."

"You're welcome. We apologize for your delay."

As I walked away from the counter I found a bench and sat down waiting by the exit until the guys made it through.

"You get everything we need?" - Myles

"Yeah. All good through customs?" - Patrick

"Yup. Come on man. I'm not that stupid."

"Good. Here. Don't lose these."

I handed him their voucher and began walking toward the exit where we found a line of people waiting in the cold for their shuttles to the hotel.

"You guys want to go for some food once we get to our rooms or are you gonna call it a night?" - Patrick

"I'm beat man. I'm using mine for breakfast." - Wes

"You're ass isn't gonna wake up early enough for breakfast. Me and Pat are splitting your voucher tonight." - Myles

"Fuck you dude this is mine." - Wes

"If you wake up I'll buy you breakfast. Just gimme that one for now dude." - Myles

When we arrived I exchanged my voucher for a keycard and used it to swipe myself into room 815 where I was greeted by a king-sized bed and a large desk occupying the majority of the room. To my left a small dresser sat with a wall mounted television and a mirror facing the foot of the mattress while only a few feet to my right a large bathroom with an impressive jacuzzi sat rivaling the size of many urban apartments. I placed my bag down next to the dresser and took myself to the desk. I knew if I sat on the bed I was likely to pass out so I sat down in the office chair and adjusted my eyes to the view of the skyline outside. As I did I twirled a pen between my fingers and shifted my focus to how much this city had called to me over the years. Even if only from movies. It had always looked like a place filled with opportunity. And if I had used my mind more deliberately after graduation I might have realized this city had everything someone my age could have wanted out of life back then. I could have traveled through all of the cultures and foods I wanted to while finishing up the last leg of school. Being here could have been so opportune knowing my tendency to bounce around. It might have been the closest I could have come to taking a different path after college and still winding up as the person I am today. And while I didn't necessarily believe in signs, I did believe in convenience, so I did a quick search to see what it would take to get me back to D.C. before the end of the weekend. In that search I found a bus ticket for $28 so I made a reservation and decided to look into the rest after I ate. From there I changed my clothes and went downstairs where I found Myles sitting with the remains of a pepperoni slice crumbling in his hand as the rest sat untouched in the center of the table. I joined him and we sat in silence absorbing the long missed headlines running along the bottom of the screens around us. Reminding us who won and where the next game was.

"What you gonna get?" - Myles

"I'm gonna chill on this pizza for now. Might save mine for the morning."

"Why? You're not gonna have time to eat again before we leave. We gotta be outta here before the fucking sun comes up like always."

"Maybe you do. I still have two days off so I'm gonna stick around and explore the city for the weekend."

"You're staying here? What about your car?"

"I'll manage. I'll call ya when I'm coming down so we can meet up."

"Well fuck. Guess that's that. Make sure you write down those passwords before we leave and I'll see if I can get everything on the cloud by the time you get back."

"I would appreciate that."

"No problem. And the money will be in your account tonight. I threw in extra for the headache. Text me if I owe you anything else."

"You're good man. It was just some food. You need a wake up call?"

"Nah I'll be fine."

"Aight cool. I'll see you soon. Tell Wes I'll see him when I come down next week."

"Will do man. You got a place to stay any time you're around. Oh and you gotta make sure to make it for my big pig roast in May."

"I could be talked into that."

"Awesome. Welp Patty, I appreciate you coming along."

"I appreciate you paying me."

"Oh come on now, you woulda said yes if all I offered was the plane ticket."

"Perhaps. Try me on that one another time. This time only two seats."

As we finished our pizza we left our vouchers and some cash before making our way through the lobby and back to our rooms. As he went upstairs I continued on to the front desk where I found a woman handling her closing duties.

"Excuse me. Quick question. How do I get to the subway from here?" - Patrick

"Are you trying to get into the city?"

"Yes mam."

"Well we don't actually have a station around here. You have to take the Q70 bus and then cross the bridge. From there you can catch a train downtown."

"Okay. Thank you."

After grabbing myself a map I shuffled through the lobby and made it back upstairs where I found my room cooled to the perfect temperature. When I walked in I tightened the blinds to make sure I would sleep through the night and set my alarm for an hour before check out. That way I could take advantage of that bathtub prior to departing. Before sitting down I flipped on the lamp at the far end of the desk and brought out my notebook. As it hit the table it opened to reveal a series of pages filled over the last few weeks. When the frayed edges began to settle one page with a paragraph in thinly scribed gibberish suddenly caught my eye. As I brought out my phone to translate it's meaning my screen lit up with an alert from my bank telling me a large transfer had hit my account. At that moment I remembered how I had once read the cost of anything was the amount of life you exchanged for it. And of all exchanges in my life I don't know that I've ever had one more fruitful. Especially not now as I look back at all it led to far beyond the words of this story. In my mind the extra money would make the weekend in the city a little less stressful. Not that I needed to spend it all, but knowing it was there I would have a bit more breathing room than usual. With that thought I reopened my phone in search of somewhere to stay over the weekend. At first glance more options popped up than my phone could properly pixilate. Given the abundance of availability I decided to leave finding a spot til the next day when I had a better idea about what area of the city I wanted to be in. After-all there's always hostels.

Laying there I kept trying to think of where I was gonna go once I got in the city. This was a walking city and I was back in the realities of winter so I couldn't afford to waste too many footsteps. And while I preferred the idea of exploring alone I needed to map out my weekend with the help of a local if I was going to maintain the same momentum from the last two weeks. Instead of guessing where to go I needed someone who could point me in the right direction. Unfortunately New York City was one watering hole I had managed to neglect during my twenties and I didn't have many faces coming to mind. From there I drew down my covers and turned off the light to the side of my bed. It was only before passing out that my mind brought back the memory of a suite-mate from my freshman year who had moved to Hollywood after graduation. He was a really cool dude and we probably woulda hung out a lot more if it weren't for our majors being so far apart, both figuratively and literally. He was always around the art department and I was located on the other side of campus. He was the only person in the dorm willing to walk all of the way across town for the pizza shop that didn't deliver. We hadn't spoken much since then beyond the mutual happy birthday we sent each other each April 14th. One of the more recent of which revealed he was now on the east coast. Other than that I remembered him being notoriously difficult to reach the few times I had tried when I was out and about on the weekends. Nonetheless, he would be the perfect person to show me around a walking city like New York which is why I spent my last few moments sending him a message before fading off. And despite my memories of his relationship with technology, he managed to answer before my night ended with a response that would send me into the next spiral of my existence. Eventually opening doors that would teach me an entirely new type of language, from a rather untraditional type of translator.

"Hey man you still around New York?"

"Damn is it April already?" - Jax

"Nah man. Just checkin in with ya."

"Yeah man. I'm still here. Where you at these days?"

"These days I'm a lot of places, but this day in particular I find myself on the outskirts of NYC. Got stuck at the airport. Think I'm gonna stay for the weekend. Any time to meet up?"

"Yo for real? Yeah man I'd love to meet up. I've got a mic Saturday night, but I'm free anytime before or after after."

"A mic?"

"Yeah bro. You gotta hear my shit."

"That's badass, I'm down for that. Let's meet up before. Where can I find you?"

"Meet me outside The Comedy Cellar. It's off the West 4th Street stop. Doors open around 7. Should be wrapped up before 10. We can go explore the city after or hit up another mic. They'll be going all night."

"That sounds awesome. I'll see you there."

Where To Next?

*"EVEN WANDERLUST
TAKES YOU SOMEWHERE..."*

Where will you go?

————————————

Where To Next?

WHAT WERE YOUR THOUGHTS ON THE STORY?

REVIEWS HELP AN AUTHOR KNOW WHAT
THE READERS THOUGHT.
OK, SO HERE'S HOW YOU START:
OPEN THE CAMERA ON YOUR PHONE.
OK GREAT.
NOW SCAN THE CODE BELOW[4]…

From there it should take you to the Amazon sales page
where you can leave a review[5]. If it doesn't, idk what to tell
ya, this world is weird sometimes. Regardless, you should
still tell your friends.
& AS ALWAYS…..
THANK YOU FOR YOUR SUPPORT.
NOW ONTO THE NEXT PAGE WHERE I'LL TELL YOU A
LITTLE BIT ABOUT MYSELF…

---

[4] Instructions are not to be used or considered as coercion for higher ratings.

[5] Provided that you have an iPhone, otherwise I can't be certain.

Where To Next?

WHAT MAKES THE WANDERER?

Where do I start with this? Well, my name is Patrick DiMarchi and I came along somewhere close enough to the end of the eighties to be considered a millennial, but not enough so that I can remember what the eighties were like. Somewhere in the 90's I started writing and since then I've scribbled my way through a little bit of everything from contracts to comedy. Although I think I should have just given in and written a book years ago. I grew up in the Shenandoah Valley and attended James Madison University, where I studied Political Science. And while I loved the classes, teachers, and the abundance of discussions, I probably should have gone another route. What route you ask? Well, had I been more in touch with myself back then I would have gone towards studying linguistics. It's one of the only topics which has constantly fascinated me, and the patterns of my life would indicate I have a tendency to place myself around some sort of international watering hole every chance I get. And in doing so I inevitably pick up a bit of whatever language

I realize the cup in my hand is empty. I was looking for a recycling bin somewhere in NYC when this random photographer pulled me aside and demanded a photo. Odd, I know.

dominates the area or people passing through. This of course led to traveling. And now has led to books. The first of which you have in your hands. With at least four more on the way. Do stay tuned.

Now If you wanna know a few random things about me. Uh, I've driven cross country seven times, which I'm sure sounds reasonable. I've never owned a vehicle with an automatic transmission, in-fact even driving one makes me nervous. I always end up speeding when I do. Despite the fact that I'm now seen as *well traveled* I didn't actually step foot on a plane until I was almost twenty-years old. And as embarrassing as it is to admit, I literally have zero frequent flyer miles stacked up from all of my years of traveling. Like zero. Keeping track of stuff like that is more annoying to me than a few seemingly far more difficult tasks like writing and editing a book. Speaking of books, I enjoy reading (though most of my books are consumed on audiobook these days) and I've loved documentaries since way before it was cool to talk about them. Okay I think that's enough for now.

Thanks for taking an interest and check out the rest of my work at my website www.PalabrasByPatrick.com. And keep up by following me on Instagram @**PatrickDiMarchi.**

Travel Well, Travel Often.
Patrick DiMarchi

Bryan,

Here's a New Take on travel writing.

Hope You Enjoy.

Best of Luck in Your own writing,
just remember, the work adds up.

Sincerely,

3/25/2021

Made in the USA
Middletown, DE
19 March 2021